MIND
FUEL

MIND FUEL

An exclusive signed edition

BEAR GRYLLS

HODDER &
STOUGHTON

MIND FUEL

SIMPLE WAYS TO BUILD
MENTAL RESILIENCE EVERY DAY

BEAR GRYLLS

AND WILL VAN DER HART

HODDER &
STOUGHTON

First published in Great Britain and the United States of America in 2022
by Hodder & Stoughton
An Hachette UK company

1

Copyright © BGV Global Limited and Will Van Der Hart, 2022

The right of Bear Grylls and Will Van Der Hart to be identified as
the Authors of the Work has been asserted by them in accordance
with the Copyright, Designs and Patents Act 1988.

A CIP catalogue record for this title is available from the British Library

Hardback ISBN 978 1 399 80509 4
Trade Paperback ISBN 978 1 399 80742 5
Ebook ISBN 978 1 399 80510 0

Typeset in Avenir by
Palimpsest Book Production Ltd, Falkirk, Stirlingshire

Printed and bound in Great Britain by Clays Ltd, Elcograf S.p.A.

Hodder & Stoughton policy is to use papers that are natural, renewable
and recyclable products and made from wood grown in sustainable forests.
The logging and manufacturing processes are expected to conform
to the environmental regulations of the country of origin.

Hodder & Stoughton Ltd
Carmelite House
50 Victoria Embankment
London EC4Y 0DZ

www.hodder.co.uk

To all of you who are both brave and strong enough to acknowledge that protecting your mental health and building positive mental fitness is a battle worth fighting every day.

We hope this book equips you with great tools to do this. You deserve wonderful things in your life.

Claim that.

And never give up.

Bear & Will

WISDOM

BATTLES

MOTIVATION

COURAGE

RELATIONSHIPS

SELF-CARE

SPIRITUALITY

DETERMINATION

HOW TO READ THIS BOOK

There are nearly two hundred mental fitness topics covered in *Mind Fuel*. They will help to equip you for life's daily challenges, building self-awareness, resilience and confidence. Just like our physical health, we all need to look after our emotional health.

Our daily insights take you through the whole year, but each topic is explored across two days to give you more space to think things through before moving on. Each day closes with two or three reflective questions to help you engage more personally with the concepts we raise, so that you can apply them to your own situation.

We have tried to create a book that gives you the flexibility to read in a way that works for you; each of the 365 entries is undated, so you can access them in any order, depending on what's most helpful for you on any given day.

If you want to read in a more thematic way, we have divided our topics into eight broad themes: Wisdom, Battles, Motivation, Courage, Relationships, Self-Care, Spirituality and Determination. Each theme has an associated icon displayed at the top of the page to show you what to expect.

While *Mind Fuel* may complement your personal journey, it is not a substitute for professional mental health support, should you need that, and at the back of this book there are a few short pieces by mental health professionals that might point you in the right direction.

Mind Fuel is to help you build day-to-day mental resilience for the challenges of life. And however you read it, we hope you find the encouragement to never give up.

Bear Grylls
Will Van Der Hart

MIND
FUEL

DAY 1

MENTAL FITNESS

AS BASKETBALL SUPERSTAR LeBron James says: 'Mental fitness is just as important as physical fitness.' It's developing an awareness of how we think and feel, coupled with effective tools to sustain (and hopefully improve) our wellbeing.

In the same way that physical fitness generates an awareness of our body, its strengths and vulnerabilities, so mental fitness can help develop an awareness of our thinking, processing and relating – giving us strategies to manage turbulent times, and to seek help if we need it.

Imagine your mind as a car. Looking after the engine keeps it working well, ensuring it won't break down unexpectedly. The more we help the engine function well, the more we protect it from developing problems later on.

Being mentally fit doesn't mean that we won't ever struggle with mental illness, just as being physically fit doesn't mean that we won't ever get physically ill. But the good news is that mental fitness principles are positive habits that can play a vital role in our lives, whatever we may be going through.

- *Have you avoided thinking about the way your mind works simply because you've never struggled mentally?*

- *How could an increase in self-awareness help to increase your mental fitness?*

- *If you were going to recommend developing greater mental fitness to a friend, how would you explain it to them?*

*'Part of the journey is to be aware
of emotional challenges before they
become too much'*

THE WORLD HEALTH ORGANIZATION defines good mental health as four attributes, in which 'the individual realises their own abilities, can cope with the normal stresses of life, can work productively and fruitfully, and is able to make a contribution to their community'. It is an holistic state of being. I have worked with people who have fulfilled all of these criteria at the same time as managing a diagnosed mental illness. It's inspiring and it's possible.

But we all need different sorts of support at times, depending on our situation. Having the effective tools to achieve these 'Big Four' is what mental fitness is about.

Most likely, we'll be training for mental fitness while suffering. Life is full of emotional challenges like stress, overwork and financial pressure; part of the journey is to be aware of these before they become too much. That's called wisdom.

If we can see challenges as an opportunity both to observe how we react and to choose better responses, then we give ourselves a good chance of building true mental resilience.

- *Which of the 'Big Four' criteria do you feel most confident about in your life?*
- *What preventative steps can you take to protect your mental health when you're feeling overwhelmed?*
- *Are you facing any challenges that could be an opportunity to improve your mental fitness?*

HINTERSTOISSER TRAVERSE

ONE OF THE most iconic climbing moves in history opened the north face of the Eiger to climbing. Andreas Hinterstoisser used his body as a pendulum to swing across an impassable section of rock, setting up a route and establishing a technique that is used worldwide today.

We all face obstacles in life that can seem impassable. Whether big or small, at work, in relationships, with finances, or health. Everyone is battling with something.

When progress grinds to a halt, it can be tempting to keep hammering away with the same old strategies to break through. But sometimes all this achieves is to burn up energy and we end up frustrated.

Sometimes the smart thing is to stop and think and amend. To adapt the way we are approaching something, so we don't give up on the thing itself.

- *Do you feel blocked from progress because of a specific obstacle?*
- *Has your approach to resolving the issue changed or remained the same?*

'Creativity is a muscle, too. The more we use it, the stronger it becomes'

HINTERSTOISSER HAD TO set aside his traditional techniques so that his imagination could find a way to adapt and find a way past the 'impossible'. He needed to look up the mountain before he could find a solution to the gap in their route.

We all have the capacity for incredible creativity but at times we need to step back from the way we have always done things to find it. Remember: creativity is a muscle, too. The more we use it, the stronger it becomes.

When we find a way to overcome an obstacle in life, it gives us a real boost. Not only is the way ahead open but we also feel the esteem of having achieved something hard.

- *Have you been looking at the problem from the same angle for too long?*
- *What would it be like to 'look up the mountain' and change your perspective?*
- *How could you engage your creativity to begin to make progress?*

AIM UPSTREAM OF WHERE YOU WANT TO LAND

CROSSING FAST-FLOWING RIVERS is one activity that always requires extreme caution. It doesn't matter how close the other bank may seem; it's never as straightforward as just getting in and climbing out on the other side.

I have had more close calls crossing rivers than any other obstacle in the wild: there is always more going on under the surface than you can predict and the flow is always stronger than you might imagine.

Change can be a bit like that too. We might be looking 'across the bank' to where we want to be. It may seem really close and achievable but there is often a major current driving against us.

This resistance to change is known as 'inertia' – and it is an all-too-common human trait to resist anything that might upset the status quo. Inertia always works to keep things the same, however much your heart longs for change.

- *Have you anticipated a simple change that turned out to be unexpectedly complex?*
- *What have you noticed about the force of inertia in pushing you back to the status quo?*
- *How have your previous struggles to achieve change enforced the idea that you won't be able to make progress in the future?*

'We should aim bigger and push harder than we think necessary'

I HAVE LEARNT that if we want to fight the current and achieve change, we have to really commit upfront. Anticipate the resistance. Recognise it and embrace it. Let it be a reminder that we are on the right track. As Corrie ten Boom said, 'Expect resistance but pray for miracles.'

It helps to aim further upstream than the destination that we've chosen, because we're going to get pushed back from our goal. So we should aim bigger and push harder than we think necessary. It just might be the extra energy we need to achieve the mission where others might not make it.

While we may want to reach that point across the river, we need to manage the various forces that stand in our way. For example, it may be a lack of confidence, an emotional connection to the present or a fear of failure. If we don't anticipate it, the force of the current can easily wash us back onto the bank we were hoping to leave, feeling exhausted and disappointed.

- *How does anticipating resistance impact your approach to making a change?*
- *What would it look like for you to 'aim further upstream' and go for more than you hoped, so that you achieve your ambition?*
- *What internal forces might be standing in your way . . . a lack of confidence or assertiveness, commitment or a connection to the status quo?*

HALT – MAKE BETTER DECISIONS

SOME OF THE most extraordinary survival stories I've ever heard started with one small, bad decision. Eric LeMarque reflected on eight days lost on Mammoth Mountain, which led to the amputation of both his legs due to frostbite: 'I made several mistakes, and the first one was the attitude that I brought up on the mountain. Even though I had ridden Mammoth hundreds of times, I kind of took it for granted . . . thinking, "It's just Mammoth".'

Maybe a person is distracted, or cold, or disorientated and rushes in without thinking. Inject a little fear into the mix and bad things can happen super-fast. Suddenly an already risky situation becomes life-threatening.

We all make bad decisions from time to time in life too. Frustration boils over and a harsh word stings those we love; we are in a corner and tell a lie; we don't listen when we should. The list goes on.

We cannot ever totally avoid making bad decisions, but I often wish that I'd been more aware of factors that precede them.

- *What do you notice about the things that have preceded bad decisions in your life?*
- *Is there anything that you could be more aware of in the future?*

'Give big decisions some space and time'

MOST OF US can look back at a moment in our lives and think: 'If only I'd waited for an hour, I'd have done it completely differently.' Or: 'If only I'd asked so-and-so for some advice first.'

Knowing when we're likely to make a decision we'll come to regret isn't an exact science, but I've found the acronym HALT to be useful. When I'm **H**ungry, **A**nxious, **L**ow or **T**ired, I know it's probably not the best time to decide something important or resolve an argument. This applies not just in practical situations, but also at work or with family and friends. If I HALT and take a moment or go for a quick walk, it's amazing how much more measured my reactions are.

So if you're not sure, HALT, take a break, talk to a friend you trust, give big decisions some space and time, then come back to the issue with fresh eyes and a new perspective.

- *How does the HALT acronym relate to your experience?*
- *How does taking a step back impact your decision making?*
- *What could you do to broaden your perspective on an existing frustration?*

FAIL
FIRST

WE HAVE ALL chalked up failures in life. In fact, if we haven't, we aren't aiming high enough! Failures are a by-product of going for things that inspire us. We all have those moments that, at times, come back to haunt us. The failed expeditions, the failed projects, the near-death moments. But the truth is, failures can also be the making of us. They are opportunities to build up resilience, they force us to adapt, to grow stronger. Inside and out. There is no shortcut to our goals that avoids failure. Failure is the doorway to success that we must pass through to get to the good stuff.

'Returned To Unit' are words that I never wanted to hear – the official term for 'failure' during the SAS selection process. First time around, those words came my way. And they stung deep. But I tried again, and by the end of my second attempt at SAS selection, only four of us out of the ninety who started were still standing.

Here is the irony. Out of those four, three of us had failed in our first attempt but got in the second time round. In other words, that first failure had been the key to eventual success.

- *Do you tend to look back on failure in wholly negative terms?*
- *Can you identify a 'failure' in your life that was a key turning point for a future success?*
- *Can you think of a person you know who has persevered in the face of failure and ultimately achieved inspiring things? How does their story inspire you?*

'Moving forward from failure takes courage'

NBA BASKETBALL SUPERSTAR Michael Jordan said, 'I've missed more than 9,000 shots in my career. I've lost almost 300 games. Twenty-six times I've been trusted to take the game-winning shot and missed. I've failed over and over and over again in my life. And that is why I succeed.'

It's human nature to overfocus on failures and assume that's all anyone else sees. As a result, we end up hiding our failures, and avoiding situations where we might fail again. But taking the next 'shot' is where yesterday's failure becomes today's success.

Moving forward from failure takes courage. But, as Henry Ford wrote, 'The only real failure is when we learn nothing.'

Failure has a habit of showing us four things: 1. where we are weak; 2. where we are strong; 3. what we are afraid of; and, 4. what we need to succeed.

Remember that just because we fail a little along the road to success, it does not mean we are a failure. Take what you have experienced, be kind to yourself, praise yourself for effort, and go again.

- *Are you at risk of backing away from something because of the fear of failing a second time?*
- *Which of the four things, weakness, strength, fear and need, have you learnt from your experience of failure?*
- *Can you see how these will, in turn, make you stronger? How could you apply what you have learnt to your next steps?*

CONNECT DEEPLY

N THE THIRD century AD, a rough group of monks, wanting to strip away unnecessary distractions, went into the Egyptian desert, seeking a place where they could better connect with the Divine. These 'Desert Fathers' were pretty radical – early survivalists who thrived in the simplicity of the barren landscape.

Their commitment to pursue a deep sense of connection is inspiring. Father Dioscuros wrote, 'But in the desert, in the pure clean atmosphere, in the silence – there you can find yourself. And unless you begin to know yourself, how can you even begin to search for God?'

When I get into the wild, it takes my ears (and my heart) time to adjust. At first you think it is just silent, but then you start to hear a different sound. The thrum of the jungle floor, the faint movement of desert dust or even a deeper voice within that offers words of light and strength.

We can find that same spirit wherever we are outside. Not only a jungle but also in a green city park. It's about slowing down enough to listen to the beat of the natural.

- *Do you find your life too full of 'the next thing' to be able to listen?*
- *When things get really 'quiet', what do you hear?*
- *What would it look like for you to carve out more space to be still and listen?*

'Our bodies and our minds want to heal, and oftentimes we just need to let them'

ANTHONY, THE ORIGINAL Desert Father, set out into an arid area of Egypt to seek solitude. He was soon joined by others who formed themselves into small communities. Ironically, the desire to be alone led to the formation of villages in the desert. This was then followed by the arrival of pilgrims who wanted to meet the Desert Fathers.

One of these monks, Simeon Stylites, was so frustrated about getting constantly interrupted that he started to climb up high poles so the pilgrims couldn't reach him to ask for advice. In the end he found an inaccessible ruin and lived for thirty-seven years on a little platform on top of a single pillar. That's extreme commitment to solitude.

At times I get it. I remember as a kid always having this one tree in our garden that I would climb when I needed some space. Community and relationship are the most precious gifts of life, and yet, our ability to constantly connect means we are never alone to hear that deeper voice. Our bodies and our minds want to heal, and oftentimes we just need to let them.

- *When were you last really alone? How long did it last?*
- *What do you notice about being on your own? How comfortable do you feel?*
- *Do you find it difficult to dedicate time for your spiritual needs?*

DAY 13

EXPECT THE BEST; PREPARE FOR THE WORST

THE 1979 FASTNET Race was the deadliest yacht race in history: twenty-four boats had to be abandoned; five boats sunk; 136 sailors had to be rescued; fifteen sailors and four rescuers lost their lives.

The disaster was precipitated by a storm blasting the race with 80-knot winds, and waves as high as 50-foot, and initiated the largest maritime rescue operation ever mobilised.

Why it happened is a catalogue of improbabilities. But an important factor was simply that, in British and Irish coastal waters in August, a storm of such devastating proportions just wasn't expected. Assumption, as we all know, is the doorway to disaster.

In familiar environments, we can easily make assumptions that get us in trouble when there are threats that we should be alert to. It's not that we should spend our lives over-anticipating risk, but it's about living with a healthy recognition that feeling safe and being safe can be two different things.

Being alert, especially in a setting where familiarity can blind us to danger, is smart. As we say in the wild: complacency kills.

So stay alert. Expect the best. But prepare for the worst. Be ready.

- *Do you find the more familiar you are with something, the less you consciously consider the risks?*
- *How could you make a habit of staying alert and being prepared even in the most familiar environments?*

'When activities are second nature, our mind shifts into autopilot'

AUSTRALIA IS HOME to some of the most poisonous creatures on the planet, including the Sydney funnel-web spider. Modern, effective antivenoms mean that funnel-webs have reportedly only killed thirteen people, but their potential to terminate life is terrifying.

The spiders love dark places, which is why Australians make a habit of knocking out their shoes before they put them on. It can be hard to imagine something as basic as putting on your shoes demands a potentially life-saving check before you do it.

And it is so easy to overlook doing it, because your mind is on other things. Activities that we feel are second nature are often times when our mind shifts into autopilot. Being 'mindful' is not just about avoiding hazards, it's about living in each moment with a calm awareness. Never in neutral, but always tuned in. It's a skill.

Learn from the past, hope for the future, but be in the present. It's all we really have.

- *Do you find your mind drifting to the past or the future a lot of the time?*

- *Does this mean you miss things of value in the here and now, or that you are disengaged from important tasks?*

- *What can you do to be more mindful, to hone your consciousness in the present moment?*

EMPOWERING TEAMS

EVERY TWO YEARS, the best 'castells' gather in Tarragona, Spain to compete to make the tallest and most complex human towers. Each team spans all ages and social backgrounds and involves hundreds of people. The best castells form human towers nine or even ten stories high.

At the base of the tower, the strongest men grip each other tight. As the tower grows, smaller, lighter men, women and then finally children form each tier. To complete the tower, a child of seven or eight clambers up the stack of human bodies to take their place at the pinnacle. Only the physically strongest members can hold the foundation of the tower – but their true power is in enabling the physically smallest to climb to the top. They are a beautiful example of 'together stronger'. A castell's success is not built on an individual's performance, but on the quality of the grip between the individuals.

It is only when we can support each other, and depend on each other, that we create the culture of a winning team.

- *Have you experienced an ineffective team where the strongest trample over the weakest to reach the top?*
- *What do you find inspiring about the principles of the castells?*
- *How strong is the 'grip' within any team you are part of? How could you help strengthen it in how you participate?*

'Inspiring leaders give those around them the strength and courage'

THE ANGLICAN CHAPLAIN Geoffrey Studdert Kennedy, aka 'Woodbine Willie', volunteered as a chaplain to the army on the Western Front at the outbreak of World War I.

Studdert Kennedy was fearlessly committed to the men he served. He carried no gun, just Woodbine cigarettes that he would give out to any who asked. He would crawl out into the notoriously lethal no-man's-land to lie with fatally injured men in the mud, so they did not have to die alone. In 1917, he was awarded the Military Cross for his courage under fire, and it was said of him that 'his cheerfulness and endurance had a splendid effect upon all ranks in the front line trenches'.

Inspiring leaders give those around them the strength and courage to achieve their objectives, no matter the costs. Willie's 'cheerfulness and endurance' empowered whole companies of soldiers to keep up their spirit and fight in horrendous conditions.

Ultimately, the fact that Willie was alongside them, at every turn and danger, set his leadership apart at the highest level. Great leadership can be summed up in three words: example, example, example.

- *What inspires you about the way Woodbine Willie stood alongside those he led?*
- *Can you recall a leader who empowered a team to persist despite huge challenges?*
- *Could you have a greater eye for people left behind in a team?*

CHARACTER IS KING

LEGENDARY UCLA BASKETBALL coach John Wooden won ten national titles, but he was much more than a brilliant strategist. Wooden was interested in developing his players beyond the 'wooden boards'. His premise was that 'ability may get you to the top, but character keeps you there: mental, moral and physical'.

The word 'character' comes from the Greek *kharakter*, meaning 'an engraver's mark'. Character is a sign of a deeper set of values and ideas that are more than what may be apparent on the surface. In the same way that a hallmark speaks about the quality of the gold, character speaks about the quality of the heart.

Character shouldn't be mistaken for personality or reputation. Those things may express something about us, but they aren't really what make us 'us'. Character is not found, it's forged. And, it's often in those moments when we are under pressure to keep quiet or go with the flow that we get to build and test and strengthen it the most.

- *Can you think of someone you know who has good character? Could you spend time with them to 'catch' something of that?*

- *How would you describe your character (aside from your personality or habits)?*

- *How would you like to forge your character further in the year ahead?*

'Character may be revealed in the big moments, but it is developed in the small ones'

BEFORE THE WAR, Richard Davis Winters was working part-time jobs to pay his way through college. He then volunteered, and soon found himself as a Lieutenant in charge of a platoon within the elite 2nd Battalion, 506th Parachute Infantry Regiment, 101st Airborne Division. Winters went on to become one of the most respected military leaders of his time, awarded the DSC, Bronze Star and Purple Heart. He said, 'I know of no man who lacked character in peace and then discovered his character in combat.' The story of 'Easy Company' became immortalised in the television series *Band of Brothers*.

When the battles come, character is forged. Winters truly led by example. He was reflective and modest. He gave credit to others. He was self-aware and resourceful. He understood and cared about the needs of his team. Under pressure, he just did what he knew was right.

Character may be revealed in the big moments of life, but it is developed in the small ones. It's often in the decisions we make when nobody's looking, the way we treat the people who haven't got power or influence.

Aim for character and you will get reputation as well. Aim for reputation and you will have already missed character.

- *What character qualities do you admire in others?*
- *What example are you setting to people around you?*

MANAGING YOUR 'ELASTIC LIMIT'

I DON'T REMEMBER A huge amount about my physics lessons at school but one experiment I do recall was called Hooke's law. This involved hanging weights on fixed springs in the lab and watching what happened. It was a recipe for classroom chaos.

Hooke's law states that 'the extension of a spring is proportional to the load that is applied to it'. The experiment worked so long as you stayed within the elastic limit of the spring. Overloading the spring with too much weight had our springs snapping and uncoiling all over the place.

Equally, people are stretched proportionate to the pressure that they are under, and we all have an elasticity limit. Being smart enough to accept this reality can prompt us to make better decisions about what we are willing to take on and what we turn down, as well as asking for help if we need it.

- *If you were going to describe yourself as a spring, are you underloaded, overloaded or do you feel that you are carrying the demands of life well?*

- *How would you describe your 'elastic limit'? What does it feel like when you start getting near it?*

- *Which weights of responsibility that you are carrying are fixed, and which could you take off, at least intermittently?*

'Only we can create boundaries for ourselves'

ONE THING MY work life has taught me is that success doesn't respect your limits. There is never a point at which anyone sits you down and says, 'I think you are close to your limit so we are going to stop giving you opportunities.' In fact, the opposite is often true: the more you do well, the more you will be asked to do. At the end of the day only we can create boundaries.

The riskiest moment for a pilot is not at the start of their flying career, or even once they are allowed to start flying solo. Their greatest risk of error, according to the Federal Aviation Administration, is at around five hundred hours of flight time. It's the exact point at which the pilot begins to feel competent and successful.

Previous successes pose many risks. One is the temptation to take our eyes away from our vulnerabilities and to assume everything is OK. But when we achieve any of our goals in life, that is also the time we need to pay close attention to our limits and boundaries.

Saying no to something good is hard, but it is often also wise to protect ourselves and our relationships. This is especially true as you start to see positive progress in your career.

- *What is it about success that makes you willing to compromise your own boundaries?*
- *What would it look like for you to protect your own boundaries and say 'no' when you are over extended?*

FACING PRESSURE

I N 2019, THE deepest ever dive was achieved by a submarine, operated by Victor Vescovo. He reached a depth of 10,925 metres, where his craft had to endure the massive pressure of eight tons per square inch. The 'crush depth' of most ordinary submarines is only around 500 metres below the surface.

In contrast to ordinary steel-hull submarines, Victor piloted a 90mm-thick titanium hull that enabled it to withstand those extra-ordinary pressures. He had to trust that its structural strength would keep him alive.

Life can feel extremely pressurised, at times unbearably so. Like the steel-hulled submarines, when we rely on our own strength, it can feel like we are going to be crushed. Our steel isn't strong enough. But there are other strengths in life that can make a critical difference and take us to greater depths: friends, family, our communities and even professionals.

Another strength I have found when under pressure has been my faith. King David also knew this quiet confidence well before the era of submarines. He wrote: 'If I make my bed in the depths, you are there . . . even there your hand will guide me'. That's truly empowering in times of pressure.

- *Have there been times in your life when you've felt the pressure and feared you were being crushed?*
- *Are you relying on yourself to withstand them? Are there other people in your life you could reach out to?*

'When we rely on our own strength it can feel like we are going to be crushed'

OLYMPIC RUNNER LOUIS ZAMPERINI crashed into the ocean when his World War II B-24 plane's engine failed. He endured forty-seven days adrift in a life raft at the mercy of sharks, starvation and dehydration. He was finally captured by the Japanese in sight of land.

As a Prisoner of War, he endured levels of hardship, torture and humiliation that defy the imagination. Yet, somehow, Louis survived.

For years afterwards, he was filled with thoughts of hate and revenge. Until Louis remembered a prayer he had said when adrift in the Pacific. 'If you save me, I'll be yours forever.' Suddenly Louis was aware that he had the power to forgive his persecutors. The following year, he visited Japan to meet many of his former guards to forgive them face to face.

Louis was under unremitting pressure, both during his survival experience, and afterwards as he dealt with the emotional scars. In forgiveness, he exercised a power far greater than his tormentors'. Louis's story speaks to the truth that love relieves us from the pressure of hate and revenge. And love always wins.

- What do you find remarkable about Louis's survival story?
- What is surprising about his journey to forgiveness and the freedom it gave him?
- Has forgiveness ever relieved pressure in your life?

ADVERSITY AND CONNECTION

IFE CAN BE hard, at times brutal. We all have to face pain, loss, grief, broken relationships or ill health at some point, and many other types of adversity besides. Christopher Reeve, the original Superman actor, broke his back in a riding accident. He reflected: 'At some time, often when we least expect it, we all have to face overwhelming challenges. When the unthinkable happens, the lighthouse is hope. Once we find it, we must cling to it with absolute determination.'

On one hand, adversity can stretch us in a positive way. After all, kites only rise against the wind. But there is also the reality that adversity can turn into trauma if we experience too much, for too long, on our own and with no help.

Looking back, whenever I've had some long periods of what felt like tough times, whether with work, relationships or injury, I know I would have struggled to get through if I hadn't been able to share honestly how I felt with friends and family. Sharing our experiences can profoundly reduce the negative impact they have on us.

- *Are you facing an overwhelming challenge alone?*
- *What is stopping you from sharing your experience with others?*

'The first step towards connection is always worth it'

WHEN WE ARE isolated, difficult experiences can all too easily become traumatising and confidence-sapping. Psychologist Peter Fonagy says, 'Adversity turns into trauma when you experience your mind as being alone. If you have good relationships they actually help you assimilate that experience.'

Breaking out of isolation can be hard, I know. But taking the first step towards connection is always worth it. In life, in adventure, in times of battle, you don't have to go it alone. Because together we are always stronger.

Are you going through something tough right now? If so, talk to a friend about it. Bring in others to help you carry the load. As my mum used to say: a problem shared is a problem halved.

- *Have you believed that you 'have to go it alone' on an issue?*
- *Who could you talk to about what you are dealing with?*
- *What would it feel like to halve the load?*

FIND A
MENTOR

WHEN I LOST my father in my mid-twenties, I felt so adrift without someone older to chat to and to ask advice from. I missed someone who I admired and trusted, who could be there for the key life decisions I was facing as a young man.

I did eventually find a mentor called Nicky, and I am genuinely grateful for all the kind, sage advice that he has given me over the years – for the wisdom and the time he invested when I needed it most.

Mentoring is not about giving control to someone else. It's about getting better control of your own life by increasing your access to wisdom, fresh perspective and broad experience. My best mentors have been people who have shared their experience, not their advice; they have left the responsibility to act entirely in my hands, without obligation: I respect that.

Getting a mentor is one of the most helpful tools for growth. Look for character and skills you admire. Give permission for honest feedback. Keep meetings light, short but honest. Be grateful and then get going.

- *What appeals to you about getting a mentor? What makes you feel nervous?*
- *Have you seen a great mentor/mentee relationship, and what results did it yield?*
- *Is there someone in your world who could offer you some mentoring?*

'It isn't just for you, it's for the people you will mentor in the future'

MENTORING IS A beautiful way to 'pay it forward'. When somebody has shared their wisdom with us, we, in turn, can offer ours to others.

The climbing world is a perfect example. I was a 23-year-old rookie when I started climbing on the bigger Himalayan peaks. At the top of my mentoring mountain were the Nepalese Sherpas. They had knowledge and such a generous and gentle disposition. They helped me so much, at every stage and on every mountain. There was also Neil, a Special Forces officer who went on to summit Everest alongside me. He believed I had what it took, even when I doubted myself.

When you come down one of the world's highest mountains, it becomes your turn to answer the questions. As a mentor our role is to be encouraging and honest, and to listen – never proud or showy.

It's a great calling and can be so rewarding, and it is a gentle way to keep the positive cycles of life turning.

- *Can you think of a time when you received wisdom from a mentor and then directly passed it onto someone else?*
- *Are there people who are already acting as mentors to you without you realising the role they are playing?*
- *What excites you about mentoring somebody else?*

MINDSET FOR THE IMPOSSIBLE

I N 2017, AMERICAN climber Alex Honnold shocked the whole world when he made the first free-solo (without ropes or protection) ascent of El Capitan, a 3,000-feet vertical rock slab, in Yosemite National Park. Until then, professional climbers had reckoned it was next to impossible. Alex achieved it in under four hours.

Achieving something 'impossible' is no mean feat. Climbing coach Pete Whittaker believes it was Alex's ability to control his mindset that set him apart. He understood how to keep a *relaxed* mindset on the easier sections. And an *engaged* mindset, absolute focus, on the harder sections. It was Alex's ability to flip from one to the other at will which enabled him to achieve the 'impossible'.

Free climbing requires more focus than probably any other sport; a momentary lapse of concentration is the difference between life and death. But by actively oscillating between being engaged and relaxed, Alex used his deepest concentration when he needed it most.

When it comes to achieving something 'impossible', focus is everything. And if failure isn't terminal – as it would be on El Capitan – what do you really have to lose?

- *How could oscillating between a relaxed and engaged mindset help your own concentration?*
- *Can you think of a time when your focus enabled you to make exceptional progress?*

'One of the greatest obstacles to achievement is focus, not talent'

MOST OF US have been told we can do anything we put our minds to. It is sometimes hard to believe it, but there is a lot of truth in it. One of the greatest obstacles to achievement is not talent, but focus. Research suggests our attention spans have actually dropped by four seconds since the mobile phone revolution. If this is true, what sets people apart will be their ability to focus.

Alex Honnold used two techniques: the 'novelty method', switching between relaxed and engaged, making every engaged moment 'feel' new and, therefore, attention-grabbing. The second was harnessing fear. Alex says it 'is pretty close to warrior culture, where you give something 100% focus because your life depends on it'. You believe it is possible.

Being 2,000 feet up a rock face without a rope is going to improve our focus, but it is also solitary and darned scary. I have learnt with scary situations that I not only need to be intentional about the way I think but also put myself in a situation *where* I am able to think. That means putting all superfluous distractions to one side. It is why focus is king to those who can master it. Do this consistently and you can achieve the 'impossible'. Ask Alex.

- *Which positive mindset method might you try to extend your focus and concentration?*
- *How do distractions change the level to which you can engage? What can you do about them?*

CAMP OUT

I T'S EASY TO think that camping is something you do because of another activity: 'I'm camping out because I am walking, fishing or on an expedition.' But camping is an activity in its own right. It's a physical, emotional and spiritual reboot.

Since I was really young, the excitement of sleeping outside was something I felt deep within me. Something natural and right. Lying under a night sky and breathing cool, fresh air can be intoxicating.

Camping is a great exchange; we swap all of the things we think we need, for all of the things we really need. When people camp for the first time, it will often feature some complaints, especially if it's raining. Fear of doing new things often elicits that response. But even reluctant campers find it hard not to be touched by the simplicity of being under the night sky.

American naturalist John Burroughs wrote, 'I go to nature to be soothed and healed, and to have my senses put in order.' That's why we do it.

- *Have you decided against camping? What things have put you off?*

- *What do you think about camping as a sort of natural 'therapy'? Could a little discomfort be part of the journey?*

- *What might it be like to give it another (or first) go, with a deeper willingness to let nature set the pace? Perhaps with a bigger tent and thicker sleeping bag?*

'It seems to call out something ancient and instinctual within us'

MOST PEOPLE WHO say they don't like camping are often simply reluctant to let nature be in charge. I think this resistance to nature's wisdom is one of the reasons so many people are so stressed and unhappy. The greatest challenge of technology is that it makes everything faster. And speed can be the killer of calm.

Camping is a sort of deliberate regression. It's about getting back to when fire, food, water and shelter were the determining factors in human survival. On that level, it seems to call out something ancient and instinctual within us. Maybe that's why food tastes better when you cook it on an open fire. It feels like more than food, it feels like triumph.

Pippa Middleton wrote, 'Whatever form it takes, camping is earthy, soul enriching and character building'. My top five tips for a 'soul-enriching' trip are: 1. Leave unnecessary technology behind; 2. Keep your plan as simple as possible; 3. Take only what you can carry; 4. Focus on the camp not the activities; 5. Let everything take the time it takes. Less is more. In terms of people, gear, time – you don't need much to get so much.

- *How is living life in the 'fast lane' impacting your wellbeing?*
- *Could camping reboot your sense of perspective?*
- *Could you put up a tent in your back garden this weekend?*

A SECURE BASE, A SAFE HAVEN

THE PRINCIPLE OF establishing a secure base is at the heart of nearly every activity that requires us to venture into the unknown: mountaineering, humanitarian work, military operations. Even staff rooms at work. They all echo our need to embrace adventure from a place of security.

Camp Bastion was a British Army airbase in Afghanistan, the largest British overseas military camp built since World War II. It provided a crucial, secure base for up to thirty thousand service personnel, in a very uncertain environment.

In life, operating out of our inner 'secure base' equips us to venture into the unknown and to take risks. It is about knowing we always have a safe place to regroup, recover and to go back out from.

I have found great security in my life from the non-judging relationships around me, from my Christian faith and in the memories of some of the harder experiences I have made it through.

Wherever you find it, use it and lean on it.

- *Are there physical 'secure bases' in your life?*
- *To what extent do you carry a secure base within?*
- *Are you acting as a secure base for others?*

*'The secure base, which launched us
into the adventure, needs to be matched
by a safe haven when we find ourselves
in a recovery phase'*

EVEREST BASE CAMP in Nepal is a hive of activity, like a mini city at 17,598 feet. I experienced a palpable sense of energy in the high altitude as determined, focussed climbers organised their equipment and discussed strategies.

What people don't tend to see about the camp is that it is also a 'safe haven' for exhausted, disheartened and sometimes grieving climbers.

We all need such a place at times. When plans haven't quite worked out as we hoped, or when we are bruised by life. The secure base, which launched us into the adventure, needs also to become a safe haven when we are in need of a recovery phase.

Safe havens can include a set of relationships in which we feel protected and able to share our struggles freely. Or it can be mindsets and attitudes, like self-compassion and forgiveness. It can have tools we adopt to help us recover, before we embark again onto the high mountain of life. Mount Endeavour.

- *Can you think of an example of a safe haven in your life, or a time when you were held and comforted by others?*
- *How could you be more intentional about leaning on your safe havens? How could you be a safe haven to others?*

FINDING
THE FIRE

FOR A LONG time, the unwritten motto of the British Special Forces has been: always a little further. At the end of one particularly gruelling mountain march, when we were at the limits of our endurance, the trucks that were waiting to collect us at the final point just roared into life and drove off into the darkness. We were told to turn around and go back over the mountains once again, with all the weight still on our backs. But we could hardly move at a shuffle, we were so exhausted.

Several recruits slumped to the ground and said they were done. They quit. But others just quietly shouldered their loads and turned back towards the mountain and kept going.

It's an attitude that says: when people around you are throwing in the towel, make that a trigger to give more. We can all find that spirit, if we choose. The fire to keep moving forward against the odds. To hang on and endure beyond the norm. A stubborn resolve that refuses to give in.

Life isn't about being brilliant all the time. It's often more fundamental than that. At times it is simply about giving that little bit extra when it really matters.

- *Have you ever felt that fire to give that little bit more?*
- *Who has inspired you by their resolve to keep going?*
- *What would it look like for you to turn back towards the mountain and go again?*

'Sometimes an ember
is all it takes'

PEOPLE OFTEN THINK that they aren't strong, when in truth they are. When the storms of life come they tend to strip away the fluff. What we often find underneath is raw and unshaped, but it is powerful. Sometimes it's well buried – no more than a tiny ember glowing in a heap of ashes. But that fire is always there. And it can change everything.

In our hardest moments, there'll always be that little voice of doubt: give up, it says. The temptation is to bow to its command. But remember: sometimes an ember is all it takes. That tiny refusal to give up. So, keep going . . . one small shuffle at a time.

That fire inside is our most valuable weapon in life. Use it. Be proud of it. It's a gift from above.

- *Have you believed that you aren't strong?*
- *When have you had to hold on and what has it shown you?*
- *How could you harness the fire inside?*

CHARGING LIFE

NAZARÉ IS A sleepy harbour town in Portugal. It's also the big wave surfing capital of the world. The giant waves at Nazaré form due to the presence of a huge underwater canyon that funnels the incoming ocean swell inland, dramatically enlarging the waves' height.

Watching the waves at Nazaré, you might wonder why anyone would risk paddling out. But the surfers are more like Gladiators than athletes, battling giants under the gaze of the crowds who line the Fort of São Miguel Arcanjo.

As humans, we are designed to be stretched. Without challenge we deteriorate. 'Predictable' isn't always challenging, and 'totally safe' isn't always fulfilling. Sure, there will be some scary moments when we have to commit. Big wave surfers feel this every day. But they embrace that daunting, creeping nervousness – turning those nerves on their head and choosing an 'all-in' attitude. They call it 'charging'.

There is a deep primal joy in these moments. You don't know the outcome – that's the whole point – but you surrender to the adventure. That's life at its best.

- *Have you developed a tendency to avoid being out of your depth?*
- *Can you recall a moment when you 'committed' anyway? How did it feel?*
- *Might there be opportunities for you to live more whole-heartedly and 'charge' life?*

'Charging in life isn't a moment, it's a state of mind. And it can change everything'

IN 2013, BRAZILIAN Maya Gabeira was towed-in by jet-ski to an incredible wave of around eighty feet, during a monster swell at Nazaré. It would have been a record-breaking ride.

As she dropped down the huge face, the worst happened. Maya was crushed under the huge power of the wave and, in the fall, her life vest was ripped off. She broke her ankle and nose, sustained spinal injuries and was knocked unconscious. It was nine minutes before a rescue jet-ski could pull her from the water.

Seven years later, Maya broke the women's world record for the largest wave ever surfed, at 73.5 feet, back at Nazaré.

Sometimes, the knock-downs in life can feel utterly brutal, but they are also opportunities for growth. Maya said, 'I had to find the humility within me to be around the ocean . . . and watch everyone shine, knowing it wasn't my time to be'.

There are times when life will humble us all, but we can decide either to fade into the shadows or start 'charging' again. Maya came back stronger, both physically and mentally, but she also came back wiser, ready to make her humility count when it mattered.

- Is there an experience in life that really humbled you?
- What did you learn and how did you become stronger as a result?
- What would it look like for you to follow Maya's example and 'paddle back out'?

KNOW YOUR MISSION PLAN

OPERATION OVERLORD WAS the name of the Allied plan to liberate Europe. The iconic images of D-Day are familiar to many of us, but the Overlord mission plan involved much more than D-Day itself.

The detail and scale of the plan were phenomenal: millions of tons of fuel, munitions, food, equipment, support vehicles. In truth, Operation Overlord delivered a victory of planning well before it delivered a victory on the beaches.

Sometimes when we ask for people's plans, they give us their goals: 'My plan is to become the first member of my family to go to university'; 'My plan is to earn enough to retire early'. It's essential to have a goal, but the plan that we put together is made up of the steps we take between here and that goal.

There are two sorts of plans: 'action plans' cover those concrete steps; 'method plans' are about how we will behave along the way. My method plans tend to be: Aim big. Empower others. Keep disciplined. Never give up.

If you develop a detailed action plan, backed up with your method plan, you are going to make solid progress, even if you face many obstacles in the road.

- *Can you distinguish between your action and method plans?*
- *How might spending more time shaping and defining your goals and plans increase the chances of you getting there?*

'Circumstances might mean my "action plans" have to change, but the method stays consistent'

WHEN ASKED ABOUT his fight plan against Evander Holyfield, Mike Tyson said, 'Everyone has a plan until they get punched in the face.'

I love that quote because it is so true about life and survival. It's only when your plans make contact with the real world that you can see their real value. It's also where our adaptability is important.

It's why I like running the twin tracks of action and method planning. Circumstances might mean my 'action plans' have to adapt and change, but the 'method'? That stays consistent.

My time in 21 SAS taught me both the value of careful planning and the value of adaptability. We tend to be far too quick to say, 'My plans have failed.' Actually, the steps to the goal might simply need to be adapted – but that doesn't mean all is lost. The action says: let's tweak the timelines and modify our steps; the method says: keep going.

The best plans are 'working documents': they aren't a 'last will and testament' on how it's going to go.

Define your goal. Decide your method. Devise your actions. Edit as necessary.

- *Does breaking plans into different aspects increase your confidence?*
- *What would it look like for you to be more adaptable and less rigid while staying committed to your goal?*

FIT YOUR OWN MASK FIRST

EVERY IN-FLIGHT SAFETY briefing includes the instruction, 'If the oxygen masks are released, put on your own mask before helping anyone else'. The reason they state this so clearly is because, for many people, it is counter-intuitive.

As a parent, I know how tempted I would feel to start helping my family first. It's human nature. And, sometimes, it feels easier and safer to look elsewhere rather than looking after ourselves.

But in so many circumstances, helping yourself is helping others. In this in-flight scenario, you can see how a 'helper' who has fallen unconscious is no help at all. Instead, they leave their family worse off and create massive challenges for airline staff!

When we seek to help others, unaware of our own need for help, the risk is that we create even greater damage, including to those who are relying on us.

- *How comfortable do you feel about helping yourself before helping others? Is it counter-intuitive to you?*
- *Can you think of a time recently when you received help from others without feeling the need to return the favour?*
- *How might getting help enable us to be better at helping those around us?*

'Making sure we are well-resourced is important'

IT'S OK NOT to be OK. Even if you are a person with a high level of responsibility for others. We all have moments. I definitely do. And every helper needs help sometimes.

Cancer-survivor and self-care expert Les Brown writes, 'Regardless of what challenge you are facing right now, know that it has not come to stay. It has come to pass. During these times, do what you can with what you have, and ask for help if needed. Most importantly, never surrender. Put things in perspective. Take care of yourself. Find ways to replenish your energy, strengthen your faith and fortify yourself from the inside out.'

Prioritising self-care can be as basic as taking some time in our day to be alone, or it might be something more defined – like seeking out a professional counsellor to talk to. Helping others is one of the most crucial, empowering and best things we can do in life, so making sure we are well-resourced to do it is important.

- *Do you feel able to take time to get replenished when you are in a caring role?*
- *When you explore your emotional resources right now, are there enough inputs to keep your resources for your role?*
- *What do you need to change, or who do you need to speak to, to make sure your voice is heard and your needs are met?*

HOPE AND HUMOUR

'IT'S BEEN A bit of a long shift,' joked Luis Urzúa after seventy days underground. Luis was the foreman of the thirty-three Chilean miners trapped inside a mine in 2010. His level-headedness and good humour are credited as a major factor in keeping their morale high, ensuring they stayed focused on survival.

Low on food and water and suffering in extreme heat, it would have been easy to despair. Not knowing if rescue is coming is one of the greatest survival challenges. It requires both a deep level of courage and some optimism. Without the hope that help is coming, people can easily neglect the everyday steps needed to remain physically well – and without humour it's hard not to become pessimistic.

Our own crisis moments may not look as dramatic as the Copiapó mining accident, but they are still significant. And in those times, hope and humour are bedrocks for a resilient mindset. Whether you are trying to be a friend in a crisis, or going through a tough time yourself, remember Luis Urzúa's hope and humour. They can conquer all.

- *Can you remember a moment when a well-timed joke in a difficult situation changed the atmosphere for the better?*
- *What do you notice about the need for both hope and humour in crisis situations?*
- *Have you got a funny friend in your life that you could draw inspiration from?*

'Laughter should never be far from our sides'

WHEN I LOOK back on many adventures, I am amazed at how often humour has turned a stressful near-death event around.

When I was totally stuck in mud, and when I might have appreciated sympathy from one of the crew, instead what I got was some quip about how inefficiently I was moving.

At times, a little black humour can lighten a hellish moment. Yet despite humour being such a powerful force for good, it often gets sidelined for use by children and comedians only. That's a mistake. Laughter should never be far from our sides, especially against ourselves. The best sort.

Cindi May, writing in the *Scientific American* says, 'Humour plays a powerful and important role in the human experience.' It is free, and yet it can be the most generous of gifts. If we can see the enduring value in humour, not only do we get to see the funny side of many tough situations, but we give ourselves a resource to look back on with fondness and a smile as we remember those times.

- *How has humour impacted your mood or stress levels?*
- *When did you last laugh uncontrollably? If it's been too long to remember, what could you do about it?*
- *Is there someone who needs your help today? You may not feel like a naturally 'funny' person, but what joy or lightness could you offer them?*

THE CHALLENGE OF INTIMACY

WHEN IT COMES to building deeper relationships with people, I have found that we connect most powerfully with others through our weaknesses, not through our strengths.

Intimacy is a circular experience: we are most prepared to share our weaknesses with people we trust. In turn, they typically match our trust and counter with their own struggles. This process builds a powerful sense of mutual acceptance and closeness.

The challenge of building intimacy is often found in the courage to take those first honest steps.

I've heard intimacy being described as 'into-me-see'. That can feel very exposing, especially if you come from a background where people have tended to be private or only share their strengths. We may fear people will judge us, but we will only know real friendship when we allow people to see who we really are. The good, the bad, the real and, at times, the ugly.

With great relationships, the risk of vulnerability has always been worth taking. Intimacy takes courage to share and build. But no risk, no reward.

- *Do you find yourself backing away from intimacy because of the fear of being rejected?*
- *Can you think of an example of a relationship that is built on mutual acceptance and trust?*

'The sooner we share our true selves, the more likely we are to build powerful, enduring relationships'

WHEN IT COMES to building real intimacy, our greatest barrier is often rooted in a fear of being rejected. So we 'put our best foot forward' whenever we meet new people, only showing our winning, successful, confident side. In truth, those parts can be the least interesting parts of us, and only sharing our 'good' attributes actually creates the weakest of connections. This is often seen most clearly online; the less secure the relationship, the more likely we are to over-promote ourselves.

But great relationships demand vulnerability. The sooner we can share our true selves, including our fears and struggles, the more likely we are to build powerful, enduring relationships. It's a decision to do our best to be real; not to over- or under-sell ourselves. Think of it like a boiled egg. The outer shell is hard, the superficial white layer is quite bland, but the heart of the egg, the yolk, is like pure gold.

- Have you got a tendency always to 'put your best foot forward'?

- What would it feel like to be more transparent about who you really are, despite the risk of rejection?

- How would you describe the part of you that you tend to share most, in terms of the boiled egg theory?

SLOW TO
SAY YES

YES IS A small word that has massive implications in our lives. Those three letters are all that is needed to commit to a marriage, climb a mountain, choose a home or start an adventure. It feels good to say 'yes' but our decisions can have big repercussions. I've learnt in life that it's better sometimes to say 'yes' a little slower and 'no' a little faster.

Saying 'yes' too fast is often tempting. Especially when we want to avoid letting other people down. But this can leave us feeling a little stuck. We can find that we have made a commitment that we feel obliged to keep, but maybe haven't got the time, skills or resources to achieve. The result can be we end up having to disappoint people or struggle to meet our commitments.

Asking for more time to decide on something is a good call all round. Not only do you get to consider whether it is something that you want to do and have the capacity to do. It also says something positive about your character – that you are a considered and thoughtful person. Whether you say yes or no in the end, the extra time will have helped you.

- *Have you felt tempted to say 'yes' quickly?*
- *What are you afraid will happen if you take your time to respond?*

'People are far more generous and understanding than we might fear'

ENTREPRENEUR JIM ROHN said, 'Don't let your mouth overload your back'. It's wise to allow some thinking space before we give our 'yes' and make sure that we really have the resources for what we are being asked to do.

On the other hand, when it comes to saying 'no', I've found it's easy to procrastinate while we wait to see if a situation or relationship might come good in time. Or else we delay, wondering if doing something we sense is 'short-term-nice-but-long-term-damaging' is really such a bad thing after all.

In those cases, it's always better to say a clear, firm 'no' early on, than end up in a tricky situation further down the road. People tend to respect honest clarity, and a gentle, unapologetic 'no' is always OK.

I've learnt that people are far more generous and understanding than we might fear. Like many things in life, when we communicate humbly, clearly and kindly, even difficult conversations can be well received.

As the saying goes: 'Fools rush in where angels fear to tread.' And a clear 'no' without lots of convoluted explanations is just fine as it is.

- *How do you feel about saying 'no'?*
- *Do you tend to backtrack, or weaken your resolve after giving a firm 'no'?*
- *How could you communicate humbly, clearly and kindly?*

DAY 47

BEYOND ACHIEVEMENT

FOR ERIC LIDDELL, the prize was not a medal. It was something much bigger. Liddell was already a Scottish international rugby player and a record-breaking athlete when he went to the Paris Olympics in 1924.

Declining to run the 100 metres on a Sunday, because of his faith, he ran and won the 400 metres and achieved bronze in the 200 metres. Reflecting on his achievements Liddell said, 'God made me fast. And when I run, I feel his pleasure.' That was his prize.

Expressing our gifts, through effort, and in line with our hearts, is a mountaintop experience. It is how we connect with the best of ourselves. Those fully alive moments are how we are called to live. And we can create those moments every day.

We might not be a champion athlete, but it's not about that stuff. It's about doing our best, following our hearts, being kind along the way, and having a never-give-up spirit.

As Liddell said: 'In the dust of defeat as well as the laurels of victory there is a glory to be found if one has done his best.'

- *Are you aware of a greater sense of delight in your life when you are doing what you love?*
- *Has winning or losing had too much influence over your sense of fulfilment?*
- *What would you choose to spend your time doing if 'fully living' was the prize?*

'Treat every moment as "bonus time" and you see the world differently'

AUSTRALIAN NAVY DIVER Paul de Gelder was doing his dream job after years of feeling unfulfilled. In 2009, Paul dived into the sea to test a piece of naval tracking equipment. He was attacked almost immediately on the leg and arm by a bull shark weighing around 600lb.

The shark severed his right hand and mauled his right leg, which was amputated later. Paul had to put in extreme effort to rehabilitate and adapt to his injuries so he could continue in professional diving. Yet, despite the attack, after finding out more about the plight of sharks, Paul felt convinced to champion shark conservation. He now dives with sharks all over the world and promotes their protection.

Paul's true gift is his attitude. 'I'm on bonus time,' he says.

If we can treat every moment as a gift, as 'bonus time', we see the world differently. I know this as well, after my parachuting accident all those years ago. Close calls remind us how lucky we are to be alive. But the really smart person lives like this without needing the near-death part of the equation.

- *What do you think about Paul's move from shark attack survivor to shark conservationist?*
- *What do you notice about how Paul approaches diving, his effort in rehab and his love for shark conservation?*
- *How could an attitude towards life as 'bonus time' impact how you live?*

TOGETHER IN PAIN

I N MOMENTS OF pain, our instinct is often to scream, shout or swear. Research suggests these reactions have a 'hypoalgesic effect': they stimulate adrenaline production, which acts as an anaesthetic, effectively reducing the pain. Expressing pain, it turns out, reduces pain. Conversely, suffering in silence hurts us more.

During British military operations in Afghanistan, many soldiers suffered limb injuries as a result of IEDs. During rehabilitation, they learnt different techniques for dealing with acute pain. Soldiers often reported that the greatest relief actually came from the camaraderie they found with others, as well as from the nurses' care. It turns out that company, sympathy and empathy are proven effective ways to alleviate suffering.

When it comes to pain, many of us will have been told to 'man up'. As a result, many people suffer emotionally or physically all alone. This not only hurts us more, it also hurts us for longer.

If you are hurting in body or mind, talk to someone kind. Bottom line: it is proven to help. And you deserve good things in your life.

- *When it comes to reducing pain, what have you noticed about the impact of connecting with others?*
- *Can you think of a time when the care of another person made all the difference to you?*
- *Are you struggling with physical or emotional pain? Who could you express yourself to?*

'Life is never hopeless'

THIS DAY CONTAINS CONTENT RELATING TO SUICIDE

ONE OF THE toughest fights in life can be when we are in emotional pain and find ourselves isolated. Life can feel hopeless, and suicidal thoughts are much more common than most people realise. Barb Gay, a suicide survivor, writes, 'My experience wasn't necessarily that I wanted to die, I just didn't want to continue living with this amount of pain, especially because it was pain nobody could see.'

Life can, at times, feel truly distressing, but it is never hopeless. Suicide is never the solution it may appear to be. There is always a different and a better way. Just hold on and keep exploring your options. There are always things that will help, or people who will support you. Your doctor is a great starting point, but there are also lots of charities that can support you and will listen.

And asking someone you are worried about how they are doesn't make it more likely for them to act on these thoughts; instead it is often a huge relief. With the right support, many people who have struggled with suicidal thoughts go on to live happy and fulfilling lives.

- *Have you struggled with feelings of hopelessness? Have you got someone to talk to?*
- *Might it help to read about other people's experiences through either the Mind or Rethink websites?*
- *Are you worried about somebody? Can you offer a gentle listening ear?*

WANTING TO WIN VERSUS NEEDING TO WIN

ROGER FEDERER HAS won twenty Grand Slam titles and is one of the greatest tennis players of all time. He is also one of the best sportsmen you'll ever meet, not only because he is a fearsome competitor but also because of his gracious manner on and off the court – in victory and in defeat.

You cannot win in the top level of sport without courage and an absolute determination to fight. To the end. But it's important to understand the difference between wanting to win and needing to win.

Being competitive is healthy. But *needing* to win is a sign our identity is rooted in our achievement. It is very hard to lose (or win) with grace if we 'need' victory. The truth is that when we lose, we show our character.

When you can take responsibility for losing as quickly as you take responsibility for winning, then that competitive spirit is serving you best.

As Federer said: 'I enjoyed the position I was in . . . I was to blame when I lost. I was to blame when I won. And I really like that'.

- *Do you feel the need to win at all costs? And, if so, why?*
- *What do you admire about successful sportspeople? Does a loss change your estimation of them?*
- *Are you able to chase a victory just for the fun of it? How does loss affect you?*

'Be content when you've given your all, and quick to celebrate others'

CAPTAIN SCOTT'S JOURNEY to the South Pole was as tough an expedition as had ever been mounted. But Norwegian Roald Amundsen's unexpected appearance in Antarctica turned it into a competition, billed 'The Race to the Pole'. The Norwegians' victory dubbed them the 'winners', but Scott's team were by no means 'losers'; they too reached the South Pole just a month afterwards.

While the competitive element was not the only factor in the disaster that followed, it had a huge impact on the team's morale. Scott wrote in his diary: 'It is a terrible disappointment, and I am very sorry for my loyal companions.' They would never make it off the ice.

Behind unhealthy competition is an assumption that life is populated by 'winners and losers', be it the overt rankings of school exams or more subtle social judgements about who is in and who is out. True sportspeople give their all, but remain calm if others succeed first. (For the record, Federer lost his first competitive match 0-6, 0-6.)

So play the long game. Be content when you've given your all. And be quick to celebrate others. That's a winner.

- *Have you suffered as a result of being judged by others?*
- *To what extent have you found yourself falling into competition because of the competitiveness around you?*
- *Could you refuse to compete unnecessarily, seeking to encourage others to be first?*

THE DANGER OF HALF-HEARTEDNESS

WHEN IT COMES to handling dangerous snakes, my principle is 'pin it securely as close to the head as you can – carefully grip it so you control the head 100 per cent – then don't loosen that grip one bit!'

The one thing not to do is to pick up a snake half-heartedly by the body, or it will bend back on itself and bite you faster than you can let it go. In a similar way, if you're tackling anything dangerous, commitment is an essential ingredient to success.

Most of the good things in life carry risk; all our decisions and actions have consequences, both positive and negative. And like with the snake, the least effective method is tepid hesitancy in the middle area.

- *Have you found yourself making hesitant or half-hearted decisions in the past? What has happened as a result?*
- *Has a specific disappointment or humiliating experience in your past made you cautious to commit wholeheartedly?*
- *What do you notice about people who commit to a decision with conviction and determination?*

'Commitment is going for it after you have done the maths'

IF YOU'RE GOING to make a decision, then commit wholeheartedly, especially if the risks are high. I've often seen moments of indecision thwart people's progress and compromise their safety in the wild, where a tentative approach to a risky situation can increase the danger significantly.

My mother used to say this to me before I'd go and play sports: 'Remember: tentative is no power. Go all in. Then there can be no regrets.'

Recklessness and commitment are not to be confused. Recklessness is leaping before you look. Commitment is going for it after you have done the maths. You know it's doable, but it's scary. T. D. Jakes wrote, 'You cannot conquer what you are not committed to.' If you have decided to go for it – whether it's a relationship, a business venture, a career change or any other significant life decision – then back yourself and go all in.

- *What would it feel like to fully commit to a decision, and can you imagine the power it would create?*

- *In your experience, what is the difference between you being reckless and being committed?*

- *Would it help you to get an objective view on your situation from an experienced friend or colleague? What difference could their perspective make?*

GET OUT OF YOUR ECHO CHAMBER

IF EVERYONE YOU get advice from looks, dresses, speaks and thinks like you, you are getting bad advice. Ultimately, if everyone around you agrees with you, you're in trouble.

An old proverb says, 'As iron sharpens iron, so one person sharpens another.' The sharpening process isn't necessarily comfortable, it often involves conflict and sometimes sparks fly, but that doesn't mean that it's not healthy or necessary.

It's not to say we should take advice from just anyone, but the people we do trust should be able to challenge our thinking. Sometimes we should stop and ask: which important people *aren't* in the room for this conversation to be effective? We all like to be with people who have similar values. That's not a bad thing, it's just human nature. Difference suggests threat, but it doesn't have to.

Listening beyond of our echo chambers isn't about discarding old connections, but about actively soliciting the opinions and perspective of people who are different from us. Those who might well disagree or see the world in a different light.

It doesn't mean we take it all to heart, but wisdom always comes from listening first.

- *Does everyone look and sound and think like you?*
- *What has kept you from connecting with people with different backgrounds, cultures or perspectives to your own?*

'I've come to see the importance of involving "difficult" people in my life'

THE WORLD-RECORD HOLDING echo reverberated for 112 seconds. From a single sound, that's nearly two minutes of sound confirmation. Echo chambers fuel 'confirmation bias' – the tendency to favour information which reinforces our existing beliefs. Author Eli Pariser sees Internet algorithms as a self-directed propaganda machine: 'indoctrinating us with our own ideas, amplifying our desire for things that are familiar'. Of course, the greatest danger of an echo chamber is to believe that everyone actually *does* think like us.

I have discovered the importance of involving a few 'difficult' people in my life. It's not that they are actually difficult, but their views are unique. There is so much value in listening to alternative opinions. After all, our minds are like parachutes; they only work when open.

If we want the best chance of making wise and informed decisions, we need to break up our echo chambers by surrounding ourselves with voices that we might, at first, find challenging. Only then will we know that we haven't chosen to hear them just because we really just want to hear ourselves.

- *Have you found yourself confirming your own thoughts and opinions through Internet algorithms?*
- *Are you able to welcome perspectives that are different from your own?*
- *What would it be like to build relationships with people who want to offer you truth over agreement?*

FOOD FOR THOUGHT

HIGH INTENSITY ACTIVITY, expending up to 10,000 calories/day, showed me the relationship between nutrition and performance. Quality food impacts my energy and how clear-headed I feel.

If we're constipated or bloated it affects everything – nature's way of saying 'stop and have a rethink about what you're fuelling me with'.

When I'm asked about my food choices, I'm cautious because what's right for me might not be for them. We're all different. But I think about three things: 1. Timing: I eat my daily portions within eight hours, leaving sixteen to rest and digest. Some call this intermittent fasting; 2. Quality: I source local, grass-fed meat (and organs), plus eggs, dairy, fruit and honey; 3. Proportions: I am thoughtful about balancing the different amounts of food I am eating. Plus, I avoid manufactured seed oils, processed sugars and wheat-based processed carbs.

I allow for 'treats' – I have a little chocolate and alcohol now and again. I don't 'restrict' myself. Self-discipline is important. I consider an 80/20 rule of regular food versus treats. You must do your own research to take an active approach to nutrition. It's worth it!

- *Have you felt guilty about making more active nutritional decisions because it looks 'ungrateful' for what you have?*

- *How relevant might timings, quality and proportions of food be to your nutrition plan?*

'It's relentless when we're bombarded by "easy" choices, even when our conscious mind knows they do us no good'

SOME OF THE stuff I've eaten over the years makes me wince: rat brain, goat's testicles, camel intestinal fluids, bats, snakes, scorpions and tarantulas, to name a few. Often raw, often on the move, almost always terrible. But survival is rarely fun or pretty.

Luckily, for much of the world, we don't have to live in permanent survival mode. Ironically, our greatest challenge is an over-abundance of choice and low-cost processed, sugar-laden, seed-oiled snacks and meals. These foods are marketed to appeal to us when we are tired, hungry, rushed or strapped for cash, emotions which target all of our survival senses. Hence the danger.

I find this as hard as anyone to handle. It's relentless when we're bombarded by 'easy' choices, even when our conscious mind knows they do us no good.

That's why I've found that seeking out a natural diet is an achievable, sustainable, logical solution. Natural, primal-based nutrition leaves me feeling much fuller and more satisfied – so it's then easier to avoid cravings for the quick-hit foods that leave us empty.

- *Do you consider how your food and its nutritional value can impact your mental and physical wellbeing?*
- *Do you consider healthy food to be boring and treat foods great? Could you find natural foods that fully satisfy you?*
- *When it comes to natural foods, how open-minded are you to finding a more ancestral way of fuelling up?*

STRESS VS DISTRESS

STRESS IS A natural human response to change: most of the time we aren't even aware that we are 'stressed' because we are so busy coping 'confidently' with the demands of our hectic lives. People are incredible. Their ability to meet the complicated challenges of life never fails to inspire and humble me. But keep a watchful eye out for yourself along the way, and nip stress in the bud when you can, before it damages you.

Distress is what we experience when we're unable to meet those demands for change. That's when we start noticing how 'stressed' we have become. Over time the weight of multiple demands can overwhelm our ability to respond well. When this happens, it can feel like we're caught in an avalanche.

Distress is painful, but it's not final. Remember that if you walked in, you can walk out again. It can take a while to get your bearings, maybe seek some direction, but you will get there. And, when you do, you will have learnt an essential new boundary.

- *Can you make the distinction between stress and distress in your life?*
- *What does it feel like when you are responding to change positively?*
- *What are the signs that show you are moving in a more negative direction?*

'If you can break down the load, the load won't break you'

WE ALL FEEL overwhelmed from time to time, me as much as anyone. Tasks, expectations and demands stack up to a point where it feels like we are stuck solid and just can't take any more.

I have been really helped by two things at these points in my life. The gentle support of others, and breaking down the demands one ball of snow at a time. List them out and focus on ticking them off. If you break down the load, the load won't break you.

Learn to say no sometimes and give yourself permission to take some time out regularly from the madness. Maybe schedule a regular bike ride or walk with a friend, a hot bath with the door firmly closed.

Little things go a long way. But above all, stay aware of your feelings and stress levels, and don't feel bad about protecting yourself on this adventure of life.

- *Have you been able to get into the detail of the pressure you feel and break tasks down?*
- *Have you been holding on until the end of the task list for too long? What breaks could you introduce?*
- *Who is in your corner, offering support and encouragement?*

DAY 61

ALL-OR-NOTHING THINKING

MY FRIEND, MICK CROSTHWAITE, was a key member of our team attempting to summit Everest in 1998. After three months on the peak, he got within 300 feet of the top, but problems with his oxygen tank and the weather meant that he was forced to go back.

In truth, he was lucky to get off the mountain with his life. It had been a tough decision to turn around for Mick, especially when he had been so close to the summit. But looking back, his expedition was a true success: he returned alive where others died.

I know how easy it is to develop a kind of all-or-nothing mentality, especially if you don't quite reach your goal. Everything can get framed in binary terms as either a success or a failure. When we start to see life through that lens we are missing out on so much.

- *Has your vision for success become binary between success and failure? Do you struggle when you fail to achieve your primary goal?*
- *How many different successes can you see in Mick's Everest journey despite the disappointment of coming so close to the summit?*
- *Can you think of a circumstance in your own life where you missed out on your goal? Can you try to list all of the associated successes that you did not see at the time?*

'The road to success is always under construction'

THE WORST SINKING feeling I have ever felt was being 'Returned To Unit' after four months of hard, cold, gruelling SAS selection. Everything I had worked for, all that sweat and effort and pain, for nothing. But one small ember remained: I was invited back to try again.

Rudyard Kipling wrote, 'If you can meet with Triumph and Disaster, and treat these two impostors just the same . . . Yours is the earth and everything that's in it . . .'

The road to success is always under construction; littered both with potholes and imperfect views. Accept the potholes as training and enjoy the views for whatever they are. Keep the long game always in mind. True success is never just one thing or a single destination. The real success comes through the journey itself and what we become along the way.

The summit or the trophy, the degree or the promotion, is simply a mark that we reached our goal. Don't look for more in it than is really ever there.

- *Do failures dominate your vision? What have you learnt from those 'failed attempts'?*
- *What does it look like for you to keep the long game in mind? When might it be right to 'go one more time'?*

SCOUTING PRINCIPLES TO LIVE BY

T HE SCOUTING PRINCIPLES were established by Lord Baden-Powell when he founded the Scout movement in 1907. And they remain relevant and empowering for all of us today.

Be Prepared is the best-known. My old sergeant used to say if you fail to plan, you plan to fail. It's true. Listen lots. Do your research. Time spent in preparation is never wasted. A huge part of preparation is practice. And the harder we practise, the luckier we become.

Be Trustworthy. This is absolutely key to good friendships, good business relationships and a strong family life. Being trustworthy means keeping our word. If we say we are going to do something, we do it.

Be Loyal. Loyalty is something humans prize as highly as any quality. It takes strength, because it's so easy to get swayed by the crowd. A good friend always walks in when the rest of the world walks out. I've seen this happen. And the friend who has the moral courage to do this sets themself apart.

The Scouting Principles might seem old-fashioned, but it is remarkable to see how valuable they are to living an empowered life, and how they continue to be fundamental to success.

- *How do you feel about these principles for living?*
- *Which of the three principles do you feel is a natural strength and which do you find hardest?*

'Principles become
who we are'

AMERICAN NEWSPAPERMAN WILLIAM BOYCE was hopelessly lost on a foggy London street when a young boy came to his aid, explaining how he could reach his destination. Boyce went to tip the boy, but the boy refused, saying he was a Boy Scout and was merely doing his good deed for the day.

Boyce was so impressed that he sought out a meeting with the Scouting movement's founder, General Baden-Powell, who told him more about what they were aiming to achieve. Boyce returned to America, and four months later, in February 1910, founded the Boy Scouts of America.

Principles are a great starting point. But it's the determination and commitment to put them into practice that counts. When we learn to drive, we are conscious of how to change gear, when to use the clutch, indicator and brakes. But before long, we reach the point that we hardly have to think about driving at all.

Over time, principles become who we are – someone prepared, trustworthy and loyal. And what we practice the most is what we become.

- *Can you think of any examples in your life when you started by following principles and ended up embodying them?*
- *What kind of traits do you admire most in others?*
- *Could you define the principles you want to live by?*

DAY 65

HUMILITY
FIRST

ONE OF THE reasons I love the mountains is that they remind us of our place in the universe. The pecking order is pretty clear: mountain, weather, you. Sometimes the mountain and the weather swap places, but we never come out on top. The mountains keep us humble.

The word 'humility' comes from the Latin *humus*, meaning 'ground'. To be humble is about being grounded. Unlike in the mountains, the pecking order in life is partly how we rank ourselves alongside others. We can either look up to other people, or look down on them. We can celebrate or diminish, encourage or dismiss, honour or patronise.

Humility isn't about thinking less of ourselves, it's about thinking about ourselves less. Far from being about low self-esteem, humble people often know their value, they just don't broadcast it to everyone else.

How you speak about others speaks loudest about yourself. Great people not only speak kindly of other people, but they consider others before themselves. That's true humility.

- *What value do you see in being humble? How does it make you feel when you see self-importance in people?*
- *Can you think of an example of someone in your life who is confident but also humble? What do you like about them?*
- *How could you more consciously show humility? What are your next steps?*

'Humility and humanity go hand in hand'

WE ALL HAVE the opportunity to demonstrate a little more humility in our lives – but it's sometimes most obvious and beautiful when we see it in the lives of people who could easily assume a position 'above' those around them. Maybe because of their success, status or wealth, it would be all too tempting for them to misuse those gifts to over-promote themselves, and yet they choose to put other people first. When we see people like this showing humility, it is so appealing. I always remember the quote: 'if you want to see a person's true character, give them everything.'

At the end of the day, humility and humanity go hand in hand. Pride is self-interested: people become commodities to be used for personal gain. But real humility is about loving people and using things, rather than using people and loving things.

Humility celebrates our shared nature – it is 'people first'. And if you keep humility in view, you will keep humanity in mind.

- *Can you think of an example of someone who surprised you by their humility?*
- *What have you noticed about the way that humble people see themselves and others?*
- *What have you noticed about the way that wealth and status can change the way we feel about people?*

DAY 67

WE'RE NOT THE SUM OF OUR MISTAKES

SOME PEOPLE NATURALLY see their mistakes as learning opportunities and let go of what's gone wrong with ease. They are the exception. Most of us have a tendency to file our mistakes for future reference. We end up going over them again and again, and mistakes expand into regrets that gnaw away in the background of our lives. 'I made a mistake' can become 'I am a mistake'.

Being humble enough to acknowledge when we have got it wrong is a crucial skill, but constant self-criticism is something else altogether – it is the enemy of happiness and leaves us without confidence or motivation.

Remember, when we make a mistake, we're not alone. As Albert Einstein said: 'Anyone who has never made a mistake has never tried anything new.'

- *Have you found yourself constantly reliving old mistakes?*
- *How could you see events more compassionately or as failed efforts with good intentions?*

'Wear those scars with pride. They show you've been in the thick of life'

PERSPECTIVE IS EVERYTHING.

Choosing to view our mistakes within the broader context of our lives can turn them from stumbling blocks into stepping stones. Suddenly the things that were a barrier can become the very things that link our successes together.

Richard Branson says, 'Do not be embarrassed by your failures, learn from them and start again.' I would take it further. Be proud of them. Wear those scars with pride. They show you've been in the thick of life and you're another step closer to your goals.

Are you burdened by regrets or constantly reminded of your mistakes? There is no need to be. It's a state of mind. Now go turn those stumbling blocks into stepping stones.

- *How have 'mistakes' redirected you towards new opportunities?*

- *Would you be who you are today if you hadn't learnt from what you got wrong?*

- *What would a kind friend say about the things you beat yourself up about?*

DAY 69

START WITH 'WHY NOT?'

BRITISH CLIMBER GEORGE MALLORY died on Everest in 1924. He was once asked why he was determined to scale the world's tallest mountain. 'Because it's there,' was his famous response.

Lots of coaches focus on the importance of identifying your 'why'. But needing a 'why' before we launch into anything new can be misleading. Arguably it is more important to ask 'why not?'

We don't always need a bigger reason for applying ourselves to a challenge beyond the challenge itself. This is true for any opportunity in life: learning a language, taking a trip, trying a new hobby, learning to cook or climbing a mountain. If you cannot see a reason *not* to commit, that is a reason to commit. Curiosity rather than virtue drives so many of life's greatest adventures.

It's easy to get overwhelmed by the need to find a justifiable reason to do something. But sometimes there may not be a clear 'why' until you begin. There is such power in just going for things sometimes . . . throwing caution to the wind and asking yourself simply: 'why not?'

- *Do you feel the need to find overwhelmingly positive reasons to do something before you'll commit to it?*

- *What would it look like for you to commit on the basis that there is no clear reason not to?*

- *How could curiosity rather than virtue drive you into some positive new experiences?*

'It's easy to get overwhelmed by the need to find a justifiable reason to do something'

WHEN THE SPANISH vessel *Vittoria* set out from Sanlúcar de Barrameda, in 1519, its crew had no defined 'why' other than their curiosity to see what might happen if they kept sailing west. Three years later, their ship sailed into Seville. They had just become the first people to circumnavigate the world.

Preoccupation with a 'why' leaves us less likely to see all the different reasons that make an adventure unique. It is the unknown, the risk and the challenge that adds the value to great endeavour. The best things often happen when they are unpredicted.

When I look back on the best things in my life and how they have shaped me, it is rarely from the events I had anticipated. I met Shara when visiting a friend, and while in the middle of training for Everest. A new relationship was not on the agenda before leaving for three months climbing in the Himalayas. Yet thank God I did.

So why not embark and sail 'west', and take on some new adventure, whatever it may be. You never know where it might lead . . .

* To what extent do you let your curiosity direct your course rather than just your ambition?
* Do you tend to manage uncertainty as a threat or as an opportunity to learn something new?
* When you look back at the important moments in your life, had you predicted them?

THE PATH TO ENLIGHTENMENT

I N 1202, A young man named Francis, who dreamed of the glory of being a famous knight and winning himself a great fortune, saw his chance. He left his parents and marched to war. But within a day of leaving his hometown he fell ill. Abandoned by his comrades, he experienced a feverish vision, telling him to turn back.

The next morning, weak and dejected, he reluctantly set off home. Along the way, he encountered a man suffering from leprosy, a disease many were particularly afraid of. But he instantly realised that this leper was also his fellow man.

Francis leaped down off his horse and embraced the leper in what he described as a 'wild fit of love and joy'. Francis was a man whose life, from then on, embodied the idea of serving others. He learnt one of the most important lessons of life: that true joy is found in the service of others, and never in the service of self.

- *What inspires you about the story of Francis of Assisi?*
- *Can you think of a time when you found more joy in helping someone else than you did in receiving something for yourself?*
- *Is there a small change or addition you could make to your week to incorporate some simple act of service to others?*

'Faith brings out a boldness that has proved, through times, to be unconquerable'

FRANCIS OF ASSISI was a man whose life embodied the idea of serving others. He would establish a global movement of people who, since his embrace of that sick man, have met the needs of the poor and vulnerable ever since, inspired by their faith in God.

I've often heard the riposte that somehow God is a crutch for those who cannot really make it on their own. It is in part true. But life is only half-lived when we go it alone.

Faith brings out a boldness that has proved, through times, to be unconquerable. It's seen in the courage of hundreds of millions of people who have experienced persecution for their faith. And that boldness is also the courage to care, to challenge, to intervene in the plight of those who are struggling in different ways. Faith has been described as simply 'one beggar telling another beggar where they found bread'. Sharing the good stuff and loving the unlovable.

- *How would it feel to accept that we all need help? Is a crutch a bad thing?*
- *Would you love the courage to intervene in the suffering and struggle of others?*
- *Where do you look for the courage and strength to keep going?*

THE POWER
OF LANGUAGE

ACCORDING TO RESEARCH at the University of Vermont, the most positive word in the world is 'laughter', followed by 'happiness' and then 'love'.

The words we use don't only have positive or negative meanings, but psychological and even physiological effects. 'Calm', 'peace', 'relax', 'serene' – all of these have a correlating effect on the mind and body, and are often used in mindfulness techniques. On the other hand, 'threat' words, like 'danger', 'fire', 'injure', 'fear' or 'hazard', have been shown to prompt a fight or flight response.

Research shows that the brain's adrenal system gets involved just from reading a word on a page. In a threat-laden world, the language we choose can make a huge difference.

I always try to use language that has a positive, rather than a negative, association. I call problems 'challenges', and an alarm clock an 'opportunity clock', to name just two. (After all, who wants to start the day 'alarmed'?) My family tease me, but I don't apologise for it.

These are small changes, but what you speak influences so much. As they say: 'your words become your life'.

- *Do you tend to speak in negatives rather than positives? How do they make you feel?*
- *Do you notice that certain words empower, embolden and strengthen you and others?*
- *What would it look like for you to develop more positive habits of speech?*

'I focus my attention on a short reading or phrase that is positive and encouraging'

THREAT WORDS ARE attention-grabbing, and there is a place for them in life, but if they are all we hear, we will soon get exhausted. So much of life is about balance: If you take something out, you need to put something back. If you pick something up, you also probably need to put something down. So, if you're activated by threat, make sure you are also able to find some calm afterwards.

And you can be proactive in this quest, too. I find many mindfulness practices help bring me into a calm headspace. Professor Jon Kabat-Zinn says, 'Mindfulness means paying attention in a particular way, on purpose, in the present moment, and non-judgmentally.'

You can do almost anything mindfully, it's just about bringing yourself fully into the moment and staying calmly within it. I try to start each day with a simple yoga routine, which then finishes with me kneeling down and saying my prayers. I then focus my attention on a short reading or phrase that is positive and encouraging.

Find your thing, but start the day calmly and on terms that enrich and empower you.

- *Do you find that your mind is often filled with threat words or worry?*
- *How might you seek out more balance to all the highs and lows you experience each day?*
- *What would it mean for you to start or end your day by using some mindfulness techniques?*

WHEN ALL IS DARKNESS, LOOK FOR THE STARS

WHEN YOU GET out of the city at night-time it can get really dark, but only then will you get a decent view of the stars. Those same stars were helping travellers navigate their way through tough conditions at night long before we had satellite technology to do the hard work for us. Just like the stars, true friends reveal themselves in the darkest times.

Friendships take work and require commitment to nurture them. They are an investment on our part. And like most investments – whether of time or money or emotion – the more we put in, the better the dividend we get back.

True, some friendships will always be no more than superficial, and that's fine. But when life is at its hardest, that's when we see who shows up and how much we need them.

- *Has a really difficult time in your life revealed a precious friendship?*
- *What made that specific friendship stand out, and what did you appreciate most?*
- *What have you noticed about the friendships that you have really invested in?*

'Friendships are an investment on our part'

MY LIFE HAS been far better and happier because of a handful of friends who have shown up for me in tough times. And I hope I've been there for them too.

We often build friendships in the light but rely on them in the dark. When you have those tough moments together, it's the friendships, more than the achievement, that you come away with. Muhammad Ali said, 'Friendship is the hardest thing in the world to explain. It's not something you learn in school. But if you haven't learned the meaning of friendship, you really haven't learned anything.'

Valuing your friendships means staying connected: taking simple, regular steps to build friendship is always better than big gestures. A text, a call, a coffee, a walk. Simple, small, but regular: that's the key.

- *What have you learnt about the meaning of friendship through your experience of tough times?*
- *Which of your friends needs your help and how could you show up for them?*
- *Who might you need to reach out to more regularly to keep your friendship strong?*

THREE POINTS
OF CONTACT

A SIMPLE RULE FOR the novice climber is the rule of three: have at least three points of contact with the rock face you're climbing on. One hand and two feet, or two hands and one foot. The principle behind the rule is that if the climber loses their grip on any single hold or if the rock itself fails, you still have enough support with the two remaining holds to avoid falling.

In life, we can be tempted to pin all our hopes on a single hold. It could be our career, a particular relationship, our family life, a financial investment, even the fortunes of a sports team. The problem with staking our future happiness on just one thing is that it's inherently unstable; if it gives way, then we fall with it. We lose our job, a relationship disappoints us, an investment fails, our team crashes out of a big competition.

Having a clear focus and being committed to something is good, so long as it's not the only thing that we are committed to.

- *Have you found yourself committing to one thing to the detriment of everything else in your life?*

- *When was the last time something you were committed to fell through? How did it make you feel and how did you cope?*

- *What do you think are the benefits and risks of having a singular ambition?*

'Constantly keep an eye out for places to put in some protection'

WHEN YOU ARE leading on a rock climb, despite having an eye for the top, you are constantly keeping an eye out for places to put in some protection. These nuts, cams, bolts and pitons link your rope to fixed points on the rock. If you fall, your belayer tightens the rope against them to hold you up.

In my experience, happiness and a sense of fulfilment in life can never be defined by simply getting to the top of a particular rock face. Instead, it is a collection of 'holds'. Some are holding me, and some I may be holding. But in that space I feel secure and loved.

Having some breadth to life not only gives you a greater experience of living, but also means you stand on firmer footing. That can give you greater confidence to face the ups and downs of life, knowing that, when some things wobble, you still have some security that is keeping you from falling.

- *What might it look like for you to link into some protection? Who is keeping an eye out for you, ready to tighten the rope?*

- *What have you noticed about moments when you made it to the top? Did you find yourself simply moving the goalposts onto a new challenge?*

- *How would feeling 'secure and loved' impact your confidence in life? Who could be part of that journey for you?*

DAY 79

ACKNOWLEDGING
THE COST

RECKON I HAVE had around twenty-one really close life-threatening calls: unopened parachutes, rockfalls, snakebites, avalanches, near-drownings . . . the list goes on. They have all reminded me that I am very far from invincible. Just mainly lucky, with each near-escape having incidentally added to my skill and experience – which is the only positive by-product.

The irony of all these near-escapes is that, far from making me feel stronger, I have at times felt more vulnerable and less certain. It's not just me; even while I was serving with 21 SAS there was an unspoken acknowledgement that life or death moments bore a cost, often rocked confidence and occasionally needed some unpacking.

There are some real risks to the maxim 'what doesn't kill you makes you stronger'. It places an oppressive expectation on survivors: those who have battled with cancers, recovered from acute mental illness, survived traumatic injuries. Not only are they reconciling themselves to their experiences, but also now they need to manifest some great new strength. Such a culture makes it even harder to get the help a person needs.

- *Have you been told not to worry; 'what doesn't kill you makes you stronger'? How did it make you feel?*

- *Do you feel the pressure to keep your uncertainty or anxiety hidden and simply express gratitude that you 'got through' whatever you were battling?*

- *How does an expectation that 'traumatic incidents strengthen you' misrepresent people's real experiences?*

'If we process trauma correctly we can emerge strong'

IF WE GLIBLY pass over the trauma of life, expecting to be 'fine' all the time, we risk not learning anything powerful about ourselves or our world. I look back on those many close calls and acknowledge that they have often shaken me more than they have helped me. Especially in the short term. A need to project strength or 'be OK', can lead us to pretend. This pressure can lead to further anxiety, substance misuse, isolation and despair.

Instead, I have often appreciated the kindness of my family who have, at times, said, 'That must have been frightening. How are you feeling about it now?' Open questions which give us the opportunity to say without pressure how we actually feel. We can never predict how an experience will affect us. That's why having the space to decompress without having to be 'strong' is so important.

When we process trauma correctly, in the long term we can emerge strong. But don't rush it. Let that renewed confidence regrow naturally over time.

- Do you feel bad talking about feelings of weakness or vulnerability? Have you felt the urge to pull away from others as a result of your feeling of disconnection?

- Who would be a kind and safe person to express your true feelings to?

- What might it look like for you to allow yourself to heal slowly and regain your confidence without the pressure of being strong before you are ready?

GOING
OFF COURSE

THE 1:60 RULE states that for every 1 degree an aeroplane is off course it will miss its target destination by 1 mile every 60 miles it flies. It's a simple aeronautical rule that shows how small errors can have huge consequences. And it holds true for life.

Author John Ortberg talks about the danger of being diverted from our intended destination by a 'shadow mission': 'What makes a shadow mission so tempting is that it's so closely related . . . it's not 180 degrees off track; it is just 10 degrees off track'.

Our shadow mission may be simply 'staying safe' rather than 'achieving the dream'. Or it may be 'building a reputation' rather than 'serving others', or 'receiving the acclaim' rather than 'working as a team'.

Going off course by a degree can seem inconsequential. So often the mission looks and feels the same, but the motivation is just a few degrees off and, over time, the whole focus of what we are working towards becomes compromised.

- *Can you identify a target, destination or 'authentic mission' that you are working towards?*
- *If you were going to be diverted off course by a shadow mission, how would that potentially manifest itself?*
- *What might you do to stay on course, or correct your trajectory if necessary?*

'If we can see the danger,
we can take corrective action'

IN NOVEMBER 1979, Flight TE901 took off from an Auckland airport for a sightseeing flight over Antarctica. Unbeknown to the two experienced pilots, their coordinates were 2 degrees off course. They had anticipated flying down the wide-open McMurdo Sound. Instead, their flight path took them and their 257 passengers directly over the 12,448-feet peak of Mount Erebus, the second highest volcano in Antarctica.

The pilots, unable to see the danger below, lowered the plane to 2,000 feet so the sightseers could get a better view. The lack of contrast in the landscape further masked their circumstances. Unable to regain height in time, the plane crashed.

Our intended course in life is often thwarted, sometimes by things we can't often see straight away; insecurities within us we find hard to acknowledge. But if we can see the danger, we can take corrective action.

If you find you get diverted by fear or doubts, it may help to spend a little time working through those things, so you can stay on course for the long term.

- *Have you found that your vision often folds into doing something less than you imagined?*
- *Do you feel like things always end up in the same pattern? Could you talk to a counsellor or trusted mentor about your experiences?*

THE FOUR CUPS
OF MEANING

RATHER LIKE AN all-terrain vehicle, we can end up taking quite a beating in life. Now and then, we need a service to see what's happening under the hood and to help us stay on track. When it comes to a 'self-care check-in', I sometimes find that it can be hard to know where to start. This is a simple model you can use to take a look at life. It's called 'The Four Cups of Meaning': Vision, Value, Trust and Joy.

The idea is to take a specific area in life, say, your professional career, your involvement in a volunteering organisation or team. Then imagine a cup that represents the vision, value, trust or joy you experience in connection with that role.

The four cups act like a road map to contentment. If we examine our experience in these four core areas, we can see clearly both where we are content and where we need to change direction. If we don't feel very valued, we might mark the level in the Value cup as nearly empty. If we feel incredibly valued, we mark the level as full. Or it could be somewhere in between. The same goes for the other cups.

- *How do you feel about reflecting back on past experience? Is it uncomfortable?*

- *How significant do you think Vision, Value, Trust and Joy are in terms of your contentment?*

- *How might being really honest with yourself in this exercise open the door to change?*

'Revelation always precedes transformation'

MOUNTAINTOPS RARELY TELL us much about ourselves. It's on the climb up that we find out who we are. But, in a fast-moving world it's tempting to avoid looking back. Reaching the goal may seem to justify the struggle. We say, 'all's well that ends well' and then avoid examining the journey honestly.

The Four Cups model can help us explore that journey in more or less any context of our life: work, relationships, volunteering opportunities or our place within a team. Revelation always precedes transformation. So, if we want to live differently, we have to start with being honest about how we are really experiencing things now.

Where those cups are towards full, we feel high levels of contentment and can be quite satisfied in how things are working. Where they are less than half-full it is likely to be a source of our discontentment. Knowing this, we can then take action or make important changes.

- *Have you tended to avoid stopping until you reach an achievement milestone? How does that affect your view of the journey to get there?*
- *Do you believe that 'all's well that ends well'? What could you be missing?*
- *How do you feel about exploring your feelings of contentment or discontentment and where will you start?*

THE FOUR CUPS: VISION

MOST OF US operate best when we have a clear vision, or when we are vision carriers for something that we are part of, socially or professionally. Having a vision is a bit like flying in thick fog: you can visualise the destination ahead of you despite not being able to see beyond your immediate circumstances.

Think about your cup of vision for a particular area of life. If you are working within an organisation, how connected do you feel to the purpose of your work? If you are considering a relationship, are you living in line with the vision you set out for it at the start? Place an honest line in the cup at the extent to which you feel aligned with a positive vision.

If you don't feel content with how full your vision cup is, what action could you take to refill it? Maybe it is simply articulating exactly what it is that you're aiming for. In my experience, action and vision are mutually beneficial: vision without action is a dream, but action without vision is a mess.

- *How do you feel about the level of vision in key areas of your life?*
- *Even if you cannot see exactly where you are now, do you have a destination in mind?*

THE FOUR CUPS: VALUE

THE VALUE WE feel in life is not about what we materially acquire, it's about how valued we feel as people. This is often felt in terms of what we give to relationships, to others, to life, or simply in a desire to make the world a better place. Our sense of value is always going to be rooted in what we give, not in what we get.

We all know people who have very little and yet have a deep sense of value. Others, despite great material wealth, are still dissatisfied and insecure. I have found a good principle to strive for is to value people and use things, not to use people and value things.

When it comes to looking at our cup of value, it should be measured in two ways: are we making it our priority to value those in our world: our partner, our children, our colleagues, our neighbours, our teammates? And second: are we feeling valued . . . in our work, in our relationships, in our family, among our friends? I believe if we get the first part right, then the second will naturally follow.

When we value and encourage others, it naturally increases our own sense of value and how others see us. It is strange how often we get what we need when we give it away.

- *How well do you appreciate the people around you?*
- *Is there a difficult conversation you need to have to express a sense of feeling under-valued?*
- *What can you give away to increase the level of value in your life?*

THE FOUR CUPS:
TRUST

WE ALL WANT to live and work among people we trust. When trust breaks down within a relationship – whether a personal or professional one – the continuing interactions become exponentially harder.

All sense of security goes out the window, and so the relationship can quickly become a source of anxiety, instead of the source of assurance, comfort and strength that it could be.

As a climber, without trust in your gear and in the ropes, the whole journey of ascending and descending sheer rock faces becomes a nightmare. But with trust in those ropes, then we can climb almost anything. And the process can be amazing.

To feel that someone trusts you with their life brings with it a sense of empowerment and a desire to honour that trust in return. It becomes mutually enhancing. But if someone doesn't trust us to deliver – whether at home or at work – it makes us feel small, ineffectual and weak.

Why not take a moment to assess the levels of trust you are experiencing in different areas of your life.

- *Are you withholding trust from those around you when they deserve it?*
- *Have you done things that have damaged trust within key relationships?*
- *If so, what small steps can you take to restore and repair trust, to return those relationships to a good place?*

THE FOUR CUPS: JOY

J OY IS SUCH a precious, yet often elusive, thing. It's within the grasp of all of us, and yet often it feels like it's the first thing we allow to be snatched from our hands when times are tough. We all want to experience joy and be happy. But joy and happiness come when we stop chasing them and simply breathe and smile and stay in the present moment. Like a butterfly, they're hard to catch, but often come when we sit down and just look around.

Take a moment to mark the level of joy in your cup. Maybe in your working life – are you running on empty? If so, no wonder everything feels hard. Or within your family – does the relentless attention that children need wear you down? No wonder your fuses are dangerously short. And yet, we instinctively know children are a source of joy, if only we can slow down and tune in to their magic.

The most enlightened humans make a choice to be joyful, whatever the circumstances of life. It's a great goal for us all. Whatever we have or don't have. Whatever our successes or failures. Don't let those worldly impostors dictate your state of mind. Choose joy, even in the midst of pain.

- *What if being joyful was a choice you could make every day?*
- *What would it take for you to find some joy even in the toughest circumstances?*
- *How would slowing down and tuning in to the sources of joy change your experience of it?*

VULNERABILITY IS A STRENGTH

MOST ENGLISHMEN ARE pretty used to hearing the stereotype about being unemotional and having a 'stiff upper lip'. Maybe it comes from a generation that was emotionally more reserved, in part because of the traumas of war, and an empire culture that expected a projection of strength at all times.

I have seen, though, how that projection can create a barrier between people and how it can mask our weaknesses. On the other hand, vulnerability, which is a willingness to be honest about ourselves, reveals a deep strength. A sort of 'accept me or reject me, but this is who I am' brand of courage.

Vulnerability comes from the Latin word *vulnus* meaning 'wound'. Most soldiers have wounds, as do most high-altitude mountaineers. Many people who have experienced a form of trauma or distress have them. We all do really.

But the ability to show and share our wounds is what separates people. Without vulnerability there is rarely any true connection. But without connections and bonds, can we really consider ourselves strong?

- *Have you at times felt the need to project strength?*
- *What makes you feel uncomfortable about vulnerability?*
- *Would others warm to you if you revealed some of your 'scars' to them?*

'Vulnerability is a gift to share with those we trust'

MAKING OURSELVES VULNERABLE requires both courage and wisdom. It's offering something of genuine personal value and often pain. And when we give away something of value it carries a cost and can feel terrifying.

I used to think that vulnerability was a sort of character trait; something some were gifted at and others weren't. But it's not. Rather, vulnerability is always a choice, a gift to share with those we trust. It's not something to be shared with everyone we meet, but when we share our wounds with those we feel safe around, it is a sign of true strength.

Vulnerability is a willingness to match your openness to the depth of a relationship.

I always try to be warm and open with everyone I meet, but there are certain things I will only share with those closest to me. This principle is known as 'concentric circles of vulnerability'. In the first circle is my faith, then Shara, then my boys . . . and so it goes on. Always deepest at the centre.

- *Has your vulnerability matched the depth of the relationships you are sharing in?*
- *Who is within the first three of your 'concentric circles of vulnerability'?*
- *What would give you more confidence to open up to those you love?*

BREATHE TO COMBAT STRESS

THE NAVY SEALS are the US Navy's primary special operations force and some of the world's most highly skilled soldiers. They are frequently operating in high-intensity situations. To cope with that stress, they use a technique called box breathing. Even in combat, it can significantly reduce the physiological effects of high stress which can inhibit our performance.

Feeling afraid or experiencing stress is a normal part of being human. But the body also offers a counterbalance to its own stress response.

Having a natural breathing technique to bring your anxiety down and restore a sharp mind can be a real advantage, especially in situations where you may feel hijacked by fear. What works for Navy SEALs can work for you too.

The more conscious you are of your breathing, the more connected you will be with your body and what it is telling you. That awareness can prompt you to deploy these techniques early and bring your stress down before it becomes more overwhelming.

I have found the key is using these techniques early, as soon as I get a sense of anxiety.

- *How accepting are you of the fact that stress and anxiety are a normal part of life?*
- *What strategies have you used in the past to help you to bring your anxiety down?*
- *What particular signs or signals does your body give to make you aware that you are stressed or anxious?*

'Simple techniques deployed at the right time work so well'

ACCORDING TO HARVARD Health Publishing, 'Shallow breathing limits the diaphragm's range of motion. That can make you feel short of breath and anxious'. This can soon become a vicious circle: stress and anxiety lead us to shallow breathe, which in turn creates sensations that make us feel more stressed and anxious.

Taking control of your breathing is nothing new. Pretty much everyone has been told to 'take a deep breath and calm down' at some point or other. But what I have learnt from guiding people in stressful wilderness situations is that simple techniques deployed at the right time work so well. Box breathing is my go-to, and can be done in cycles of four, for when stress is high.

Breathe in through your nose for a count of four; hold your breath for a count of four; breathe out through your mouth for a count of four; hold your exhaled state for a count of four. Repeat until you feel a calm return.

There are other similar techniques; whichever you settle on, get familiar with it before you feel you need it so you can call on it at will.

- *Have you noticed how shallow or anxious breathing can make you feel panicked and even more anxious?*
- *Which breathing techniques would you like to explore further?*
- *How confident are you that breathing techniques can play a part in restoring calm and reducing stress?*

JUST BEGIN

'VE LEARNT THAT there is no perfect way to start something. You can pore over maps, plans, schedules and objectives hour after hour, yet be no better off.

Planning is, of course, crucial to success, but it has its limits. Planning won't enable us to foresee every obstacle along the way, the human error factor, or unpredictable weather.

Planning can become a form of procrastination. It constantly pushes us away from beginning something new because we just never feel quite prepared enough. The spectre of the unknown constantly rises in our minds, and we find ourselves researching or talking about something without ever actually experiencing it.

- *Do you have a habit of over-planning?*
- *Are there ambitions in your life that you haven't fulfilled despite having all of the information you need to get started?*
- *When you explore your reluctance to begin, what do you think is holding you back?*

'Making a beginning, however small, is so important'

JOHANN WOLFGANG VON GOETHE wrote, 'Whatever you can do or dream you can, begin it.' There is an inherent power to beginning.

An incredible 70 per cent of what we learn comes through experience versus only 10 per cent through training. That is why just making a beginning, however small, is so important. Unless we begin, we will never know.

And then, once we are in it, we find that we have the opportunity to resolve challenges on the go, something that I believe humans are naturally wired to do. Problem-solving is in our DNA if we give it the chance.

- *What would it feel like to learn from experience and potentially failure during a task?*
- *How could you trust your ability to problem-solve in the moment more than you do?*
- *Is there any other information that could help you to make a start? If not, when will you begin?*

BROADEN YOUR RANGE

WHEN YOU HEAR the name Leonardo da Vinci, most people think of an artist. But da Vinci was also a draughtsman, inventor, engineer, scientist, theorist, sculptor and architect. There's very little that he didn't take an interest in.

Life can feel like a funnel that gets increasingly narrow the further in we go. We move from multiple different subjects at school to just a few as we get older. In the online world, algorithms anticipate our interests and show us more of what we already know we like. When we do choose to try new experiences, it can often be 'for the sake of' something else, like training for a promotion or career change. But what about experiencing it just because it's there?

We may have told ourselves a long time ago that we aren't into art, music, theatre, books or performance, but it's never too late to start something new. Our cultural world is a vast landscape to be explored. So why not be adventurous? Be curious. Step out beyond what you find comfortable and familiar. The good stuff in life always happens there.

- *Have you found that the range of your experiences becomes narrower the older you get?*

- *Are you aware how algorithms narrow your horizons?*

- *What would it look like for you to expand your exposure to new things? Could you plan something in the week ahead like a cultural expedition in your local area?*

'If you haven't seen something before and don't know if you will like it, that's exactly what adventure is all about'

IN 1943, THE Monuments, Fine Arts, and Archives program (MFAA) was set up to protect cultural monuments from war damage. The 'Monuments Men' were tasked with finding and returning works of art stolen by the Nazis. Perhaps their most famous achievement was securing a Nazi hoard of art in a salt mine near the Altaussee in Austria in 1945. It contained thousands of works, including some by Michelangelo and Vermeer.

Despite the colossal devastation facing Europe, rescuing art from destruction was seen as a worthy endeavour, showing just how important art is in our shared story of humanity. Being able to view these paintings today is an incredible privilege, just like listening to live music or watching a play or a film. The fact that you haven't seen something before and don't know if you will like it, is exactly what adventure is really all about. After all, adventure truly is a state of mind. It's a bit like having a glorious mountain on your high street, just waiting to be climbed.

So, if the arts haven't been your thing in the past, why not give them a try?

- *What surprises you about the work of the 'Monuments Men'? Is art worth fighting for?*

- *Have you believed that art is irrelevant or uninteresting? What might change your mind?*

THE MEANING
OF TEARS

EMOTIONAL TEARS ARE different from what are called 'irritant tears' (ones that simply clean the eyes). Emotional tears have a different chemical composition, containing more protein-based hormones and certain chemicals produced in response to stress.

The result is that emotional tears are much more viscous. They hold their shape and track down the face more slowly. In other words, they are tears that are meant to be seen. The purpose is to make a visible expression of our emotional pain. The value in communicating our emotion to others is to share the load, the sorrow, the pain.

According to the senior curator of the Smithsonian's National Zoo, humans are unique in their shedding tears as an emotional response. They are a remarkable sign, not just of our ability to share our upsets but also of how community is so critical to our healing.

It can be hard to become comfortable with our own tears, but even more difficult to trust that they will be met with a kind response. I have learnt that only the courage to show our tears will answer that doubt – and that a kind encounter with our tears can be life-changing.

- *What have you believed about tears and their significance?*
- *When did you last cry emotional tears?*
- *Do you believe that the community around you is important in your experience of pain?*

'Hiding tears is a bit like hiding an SOS sign'

LINUS AND SABINA JACK were crossing by sea to Tamtam Island in Micronesia, but they got stranded on a tiny uninhabited island. Alone and in trouble, they wrote huge SOS signs in the sand. For seven days, the US Coast Guard searched 16,000 square miles. Eventually, on the cusp of calling off the search, they spotted their flashing lights and makeshift signs, which ultimately saved their lives.

Emotional tears are a universal human SOS. They are a visible sign to others that we need comfort. Sharing tears takes courage. Vulnerability always does. Yet it is still common to hear phrases like, 'men don't cry', or 'come on, toughen up'.

Research suggests men cry significantly less than women and that there are additional psychological pressures on men that restrict them from crying – yet men and women need support equally.

Hiding tears is a bit like hiding an SOS sign. You are avoiding rescue. I have shared tears with some of the toughest soldiers in the world. Crying doesn't make you weak, it's a sign of great trust and intimacy. Shared tears are about being real, as well as accepting that, at times, we really need each other.

- Have you felt the need to hide or suppress your tears?
- How have ideas around 'being tough' impacted your view of showing emotion?
- How could you begin to show your emotions to others and feel more understood?

WHEN ALL IS LOST . . . FINISH THE STORY

FLIGHT 571 CRASHED into the Andes in October 1972. On board were the pilots, a Uruguayan rugby team and some family members. Fifteen died on impact, leaving thirty alive but stranded in a hostile frozen wilderness. The events that followed were immortalised in the 1993 film *Alive* and, as days turned to weeks, all hope of rescue faded.

Many of the survivors died of exposure and malnourishment. It seemed as if all was lost. Except that one man – Nando Parrado – was determined to survive. He and two others made the impossible decision to eat from the frozen flesh of some of the deceased, and they determined to use that energy to seek help.

Incredibly, they managed to make the gruelling, mountainous and sub-zero journey back to civilisation and eventually trigger a rescue. As a result, sixteen people survived.

The difference between life and death in a survival environment often hinges on determination. It's the power that makes the impossible possible, and the unthinkable reasonable.

- *Do you have a tendency to assume the worst outcome is likely to happen quite quickly in a difficult situation?*
- *How does Nando Parrado's attitude surprise you, especially after seventy-two days on the mountain?*
- *What does determination feel like to you? How could you strengthen your resolve and fight that little bit harder to turn things around?*

'It is important never to give up'

WE'VE ALL EXPERIENCED moments when it feels like all is lost. A plan comes to nothing. A dream is dashed against the hard realities of life. A relationship dies. They are brutal, painful moments.

It's OK to acknowledge the devastation and loss we've suffered – to shout out our pain and frustration. But it is even more important never to give up. Nando Parrado reflected on his attitude in the Andes: 'I would walk until I had walked all the life out of me, and when I fell, I would die that much closer to home.'

Most good stories have an 'all is lost' moment, but the story doesn't have to end there: whatever dark time you may be walking through, keep walking and finish the story. It will be tough, worthwhile journeys always are, but when you look back and see what you have come through, it will be so worth it.

As Winston Churchill once said: 'When you're going through hell, keep going.'

- *Do you need to accept or acknowledge the pain and disappointment of an 'all is lost' experience in your life?*
- *Is there an empathetic, compassionate person in your life that you could share your story with?*
- *What does it look like for you to 'keep walking' like Nando Parrado, either to finish that story or to walk into a new brighter one?*

FOLLOW YOUR INSTINCTS

WISDOM SOUNDS LIKE something somehow far away, something that other people have, maybe – but wisdom is often just a fancy word for common sense. Oprah Winfrey says, 'Follow your instincts, that's where true wisdom manifests itself.' In a world in which we can access more and more information, it can be hard to trust our own instincts with things.

We all need wisdom to navigate life effectively and happily. Wisdom is about doing today what you'll be pleased you did tomorrow. I have often found huge wisdom from sources outside of myself over the years, such as simple phrases that Christ used, like 'Do to others as you would have them do to you', or wisdom and good advice from family and friends.

People often think about wisdom as a 'happy accident' that you collect on the way to old age. But it's much more than that. Wisdom is something we need to gather intentionally. It is the necessary ingredient to pretty much every success story. Wisdom is the difference between losing the things you love and keeping them. If you decide to do one thing, pursue wisdom.

- *Who or where do you look to for wisdom outside of yourself?*
- *Think of one phrase of wisdom that you value.*
- *How has this wisdom shaped your life?*

'If your instinct is speaking to you today, don't ignore it!'

INSTINCTUAL WISDOM IS within us. It's a sort of gut feeling that helps us to navigate the complexities of life with all of its challenges and opportunities. I call it the nose of the mind. That sense that you know the right thing to do. Even when it's the hard route.

When we listen to our instinctual wisdom, not only do we get a sense for what is right, but we also gain confidence in our ability to steer a good course through the obstacles of life.

If your instinct is speaking to you today, don't ignore it! The more we learn to trust our instincts, the more likely we are to make good decisions. Then, later, we get to enjoy the fruits of those choices. Remember our lives are made up of the many small decisions we make every day. Choose wisely and from the heart.

- *Have you thought about your own 'instincts' as being a source of wisdom?*
- *What would it feel like to start trusting your gut more?*
- *What would 'choosing from the heart' look like today?*

LISTEN TO
THE WARNING

THERE ARE FEW sounds in the wild that bring me to a faster stop than the sound of a rattlesnake. A bite can be deadly, and hearing that 'rattle' means that danger is close – you need to proceed with extreme caution.

I think we all carry an internal 'rattle'. Call it a moral compass, a conscience, intuition or gut instinct. It warns us we are in danger of crossing lines we know we shouldn't cross. Yet too often we ignore the warning and end up hurting ourselves or others.

In life we can all too easily find ourselves reaping the consequences of guilt and regret. Only then do we look back and remember that quiet voice of concern, that niggle of doubt in the gut. And we remember we ignored it.

We tend to hear what we are listening out for. We can tune out that sound of warning or we can tune into it. It's up to us.

When I look back, my regret is always that I hadn't listened more to that inner voice.

- *Can you remember a time when you felt that 'rattle' within?*
- *Have you ever been tempted to ignore it? If so, what was the outcome?*

'The moments I regret are when I have failed to listen'

I'M DEFINITELY NOT someone who claims to have no regrets. We all make mistakes, hurt people or are unkind at times. The moments I regret the most are when I have heard the 'rattle' but failed to listen.

My faith has taught me two key things: we aren't meant to live our lives shackled to regret, and forgiveness is available to us all.

When I was finally bitten by a viper in Borneo, it was miserable. I heard the voice of caution in my head, but gave it another pull from the branch anyway. Fortunately, it turned out to be non-venomous. Luck alone saved me that day; I cleaned the wound and lived to fight another day.

Without 'careful cleansing', our mistakes and regrets can become burdens that steal our happiness and harden us to hearing our conscience in the future.

In the Bible Jesus says, 'Friend, your sins are forgiven'. That means a fresh start to every day. It's the greatest thing I have, to help me live lightly. A daily reset from the Almighty.

- *Are you carrying the burden of regret?*
- *How has this affected your willingness to listen to the 'rattle' within?*
- *What might it be like to receive a fresh start today?*

LAUGH AT YOURSELF

THERE ARE TIMES when we all take ourselves too seriously. On the other hand, we warm to people who can honestly laugh at themselves and their foibles and failings. And often the best jokes are against ourselves. A study by Dr Ursula Beermann demonstrated that people who can laugh at themselves were more likely to feel good and worry less.

To be able to laugh at ourselves shows character, humility and grace. Great people make others feel great about themselves. They build others up and don't shoulder their way forwards into a position of superiority. How we speak about others speaks loudest about ourselves.

I've noticed that one of the best determining factors of how comfortable we are with ourselves is our ability to laugh at ourselves. And that level of self-assurance goes hand in hand with a willingness to 'talk up' others.

- *Have you noticed how the confidence to laugh at yourself is often the same confidence that can build up others?*
- *Do you have a tendency to be oversensitive or take humour against you too seriously?*
- *How could you be more accepting of your foibles and more confident about your character?*

'It is good for our wellbeing to take ourselves less seriously'

IT'S SAID THAT humility isn't thinking less about yourself, rather it is thinking about yourself less.

Finding humour in difficult things, cheering others up, seeing the funny side are all a great antidote to many of life's challenges. Being grounded enough to be the subject, as well as the author, of a joke, shows real humility. What's more, when we laugh, it's proven to have a positive impact on our memory, heart health, ability to manage pain and psychological wellbeing.

It is good for our wellbeing to take ourselves less seriously, to shoulder a joke, and, at the same time, speak well of those around us. Pastor and author Ted Loder said, 'Laughter is a holy thing. It is as sacred as music and silence and solemnity, maybe more sacred. Laughter is like a prayer, like a bridge over which creatures tiptoe to meet each other. Laughter is like mercy; it heals. When you can laugh at yourself, you are free.'

- *What do you notice about humility and humour? How does being grounded give you more space for laughter?*

- *What is the difference between humour that builds others up and humour that is critical and destructive?*

- *Do you see a relationship between laughter and freedom? How could you laugh more?*

CHALLENGE
THE SYSTEMS

HENRY FORD DESIGNED his first moving assembly line in 1913. Until then, workers brought each part to the car, rather than the car to each worker. The moving assembly line was the beginning of mass production methods around the world.

The systems you have in place in your life are 99 per cent responsible for the results you are achieving. When it comes to systems, what we put in is what we get out. Both good and bad.

I have seen how attached I become to the way that I do certain things. Survivalists might have diehard methods for starting fires, but that might not be the best method for certain woods or certain conditions. In our lives, it's amazing how over time 'my way' can become the 'only way'.

Henry Ford said, 'We do not make changes for the sake of making them, but we never fail to make a change once it is demonstrated that the new way is better than the old way.'

Don't let the way you have done something in the past be the reason you can't do something better for your life today.

- *Is there a danger that you are stuck in a system that is limiting your progress?*
- *Are you able to make an honest assessment of the way you are doing something?*
- *How entrenched are your 'systems'? Could you explore different ways of doing things?*

'If it keeps yielding the same results, I know it's time to explore my beliefs more deeply'

HUMAN THINKING IS a bit like a production line. Cognitive Behavioural Therapy leans on the idea that if a person's thinking can be changed, their behaviour follows.

This 'system' is often described through ABC: 'A's are 'Activating events'; 'B's are the 'Beliefs' we apply to the 'A's; 'C's are the emotional and behavioural 'Consequences'. (The 'C's then often feed into the 'A's.)

Imagine wandering through the jungle. A beautiful bird takes off from the canopy above, creating an explosion of noise. If your 'B' is that you are under threat from monkeys, the 'C' will be that you run in fear. But two people will react to the same situation very differently based on their 'B's.

I have learnt to observe my thinking and behaviours. If the system keeps yielding the same results, it says as much about how I am thinking as it does about what I am experiencing. Then I know it's time to explore my 'B's more deeply.

It's good to challenge, refine and improve our beliefs, habits and thinking in order to yield better, happier, kinder results at the end. After all, our minds are like parachutes. They work best when open.

- Can you think of an example of where two people experiencing exactly the same event had completely different interpretations?

- How might you challenge some of your belief systems more deeply?

CHARACTER OVER EXPERIENCE

BRITISH ARMY OFFICER Preet Chandi had never been on skis before. In fact, she hadn't really considered skiing to the South Pole until she had run the 156-mile Marathon des Sables in the desert. Preet said, 'I have been told "no" on many occasions and to "just do the normal thing", but we create our own normal. You are capable of anything you want.'

It took her two-and-a-half years to prepare for her expedition, which included learning to ski and survive in the -50°C temperature on the Antarctic. Preet completed the 700-mile challenge in forty days, nearly beating the current women's record. All this from someone who, three years previously, had no experience in ice or snow.

It's natural to limit our ambition to our experience; the things that we know we are good at. We believe that our right to do stuff depends on whether we've done it before. Preet is a brilliant example of the truth that determination, courage and a willingness to start at the beginning are far more important components to success than knowing it all upfront.

- *Do you have a tendency to count yourself out because you have 'no previous experience'?*
- *How does Preet's story challenge your assumptions about what is possible?*
- *What have you longed to try, but assumed that it wasn't for you?*

'Everyone stands a little taller when we encourage them'

THERE ARE MANY obstacles to accessing opportunities in life – external and internal. And at times we all need a little nudge.

Every trailblazer needs a little external belief and an encouraging word – it is often the first spark to our own self-belief. It was Preet Chandi's boss who first nudged her towards the Antarctic expedition. Preet couldn't see herself in the company of other polar explorers, but those around her believed that she should be.

Preet would go on to become the first woman of colour to ski solo to the South Pole. In turn, she has become a gatekeeper for others' success. As she says: 'No matter where you are from or where your start line is, everybody starts somewhere. I don't want to just break the glass ceiling; I want to smash it into a million pieces.'

Everyone stands a little taller when we encourage and help them to realise a dream. We might not all be able to achieve what Preet did, but words of encouragement and belief to those we love can go a very long way.

Helping others to see beyond their limitations, and nurturing that spirit of endeavour in ourselves, makes for empowered living.

- *Are you facing obstacles to participation because of your experience, race, ethnicity, gender or socio-economic background?*
- *What encouragement do you need or can you offer so a 'glass ceiling' gets smashed?*

GRIEF IS NOT
A WEAKNESS

GRIEF IS NOT a weakness that some people carry. It's the 100 per cent statistic. Every one of us will grieve, both for the life-changing loss of a loved one, and for the smaller losses of health, opportunity, finance or ambition. I remember when my wife Shara and I lost our fathers within ten weeks of each other; suddenly the world felt like it had been pulled out from under us.

The way we encounter grief is different for each person. Some events will create a far stronger reaction in us than others, but we can usually expect the same sort of emotions: numbness, shock, extreme tiredness, regret, guilt, anxiety, emotional overload and anger.

We all have different ways of processing these feelings, some through tears, some in solitude, others in activity, or camaraderie. There are no 'better' methods and no prescribed time frames.

- *What has been your experience of grief to date?*
- *Which of the emotional responses to grief do you most relate to?*
- *Have you believed that there is an acceptable time frame for grief?*

'We should never be embarrassed or ashamed about our grief'

SHAKESPEARE WROTE: 'GIVE sorrow words. The grief that does not speak knits up the over-wrought heart and bids it break.' Putting your feelings of grief into words and sharing them with others is a key part of processing loss.

Grief that is withheld and not recognised can have a negative impact on us emotionally as well as physically. We can experience issues such as headaches, disrupted sleep patterns, depression, anger, even stomach ulcers.

We should never be embarrassed or ashamed about our feelings of grief. I've found that when we let them breathe, in time, they will let us breathe. The key thing is that we are connecting with our own feelings of loss and sorrow.

- *Are you walking through a season of grief right now?*
- *How could you put your feelings into words and who could you share them with?*
- *Is there anything you could do to connect with those feelings and let them breathe?*

THE SWAMP
OF INDECISION

PROBABLY THE TOUGHEST wilderness I've ever had to operate survival skills in is the swampland of the Northern Territory in Australia. At nearly 100 per cent humidity, with crazy-high temperatures, the air is so stifling that at times you can hardly breathe. The ground is waterlogged, a lot of it soft, squelchy mud, making every footstep heavy-going, and the air is thick with huge mosquitoes. The landscape is deceptively repetitive and devoid of any clear pathways. The result of all this is that the survivor becomes consumed with indecision; the heat, the effort needed to move and the lack of obvious direction can leave you confused and immobile.

In the wild, indecision can be deadly. It leaves you locked in a hostile environment, with no improvement to your circumstances. All the while, your strength and resources are being used up. The biggest danger is feeling that, by not moving forwards or backwards, you are somehow safe or saving energy. This trap has led to the death of countless lost hikers in the outback.

- *Can you identify with the feeling of somehow being safe despite neither moving forwards nor backwards?*

- *When have you struggled with indecisiveness? If so, what has it felt like to be unable to make a decision?*

- *Are there any particular circumstances that make you more likely to be indecisive? Can you identify any particular threat you feel about making a decision?*

'Any decision is usually better than indecision'

INDECISION CAN PLAGUE all of us. The consequences may be less immediate or obvious than in the desert or swamp, but they are still negative and life-sapping: we end up living in worry, regret and endless procrastinating.

Humans are settlers and we naturally struggle with change. If the necessity of change is unclear, or if we think we might be worse off because of a decision, people often tend to put it off. The trouble is that you will never have all the information you need to make a perfect decision. Fortune favours the brave and, in my experience, any decision is usually better than indecision.

I have learnt that indecision is a habit, not something linked to particular circumstances. (According to the research, 20 per cent of the adult population suffer from it.) The remedy isn't more information, it's more confidence. Start small, use your gut and practise making quick decisions. These small steps can translate into a greater confidence to make the bigger decisions that you may have been previously avoiding.

- *How is indecision practically impacting your life and sapping your time and energy?*

- *Can you remember a time when you were indecisive, but once you had made a decision, you were delighted with the change?*

- *What might it feel like to strengthen your 'decision confidence', and what small step could you make towards that today?*

TOUGH OUTSIDE, GENTLE INSIDE

I'VE BEEN LUCKY enough to get to know some incredibly tough people with beautiful, gentle hearts. And when you see that combination of strength and fragility it is magnetic. But to show such vulnerability takes great strength. Yet it is always worth it. Because it is only through our vulnerability that we truly connect with people.

I have learnt that it doesn't matter how 'tough' someone is on the outside, we only really connect to the humanity of a person – not their capabilities or achievements. But to connect, we need to be able to 'see in'. Brené Brown says, 'We cultivate love when we allow our most vulnerable and powerful selves to be deeply seen and known.'

But, vulnerability is counter-intuitive, especially when we feel under threat. In the ancient world, one of the most effective defensive moves in battle was to form a shield-wall. As the danger increased, warriors would close ranks and interlock shields, creating an impenetrable barrier.

- *How have you connected with others? Through a show of strength or vulnerability?*
- *What do you find threatening about showing more of your real self to others?*
- *Have you been tempted to create a 'shield-wall'?*

'It takes real courage to be open and vulnerable'

IF WE'VE BEEN through tough experiences or feel insecure about ourselves, it's tempting to develop a tough shell to keep people out. To raise our shield-wall against all threats. But what feels protective proves destructive, and we end up hiding our real personalities and vulnerabilities from view. That ironically leaves us feeling even more disconnected.

Being tough can become a trap; it can look like it's working, but it will only ever allow for a superficial connection with others. Before you know it, you end up having to try to be 'more impressive' to keep people's attention, which is always going to be exhausting and even more isolating.

It takes real courage to be open and vulnerable, particularly if we have been badly wounded or betrayed by people in the past. But when we find the strength to share our vulnerabilities, we create connections and bonds that can be unbreakable.

- *Are there any steps you can take in an existing relationship to share more of your fragile self?*
- *Could your hurt story become a doorway to connection rather than isolation?*
- *Who might you feel comfortable starting a conversation with about this?*

STAYING
IN TOUCH

I N 1858, THE first transatlantic telegraph cable was laid beneath the ocean. In its inaugural message, Queen Victoria congratulated President James Buchanan on their countries' mutual success. Newspapers on both sides of the Atlantic applauded this huge technological achievement. But, the cable stopped working after a few weeks and in the end they realised it required a lot more effort than anyone expected to keep the communications going.

Today, we have greater means of communication than at any time in history, but this ironically leaves us in danger of not actually communicating at all. It takes effort to stay in touch, and being overwhelmed by different options complicates the issue.

One thing that has helped me is to create small contact groups for different areas of my life. Within those groups, I try to initiate, contribute and respond regularly and honestly. At the very least, it means I am keeping in touch with the people who matter most in my life, with a frequency that is good for me and for them.

- *Are you struggling to 'keep in touch' with key people in your life?*

- *Do you find that the array of communication methods makes things easier or harder?*

- *Could you create a personal communication strategy to maintain a healthy connection with people you care about? What could that look like?*

'Little miracles happen more often than you might think'

CURTIS WHITSON, HIS son Hunter and girlfriend Krystal were on a hike in California when they got stranded in a narrow ravine beside a waterfall. The volume of water coming through the river and the 40-foot ravine walls meant they couldn't rappel down, and a missing rope meant that they couldn't climb out.

Curtis wrote an SOS note on a scrap of paper. He sealed it inside a green water bottle on which he carved HELP, then tossed it into the raging waters. The bottle went straight over the falls and, amazingly, was picked up by two hikers downstream who raised the alarm. The group was airlifted to safety only a few hours later.

When we're in trouble, it can feel pointless trying to get in touch. We may think people may not care. Pessimism often takes hold when we are struggling – but pessimism doesn't need to have the last word. If you need help, get in touch with family, friends or a helpline. People like to help.

- *Do you find that pessimism or negative predictions keep you from getting in touch with others?*

- *Can you think of a time when you were helped in the past, or a time when you responded to someone else's call for help?*

- *Do you need help? Who might you try to get in touch with, as a first step forward?*

THE COURAGE TO SEEK FREEDOM

COLDITZ IS PERCHED on a rocky outcrop overlooking the River Mulde near Leipzig. During World War II, the German authorities chose the castle as the ideal site for a high-security prison for allied officers with a history of trying to escape. However, despite its 'escape-proof' label, the Gothic building witnessed 174 attempts. The challenge was immense. But so, too, was the men's determination for freedom.

Although it was not a military duty, escape felt like a moral cause to many prisoners of war. The result was that Colditz saw some ingenious escape attempts – including building a glider in the castle attic in order to fly from the rooftop. The majority of the attempts failed, but the prisoners never gave up their courageous efforts to try.

Over time, it is easy to accommodate limitations to our freedoms: we may lose our confidence to try new things, or accept negative circumstances without challenging them. Breaking out of false limitations begins with asking ourselves, 'Who says I can't?' Once we have identified a limitation as false, we begin to fight for freedom.

- *Are there limits to your freedom you have grown to accept?*
- *How could you break out of a physical or emotional limitation?*
- *When you ask 'Who says I can't?', is there a clear answer?*

'Don't hold back from life-changing decisions on the basis of what you assume other people think'

THE MOST DANGEROUS false limitations are always the ones we impose on ourselves, especially if they seem to serve the interests of others. We might say, 'I cannot possibly leave this job, the team would never cope without me'; 'My family have lived here for their whole lives, I couldn't possibly move.'

I have learnt two things about these sorts of limitations: they rarely reflect what the other party actually feels; and they make ambition appear selfish and, therefore, a non-option.

In 1944, Japanese soldier Hiroo Onoda had orders to defend Lubang Island in the Philippines. He was strictly forbidden to surrender. In 1945, leaflets were dropped to announce the end of the war, but Hiroo thought these were enemy subterfuge. He refused to give up his obligation until his former commanding officer, Major Yoshimi Taniguchi, returned. That happened in March 1974. Hiroo had fought his own war for twenty-nine years.

You can spend a lifetime limiting your freedom for the sake of obligations that don't serve you or anyone. Don't hold back on the basis of what you *assume* other people think.

- *Do you tend to limit your ambition because of feeling obligated to others?*
- *If you carry real obligations of care for others, are there ways of meeting these alongside removing the limitations on your freedom?*

THE BLESSING OF THE BERGEN

T HE COMMANDO BERGEN rucksack has been one of the most sought-after pieces of military kit since World War II. They were designed to be wide at the bottom, narrow at the top, and enabled you to carry heavy loads for long distances. They are designed for purpose. And they work.

It is incredible sometimes when we observe the heavy loads that people manage to carry through their life: high levels of responsibility, intensive duties of care, personal struggles with health or disability, and yet they remain passionate and joyful. I often wonder how they do it.

Resilience is about keeping going under unrelenting pressure or bouncing back from the things that come against us. Resilient people have a broad base of support that keeps them going: friends, faith, support groups, hobbies, self-care and good habits. They are not afraid to ask for help. These are the ballast activities that keep them upright over the long-haul. Just like the Bergen.

- *What burdens of responsibility are you carrying and how are you doing?*
- *How broad is your base in terms of friends, faith, support groups, hobbies, self-care etc?*
- *How could you build your resilience support structure at the bottom end?*

'We need to adopt the best ways of thinking that we can'

IF WE ARE to make it through the complex challenges and pressures of life, we need to know that we are founded on a broad base of support. But what about at the top end? We need to adopt the best ways of thinking that we can, a small but effective number of attitudes which enable resilience of mind as well as body.

I've noticed that resilient people often have a set of recognisable mental attitudes that serve them well: self-awareness, empathy, flexibility of thought, motivation, courage and positivity. Each of these helps us stay in the right headspace when the tough stretches come. As they surely will.

Put together with the wide base support structure and the narrow head attitudes, we become a potent piece of equipment for life.

- *Which of the 'mental attitudes' do you want to develop more?*
- *How well do you connect your 'head attitudes' to the practical activities of your support base?*
- *Are you confident that you can carry your current load, and if not, what might need to change?*

DAY 123

KNOW THYSELF

I F THERE HAD been eleven commandments instead of ten, the eleventh might well have been to *know thyself*. Because if our lives are to have purpose, meaning and to bear fruit, we need to have some sense of what we are designed for and what truly makes us come alive.

It's hard enough to make sense of the world around us, but it is harder still when we don't know our own minds and hearts. The philosopher Socrates wrote, 'Know thyself, for once we know ourselves, we may learn how to care for ourselves.'

Think about it. If we don't know our own views, our own dreams, our strengths and failings, we become like a ship without a rudder. We end up chasing after things that run counter to our nature, which in turn leads to frustration and unhappiness.

- *Have you spent time reflecting on what makes you unique, your likes and dislikes, your personality and temperament?*

- *How would you describe yourself if you had to write a totally honest biography?*

'Looking at what we inherently love doing is a good place to start'

IF WE KNOW ourselves, we stand a better chance of making decisions that will make us happier, because we'll be pursuing goals that are true to our core nature. Nelson Mandela wrote, 'Learn to know yourself . . . to search realistically and regularly the processes of your own mind and feelings.'

Listening to our hearts, discovering what we are naturally good at and looking at what we inherently love doing is a good place to start when it comes to choosing the right path. And knowing we are on the right path then gives us the confidence to run down it with all the energy and enthusiasm we are designed for.

Go somewhere quiet. Sit and be still . . . think about what you would do and how you would live if there were no barriers to entry, no peer pressure, no societal expectations. That's a good place to start.

- *Do you feel tied to the expectations of others?*
- *What would you choose to do if you could?*
- *How do you really recharge, and are you allowing yourself to do that?*
- *What gives you deep joy in life?*

BE A
TREE HUGGER

ONE OF THE oldest trees in the UK is the Ankerwycke Yew. It started growing around 2,000 years ago along the banks of the Thames. The trunk is ten-foot wide. Legend has it that the Ankerwycke Yew was the site for the signing of the Magna Carta in 1215 and a meeting place for King Henry VIII and Anne Boleyn in the 1530s.

I have a habit of placing my hand on the trunks of old trees. I imagine how other hands have touched this bark; people facing their own battles over the turbulent course of life. It grounds me and keeps me connected to something bigger than myself.

When we get stressed we can act like we are the centre of the world. But remembering that most trees have lived longer than us reminds us we're all part of this great cycle of life. We are neither the centre of everything nor in any way insignificant. We are all connected, called to do our best and to live with courage and kindness along the way.

- *Do ancient trees inspire you? What battles might those who have also touched their bark been facing?*

- *Have you found nature speaks to you about your place in the world? Does it change your perspective?*

- *Does the enduring life of the world make you want to play a bigger part in its protection for future generations?*

'I find myself quietly saying "thank you" to trees as I walk past'

STANDING ALONE IN a giant forest can be a truly incredible sensation. I love wild places for how they can make humans feel. They bring a sense of scale and time and power that's hard to describe. But I am also aware that these places are so much more – they are fundamental to our survival.

Trees are the lungs of our world, with forests globally absorbing around 2.4 billion metric tons of carbon each year. They are the front line in our fight against climate change.

This is just one of the many reasons that, from time to time, I find myself quietly saying 'thank you' to trees as I walk past. It somehow feels wonderful.

Of course, my gratitude doesn't change the tree, it changes me. It reminds me that nature is part of us all, and that we are doing this journey of life together – just at different paces.

Nature hasn't asked much from us; it has given to us without complaint. Yet many parts of our natural world are struggling right now. It's good to acknowledge that. And to do all we can to help restore it. When we help nature, we help ourselves.

- What shocks you about the vital role that trees play in the environmental battle for survival?
- How does saying thank you to trees sound to you? How could it change how you feel or act towards nature?

BUILD A ROUTINE

WE ALL OPERATE somewhere on the scale between spontaneity and never making plans, and planning our day to the very last second. Too much spontaneity can become chaotic; over-planning can become restrictive. The best balance is often achieved by blending a routine (what we instinctively find works for us) with a plan (what we specifically need to do).

I have found building a routine for daily life creates some order around which I can either schedule plans or leave space to be spontaneous. Leadership coach John Maxwell says, 'You'll never change your life until you change something you do daily. The secret to your success is found in your daily routine.'

In the wild, animals repeat the same activities at the same time of day, often in the same place. There is a positive, natural rhythm to that way of living, both collectively and as individuals.

People also benefit from existing within the same sort of rhythms. Living according to a routine is proven to reduce stress, improve sleep, help maintain a healthy diet and encourage exercise. It helps us find balance between structure and freedom.

- *Where do you sit between spontaneity and meticulous planning?*
- *Have you noticed any correlation between establishing routines and positive mood changes and an increased sense of wellbeing?*
- *How could building a solid routine give you more space both to plan and be spontaneous?*

'Routine is about forming and then performing habits that become almost unconscious'

ONE OF THE best things about living by routine is that it takes some of the uncertainty and, therefore, anxiety out of living. We start to live by instinct. What we should be doing becomes ingrained in our bodies, and we end up moving from one part of our day to the next almost seamlessly.

One study in the *Journal of Abnormal Child Psychology* showed that children who had developed a high level of routine had far fewer instances of tantrums in school. Routine helps us feel safer and more settled in the unpredictability of life, something we can carry into adulthood.

I have some real staples to my life, like walking the dogs up a small hill early in the morning; stretching for ten minutes while saying my prayers; working out and taking an ice bath every other day; fasting in the morning and then eating certain healthy foods. Whatever it is, these small things act as secure anchors to often busy, unpredictable days.

Find small actions that you love, that are non-taxing to incorporate into your day for the long term, and see if they help you – then steadily develop them into positive habits for life.

- *How much of your day is currently made up of planned versus spontaneous activities?*
- *Would your spontaneity grow if you had more structure?*
- *What routines are you already practising that work well for you?*

OPPOSITION IS OPPORTUNITY

PARAGLIDING, WHERE YOU leap off cliffs and mountains with a canopy above your head, is an incredible experience: an adventure sport that my boys and I love.

It's a combination of a lot of things: understanding the mountains, the alpine winds and conditions, the canopy and its technical challenge, the gear, the fear and the adrenaline! Besides all this, it's an example of how so many of life's exciting things also include opposition.

A paraglider can only take off with airflow filling the chute. It needs speed and resistance. Then, once you're airborne, the chute smooths out and soars away from the mountain. Suddenly the situation looks and feels very different from the struggle you might have had on the ground, trying to launch the chute. You need both resistance and speed. The wind can be both your enemy and your friend.

- *Have you got a tendency to doubt yourself at the first hint of opposition?*
- *Can you think of a moment in your life when you experienced resistance but it actually strengthened your resolve to make progress?*
- *What strikes you about the image of a paraglider and how could it inspire you in a moment of doubt?*

'Resist giving in. Opposition is rarely the blockage we believe it is'

WE HAVE A natural tendency to see opposition as a bad thing. Like that headwind we are battling against that seems to be trying to crush our plans. We may be tempted to give in, or become despondent. That's natural. But resist it. Because opposition is rarely the blockage we believe it is.

Athlete Roger Bannister said, 'Just because they say it's impossible doesn't mean you can't do it.' After becoming the first person to run a sub-four-minute mile, he achieved what the doctors and scientists said was beyond the realm of a living body. After crossing the line he concluded he must be dead.

If you can change your perspective on opposition, on resistance, on turbulence, it can become the lift you need to achieve your goals. In fact, it is essential.

* *Have you had a tendency to overestimate the negatives and become despondent?*

* *Can you shift your perspective so that you see this opposition as an opportunity – the necessary conditions to lift you to greater things?*

* *Which opportunity or idea do you want to put back on the table today that you had been tempted to give up on?*

CHOOSE
NEW HABITS

OUR WORST HABITS were once our best attempts to make ourselves feel safe. Just take a moment to think about that for a second. The traits we don't like about ourselves are often a product of an earlier attempt to feel safe.

Maybe we dominate conversation, because we used to never get noticed. Maybe we go quiet in a group, because once upon a time we had a bad experience of having an unwanted spotlight on us at a vulnerable time. Maybe we get angry too quickly, or else never get angry at all. Whatever it might be, this is one reason why habits can be so hard to break. John Dryden said, 'We first make our habits, then our habits make us.'

But it doesn't have to end like this. Our story can be different. We each have the power to create positive patterns in how we act. It just takes a little focus.

- *Which of your habits of behaviours do you find most frustrating or limiting?*
- *Can you identify a way in which these habits had served to protect you in the past?*

'We can build up the courage to get free'

SUCCESS IN THE survival world is largely dependent on the ability to adapt, and it soon becomes obvious when old strategies are obsolete – or worse, holding us back. The ability to recognise when something that served us in the past may be hindering us in the present is the first step towards positive change.

Everyone is defensive about their habits, which may feel both deeply personal and necessary. At the same time, when we can accept that our habits aren't 'us' we can build up the courage to get free. (If there are any persistent and destructive habits in your life you may need professional help to address them.)

Our old habits served us well once, but if we can recognise that they aren't helping us now, we can move from saying: 'That's just how I do things' to 'That's how I used to do things'.

- *How do you feel about letting your limiting habits go?*
- *How have you defended your habits in the past? Were you realistic about their value?*
- *What would it look like for you to adapt your behaviours to fit well into your life today?*

QUIET COURAGE

IN 1997, TONY BULLIMORE was competing in the Vendée Globe race for single-handed yacht sailors when he was caught in a violent storm in one of the remotest and wildest areas of the Southern Ocean – 1,500 miles west of Australia and 1,000 miles north of Antarctica.

When the keel snapped, Tony's yacht turned turtle and he was trapped in an air pocket inside the boat. In the freezing, dark and icy water, with little evidence that he was about to be rescued, Tony made a decision to endure with courage to the end, whatever his ultimate fate was to be.

In total, he was trapped for 89 hours. When divers located him, Tony had little oxygen or strength left. He was on the edge of death. His first words were, 'Thank God. It's a miracle.'

It's easy to think courage is about spectacular actions in the heat of the moment, but courage is often more about a quiet resolve in the face of overwhelming odds, about what we don't do, rather than what we do. Tony said he survived on 'sheer determination, a little water and a little chocolate'.

- *Can you put yourself in Tony's situation and imagine the temptation to give in to fear and despair?*

- *Have you gone through experiences that have taught you quiet courage?*

- *What are you facing today that demands you stand your ground and find your courage?*

'You might not always be celebrated for quietly persisting, but you will make a difference'

WILD PLACES AND survival situations rarely demand 'battle cry' courage, more often they demand a quiet courage that has much more to do with persistence. 'Courage doesn't always roar,' said Mary Anne Radmacher.

Often unseen and uncelebrated, quiet courage can be easily overlooked. And yet it is one of the most powerful forces for good.

The power of a river to cut through sheer rock is all about persistence and time. We can all be agents of change in difficult, unjust or painful situations by having the courage to quietly persist.

American civil rights leader, theologian and author Howard Thurman notes, 'There is a quiet courage that comes from an inward spring . . . such courage is an underground river, flowing far beneath the shifting events of one's experience'.

You might not always be noticed, celebrated or championed for quietly persisting, but you will make a difference. Power and change in nature, whether it's with a glacier or a river, always comes through small persistent actions over a long period of time. And one human alone can truly change the world.

- *Are you questioning the difference you are making to a situation because of the lack of perceptible change?*
- *What positive changes are going to take persistence?*
- *What are the rewards of keeping going even when we don't see the spectacular breakthroughs that we might hope for?*

KEEP COMPANY
WITH ME

EVERYONE IS CARRYING something heavy. A lifetime spent with people of so many diverse backgrounds, faiths and responsibilities has shown me this, time after time.

Filming *Running Wild* has been a privilege in so many ways, but perhaps the greatest privilege of all has been the personal, intimate conversations with guests like Barack Obama, Roger Federer or Kate Winslet. Chatting about the stuff of life, their children's aspirations, the weight of work, personal struggles or bigger anxieties they might have about the environment or politics. Nothing makes you immune to the pressures of life or the need for help.

In the first century, Jesus was having some of the most powerful and often-quoted conversations in history, with a small band of misfits, each with their own struggles, burdens and hopes. These were the sort of people who would have been kept at arm's length by the religious folk of the time. Yet he told them simply: 'Keep company with me and you'll learn to live freely and lightly.'

- *How does knowing that 'everyone is carrying something' make you feel towards people who may look like they are in an amazing situation in life?*

- *What strikes you about comfort and companionship that is offered across social, political or religious barriers?*

- *What would living 'freely and lightly' look like to you?*

'The company you keep affects the weight of the burdens you carry'

IN 2016, DURING the World Triathlon Championship Series, British Olympic champion Alistair Brownlee was in position to win the race when he spotted his brother in trouble. Jonny was immobile, only a few hundred yards from the finish. Alistair stopped, put his arm around his brother and walked him across the line, handing victory to another competitor. Jonny wrote from his hospital bed after the race, 'Thanks @AliBrownleetri, your loyalty is incredible.'

For millions of people around the world and throughout history, the simple words of a lowly carpenter from Nazareth have transformed their lives for the better; lightening their load and carrying them when they cannot go on alone.

Faith is not about being 'good enough'. It's simply handing over your burdens, mistakes and insecurities every day. It's about having a loyal friend who is always there to hold you up when your legs give out. It's about living freely and lightly.

- *How is your company affecting the weight you feel – for good or ill?*
- *What might it look like for you to hand over some burdens, and start living 'freely and lightly'?*
- *Is there someone that you can keep company with today, lightening their load and giving them support in a difficult moment?*

CALL TO HUMANITY

ON CHRISTMAS MORNING 1914, British soldiers, who were huddled in their trenches, heard German troops across no-man's-land singing carols. Calling out to one another, they agreed an impromptu truce and the soldiers started climbing out of their trenches and walking towards each other. They met, and swapped gifts, food and drink. Famously, there was even an improvised football match.

For a brief time, beneath the realities of the war, these soldiers were simply people. United in their common humanity. Tragically, it didn't last long before they resumed their efforts to shell one another.

Our digital world has made it easy to define others by their politics or allegiances. Countries, cities and even families have become divided over their views on issues that, while important, should never fracture our community. Each of us can fall into the danger of losing sight of the humanity in others, seeing them simply as competitors at work, sporting enemies, religious, racial or political opponents. And often because those people simply see the world around them slightly differently to us.

- *Have you been ostracised or discriminated against by others? How did this make you react?*

- *Have you found yourself unable to see the humanity in people who are different to you?*

- *What would you like to see in the world around you, or in yourself and your own attitudes?*

'If humanity comes first, differences can be respected and understood'

NELSON MANDELA SAID, 'No one is born hating another person because of the colour of his skin, or his background, or his religion. People must learn to hate, and if they can learn to hate, they can be taught to love, for love comes more naturally to the human heart than its opposite.'

Those are beautiful words of truth and inclusivity. And what strength it shows to try to live this out.

Each of us has the power to value our shared humanity ahead of our differences. If humanity comes first, differences can be respected and understood. In my experience, more often than not, it is our differences that are, ironically, our strengths – they make us collectively smarter, inquisitive and more open-minded.

Society should always strive to be a diverse tapestry of views that can be celebrated and appreciated.

- *How does discrimination tend to affect a person's vision compared to the person who is open, kind and inclusive?*
- *In your experience, what tends to open people up to the beauty of difference and diversity?*
- *How do you think we can learn to love in line with Nelson Mandela's vision?*

YOU NEED AIR TO MAKE GOOD DECISIONS

O NE OF THE greatest risks facing a high-altitude climber is hypoxia. It's when there's simply not enough oxygen getting into the bloodstream. The symptoms include confusion, dizziness, disorientation – exactly not what a climber needs, when any kind of misstep is potentially deadly. If a climber shows signs of hypoxia, their teammates need to get to them fast. Because the chances of them making a bad decision is very high.

Everyone wants to make good decisions. And most of the time, we are pretty good at it. But sometimes we will stray into a place where conditions themselves mean the chances of making a good decision grow radically smaller.

I've found that stress can act like high altitude in our daily lives. When normal levels of stress increase to the point that it all becomes too much, it's a bit like starving the brain of oxygen. It is easy to become confused and start making poor choices.

- *When have you tended to make bad decisions?*
- *How has stress impacted your objectivity or clarity?*
- *When have you been really satisfied with the way you approached a difficult decision?*

'We need to be wise as to when we're at risk'

AT SEA LEVEL our blood is usually 98 per cent saturated with oxygen, but on high mountains over 8,000 metres that can fall to below 40 per cent. That huge reduction in blood oxygen is a massive loss to the brain's function. Even wiping your goggles can feel like doing a crossword puzzle.

For the climber, the first response to hypoxia is always to get the sufferer down where the air is thicker. In a similar way, when we're overwhelmed by stress, we need to get some emotional space, regain our perspective and start breathing again. That could mean going for a walk, listening to music, taking time for meditation or prayer. Or simply talking to a good friend.

On a mountain, the risk is obvious. In daily life, though, it's far less obvious when we've strayed into the danger zone. We need to be wise as to when we're at risk.

* *Take a moment to check in on yourself. Have you got enough air right now?*
* *Practically speaking, what do you need to get more emotional oxygen?*
* *How can you set yourself up for long-term success where stress is concerned?*

SUCCESS DOESN'T
MAKE US SECURE

BUILDING A LITTLE dock at our small island home in North Wales was more work than I had imagined. For months, the hardest work was unseen, going on underwater. Stanchions and pylons needed to be drilled deep into the seabed before anything could begin to happen on the surface. Without depth, strength and security, there could be no outwardly visible success – no dock.

It can be tempting to believe that success is a means to security. People talk about 'making it', as if there is a destination where anyone feels like they have enough success to feel secure. What I have learnt is that nobody finds security by becoming successful, but many find their success once they find their true inner strength and security.

These aren't new problems. Success doesn't resolve our insecurities – if anything, it amplifies them. If someone is tight and suspicious before they have money, they tend to be much more so afterwards. If someone is a show-off before they win a game, they will be even worse when they hold the trophy.

Build your character first. The rest will follow.

- *Do you imagine that achieving more success in your life will bring you a sense of security?*
- *What does real success look like to you?*
- *What would it mean to build your life on secure foundations?*

'Find a secure identity, the rest will follow'

SECURITY COMES FROM the Latin *securitas*, meaning 'freedom from care'. It's easy to see how success and security have become confused: 'if I have enough money I can live a carefree life'. But success does not free you from cares, it challenges you and reveals who you are. When we achieve our goals in life, it asks the question: what is our true character?

If we can do our best to stay humble and kind when we win, it amplifies the success. When we are big-headed, proud or self-centred with our victories, it undermines it all.

The sort of security that endures the storms of life doesn't come from things – it comes from strong relationships and it comes from an identity that has nothing to prove.

Success is subjective. But what is clear, is that when we know our value, honour others and follow our hearts, we are rich beyond measure.

- *How can you turn the drive for visible success into a freedom from worrying what others think?*
- *How can you create a deep foundation of security based on good relationships and knowing your identity?*
- *What would it look like for you to be content and love what you do?*

DAY 143

SURPRISE IS
GOOD FOR YOU

RAW SURPRISE CAN bring vitality to our lives and keep us on our toes in so many ways. Once in the Everglades while filming *Man vs Wild*, I remember doing some 'catfish noodling' to catch some survival 'dinner'. This involves putting your arm, and sometimes your torso, into underwater mudholes in search of heavily muscled catfish. If there is a fish in the hole they latch onto your arm and you yank it out. It works, but it's painful, scary and often bloody. And it rewards the bold. Not unlike life.

Not being able to see through the murky water, not knowing which hole might contain a huge catfish with a vice-like jaw, not knowing if there might be something more deadly and less edible in there. All this is unknown and often scary.

Surprise comes about through the limitation of our senses and foreknowledge. We may not like 'not knowing' what will happen, but the unknown is also good for us and it keeps us firing, thinking, feeling, adapting, anticipating.

In short, surprises keep us from going stale.

- *When were you last truly surprised and how did it make you feel?*
- *Have you had a tendency to avoid surprises, and if so, what might you be missing out on?*
- *What have you noticed about coping with surprise and your ability to anticipate and adapt?*

'Surprise makes us more resilient to the unexpected'

ACCORDING TO PSYCHOLOGISTS Tania Luna and LeeAnn Renninger's book *Surprise*, we go through four important responses when surprised: Freeze, Find, Shift and Share. Initially we will often freeze when we encounter the unexpected, then we try to find out what is going on, before shifting our perspective and then sharing this new information with others.

The key thing is, surprise reshapes how we experience life, it makes us more resilient to the unexpected. Surprise connects us to new experiences and then, through those encounters, connects us to each other through story, laughter and change. It's part of the reason that encountering the unexpected in adventure builds such strong connections between people.

It is easy for life to become 'surprise-free' as technology gives us the ability to edit out the 'unknowns'. But that also makes us more likely to avoid them in the future, when more surprises might actually be good for us. As G. K. Chesterton wrote, 'Surprise is the secret of joy.'

- *Has technology led to you editing out most of the unknowns in your life?*

- *How could you become more open to surprises and become more confident in dealing with the unexpected?*

- *What have you noticed about how surprise can build deep connections between people, often leading to great storytelling and laughter?*

THE POWER
OF MOMENTUM

'YOU JUST KEEP your arms and legs moving. As long as you are progressing on something, that's all it's about. You wanna keep moving, having progress in your life.' Swiss mountaineer Ueli Steck had just shattered his own record time for climbing the infamous 'Nordwand' – the north face of the Eiger – in Switzerland in 2008.

He had solo climbed to the summit in 2 hours 22 minutes and 50 seconds. Even the best and most experienced climbers spread the climb over a day and a half. What Ueli did was mind-blowing. He had literally run up the final, almost sheer, ice field towards the summit. His climb was a masterclass in momentum.

When we lose momentum in life it can be incredibly hard to get moving again. It's why volunteering is so powerful to do if you are between jobs, or light alternative exercise if you are carrying an injury. It might not be the perfect version of what you want, but it acts like a momentum placeholder. It keeps us going forward.

So whatever you do, just keep moving. Onwards. Upwards. Make that a mantra.

- *What do you find inspiring about Ueli Steck's record-breaking assault on the Eiger?*
- *Can you think of an example of when you struggled to get going again after you lost momentum?*
- *What imperfect activities could you do to maintain momentum in the gaps of life?*

'Most goals take longer to realise than you anticipate'

CYCLISTS, WHO NEED around 160 watts of energy to keep themselves moving at 20 mph, are masters of maintaining momentum. Here are a few things they've taught me about achieving goals:

1. Find a sustainable level of output over the long haul. It's easy to set off at a sprint only to end up flagging later on. Most goals take longer to realise than you anticipate.

2. Slipstreaming behind a faster rider saves as much as 20 per cent of their energy. We may think we have to work alone, but the failure to collaborate is exhausting and inefficient.

3. When facing opposition (wind or incline), change into a lower gear, which increases your work rate but decreases the pressure. People over-focus on their achievements and under-focus on sustained progress.

4. During an uphill struggle, stand up. Legendary cyclist Alberto Contador is famed for his out-of-the-saddle hill climbs, dubbed 'dancing on the pedals'. Steep challenges need a bold attitude – it's time to rise up and be counted. The pain will pass – but the pride in a task where you went 'all in' will endure for ever.

- *Are there fresh ways that you can increase or sustain your momentum for the long haul?*
- *How could you 'dance on the pedals' during an uphill struggle?*

THE HABIT OF OPTIMISM

THE THRIDRANGAR LIGHTHOUSE stands in the middle of the Atlantic Ocean, situated a few miles west of the Westman Islands off the southern coast of Iceland. It is one of the most iconic lighthouses in the world. Thridrangar means 'three rocks' in Icelandic, representing the three jagged spurs that rise up out of the water. It is these rocks that the lighthouse is there to save you from.

You can look at the lighthouse in one of two ways – as a danger or a guide. Pessimism is the frame of vision that sees the rocks beneath the lighthouse, more than the light above it. Both the optimistic and pessimistic sailor see the same lighthouse, but the pessimist is more likely to run aground. The reason is simple: the human mind gravitates towards what it focuses on.

The more we elect to have a focus on the positive and optimistic in life, even when we don't feel like it, the more our subconscious will pull us towards those very things.

- *Have you too often taken a pessimistic outlook on things? How has this impacted you?*

- *How might choosing to tackle the hardships of today in a more optimistic way change your experience?*

- *How might you make optimism a lifelong habit?*

'Focus on the light . . . the chances are that your life will start to look brighter'

'OPTIMISM IS THE faith that leads to achievement. Nothing can be done without hope and confidence.' So said Helen Keller, disability rights campaigner, who lost her own sight and hearing at nineteen years old.

It can be hard to be optimistic. Pessimism can easily take hold if we allow the weight of past disappointments to dominate. And the pessimism of predicting negative outcomes can feel like a form of protection against being let down again. But pessimism limits us, affects those we love and *can* start to alter our destiny.

We become what we focus on, and since we know pessimism is a joy-destroyer it is smart to avoid it like the plague. If people choose the negative for long enough, then they may start to actually 'look' angry and bitter. You may know people like that. Conversely, if you choose to see the light and not just the rocks, even when you are tired and scared at the helm of your boat, then the chances are that you – and your life – will start to look brighter.

So, wherever you can, choose to adopt an optimistic spirit of hope and laughter. Focus on the light, not the rocks.

- *What do you find inspiring about Helen Keller's optimism?*
- *What would be the impact on your life if you chose an optimistic attitude when times were tough?*
- *How would choosing a brighter attitude affect those around you?*

DAY 149

PLAN FOR THE
WAY DOWN

TWICE AS MANY people die climbing down Everest than climbing up, but I have never met someone who has said, 'I'm training to climb down Everest.' Of course, everyone plans to make it safely back to base camp, but it's rarely in mind before reaching the top.

We are all naturally 'ascent focused', looking towards the next challenge or opportunity ahead of us. But what comes after success can be just as important as success itself. Sometimes, more so, because reaching the goal can make us vulnerable in new ways. George Bernard Shaw said, 'Man can climb to the highest summits but cannot dwell there long.'

Success, then, is also about getting back safely to base camp. Or reaching the muddy car park, or making it home in time for supper, or whatever it may be. After all, it's no good being able to scale the highest peak if we can't then handle the descent.

- *Have you become 'ascent focused'?*
- *What specific vulnerabilities can you anticipate when you get there?*

'What comes after success can be just as important as success itself'

IT'S EASY TO think of success as simply being about achieving our goals. But it's also about meeting the demands of what that success means. As high-altitude mountaineer Edmund Viesturs said: 'Getting to the top is optional, getting down is mandatory.' If we are aiming for promotion we need to know that we actually want the job if we get it.

Thinking about success as a package of experiences can help us to prepare for the future – which is the key to unlocking every success. Visualising what the 'climb down' will require of you means that your ambition to achieve success is matched with the resources you need to back it up.

- *What will you need to do to meet the demands of success?*
- *What comes after the summit, and do you really want it?*
- *How can you prepare your resources to back up your achievement?*

DAY 151

NEGATIVE THOUGHTS AND WHAT TO DO ABOUT THEM

THE DESERT IS full of things looking for a free ride. This is especially obvious when I get home and empty my bags. What falls out is a lot of sand, the occasional dead scorpion, but most of all burs. Burs have been called 'the ultimate hitchhikers'.

Covered with tiny hooks, they attach themselves to pretty much anything they touch, particularly fabric. They are a pig to get rid of. The result is many of them travel several thousand miles back with me to the UK.

Some thoughts can be as annoying and persistent as those burs. They might be connected to a particular doubt or worry or regret. It doesn't matter what you are doing, or where you may be, that negative thought can crop up to spoil the occasion.

All too often our response is to try to get rid of the thought by rationalising or reviewing them. The trouble is, the more you try to pull them off you, the more clingy those burs can become.

- *Are you troubled by persistent negative thoughts that intrude in your mind at moments when you are just trying to relax or enjoy something?*

- *What do you notice about the content and frequency of those thoughts? Do they tend to include some doubt, guilt or anxiety?*

- *Have you found yourself rethinking and rationalising the same thoughts over and over again?*

'Clingy thoughts tend to fall off in their own time'

YOU CAN LOOK at desert burs in two ways: a problem that needs to be fixed or nature just doing its thing. One draws in your attention and makes you act; the other reduces your attention, and you leave things be. Studies show that, rather than trying to neutralise them, if we simply acknowledge negative thoughts, they tend to fade away. It's a proven strategy for breaking their persistent power. So next time, rather than struggling to 'get rid' of a clingy, negative thought, simply allow the painful thought to be there. Acknowledge it, then release it.

Feelings and thoughts come and go. That's life. Let that flow happen. Don't place too much importance on the negative ones. Because clingy thoughts, like burs, tend to fall off in their own time when we don't attach too much importance or meaning to them.

The less attention we give the negative, then the less power it has over us.

- *What do you notice when you sit with a troubling thought without attempting to push it away or resolve it?*

- *Have you talked to other people about the sort of repetitive thoughts that they experience and how important they believe them to be?*

- *Could you be 'mindful' of the problem, but deliberately put your attention on to something else? Try setting a specific length of time (fifteen minutes for example) and see how it feels.*

THE IMPORTANCE
OF SLEEP

ALONGSIDE SAS SELECTION, the Navy SEAL training programme is probably the most feared military training that any individual can experience, in a large part because of the near three days of complete sleep deprivation.

Good sleep has many deep benefits. We're less likely to get sick and we have a lower risk of serious health problems. We experience less stress, our mood improves, we are more creative and we recover and heal physically much faster.

Studies show that even after seventeen hours without sleep your judgement, memory and hand-eye coordination all suffer. Yet nearly 70 per cent of UK adults have broken sleep and a quarter get no more than five hours per night.

Taking our quality of sleep seriously, and figuring out how to get a sufficient amount of it, is one of the best ways of maintaining our wellbeing. People tend to describe themselves as a 'good' or 'bad' sleeper, but I have learnt that we can all take positive steps towards improving the quality of our sleep. Like most things, it takes some persistence, but there is hope for those who struggle.

- *Do you respect getting enough sleep?*
- *If your physical or mental health isn't what it could be, could poor sleeping patterns be at the root of the problem?*
- *Do you have an intentional routine for preparing yourself to get a good night's sleep?*

'Make good sleep a priority'

'SLEEP HYGIENE' IS all about putting yourself into the best mindset to get as good a night's sleep as possible. I learnt many of my sleep habits in the military, where you become accustomed to grabbing some shut-eye just about anywhere, whenever you can.

I split sleep hygiene into three categories: Pre-sleep, Sleep and Not Sleeping.

'Pre-sleep' is making sure we get enough 'wind down' time, away from screens and stressors.

'Sleep': we should try to set our bedtime to roughly the same time every night, so the routine gets internalised. It helps if our body is expecting to switch off. Pay attention to the small stuff, like making sure the room isn't too hot or cold. Maybe read a 'slow' book to calm the brain down, instead of switching into problem-solving or planning mode.

'Not Sleeping': try to avoid worrying about not sleeping. Just say to yourself: 'I am going to have a refreshing, recovery lie-down for a few hours.' Maybe get up and restart your sleep routine, have some water, get back into a book, until you're relaxed.

Make good sleep a priority and you will see benefits across your waking life.

- *What do you tend to do before sleeping that gets you ready for a deep and refreshing sleep?*
- *What 'sleep hygiene' steps would you like to try?*

WHAT BEGINS BADLY DOESN'T HAVE TO END BADLY

THERE IS AN old adage: 'What begins well, ends well.' It's as if a good start is an unshakable omen for a positive outcome. But life isn't always like that and, in reality, the maxim couldn't be further from the truth. I have seen the most perfect starts turn into a gruesome fight for survival. Life just isn't always pretty or predictable.

Things had started perfectly for Joe Simpson. He and his climbing partner Simon Yates had just become the first men to summit the 20,000-foot Siula Grande's West Face, in the Andes mountains of Peru. At 7.30 a.m. the next morning they started their descent, but Joe fell, badly breaking his leg and destroying his knee. Through a series of terrifying events, including having his partner resort to cutting the rope that was holding him, Joe ended up alone, presumed dead, deep down an ice crevasse.

Despite being in unimaginable pain and impossible circumstances, Joe refused to give up hope. He would spend the next three days crawling off the mountain to safety in what is one of the most incredible stories of resolve in mountaineering history.

- *Have you been tempted to believe that how something starts is a guarantee of how it will end?*
- *How has this affected your willingness to battle through things when circumstances have changed?*
- *What was Joe Simpson's attitude towards a 'hopeless' situation?*

'See beyond the feeling that failure is inevitable'

ICONIC SCIENTIST, ARTIST and inventor Leonardo da Vinci said, 'Obstacles cannot crush me. Every obstacle yields to stern resolve.'

In a world of 'fresh starts' it can be tempting to give up early and say, 'This isn't working. I'll try something else.' Inevitably, this reinforces the false idea that 'what begins well, ends well', or 'what starts badly, ends badly'. Neither is true.

Joe Simpson's descent of the Siula Grande is evidence of what people can resolve to do when they haven't got any other choice: it's seeing beyond the feeling that failure is inevitable. The same resolve led Leonardo da Vinci to design a helicopter five hundred years before one was actually built; he resolved to see beyond the obstacles and assumptions of his day. How often do the most life-changing and life-enhancing moments come off the back of many obstacles and challenges.

- *When have you seen how 'resolve' has turned difficult situations around?*
- *What do you see as the primary obstacles or assumptions that limit you today?*
- *How empowering would it be to really believe that a bad start can become a great ending?*

OVERCOMING THE BULLY

ONE OF THE hardest things about going to boarding school was witnessing some pretty horrible bullies. Sometimes against me; often against my buddies.

I was thirteen when one of the sixth-form boys, high on something, thought it fun to treat my buddy and me as his personal punch bag. It set a pattern: whenever the boy was high, he'd come for us. And it was never fun.

I am sure some of the fears I still have come from that time. It wasn't just about being on the receiving end – what was often worse was witnessing bullies in action and being powerless to stop them.

As any parent will know, one or two bullies can make life unbearable for kids. It's why I have a good antenna for bullies nowadays. If I see it anywhere, I deal with it. Because I've seen the lifelong destruction it causes. No child (or adult) should have to rely on their wits, their luck or stature to be safe. Bullying just shouldn't be accepted as a part of life.

It is our shared duty to deal with bullying – to call it out and put systems in place to prevent it.

- *Have you been subjected to bullying?*
- *What effect did it have on your self-esteem?*
- *If you could speak any words of encouragement to your younger self, what would you say?*

'While some of my experiences were painful, I never got isolated'

TEXAS UNIVERSITY RESEARCH concluded that victimisation does the most damage to those who feel isolated. While some of my experiences were painful, I never got isolated. My buddies were a real strength to me and we bonded more deeply through some of those tough moments.

Being scared *and* alone can so often create a negative cycle. Bullies tend to pick on people who are isolated because the bullying is easier to do.

I have watched musk oxen pursued by wolves on the Siberian tundra. While the oxen were running away, those left isolated were most vulnerable. But then the oxen turned as one, forming an impenetrable circle around the stragglers. The wolves, and the threat, soon slunk away.

Overcoming bullying is not the responsibility of the victim, but of the community. It's never 'nothing to do with me' – it's 'everything to do with us'. We have to speak out against bullying. It takes courage. But do it – it's always worth it in the long run.

Remember the oxen. Never suffer alone.

- *Have you become isolated as a result of being bullied? Is there a safe friend or person you can talk to?*
- *How could you use your voice to tackle bullying as part of your wider community?*

LIVE BY YOUR PRIORITIES

A N IMAGE THAT will always stay with me is watching a good buddy, Steve Rankin, one of our executive producers of *Man vs Wild*, wading through a swamp in Sumatra. As the water grew deeper and deeper, he moved his treasured tobacco and rollies from his knee pocket to his trouser pocket, then to his chest pocket, the top of his hat and, finally, to his hand clutched high over his head. Meanwhile his radio, his phone, his notebook were all ruined by the rising waters.

It's a silly reminder that we have the power to choose what we prioritise, good or bad.

One of the most important things we need to figure out is what matters most or least to each of us. Only then can we consciously live according to the genuine order of our priorities.

You could say that the most significant thing in your life is working out what are the most significant things in your life. It's never a one-time activity, but more of an ongoing process; life changes and our priorities change with it. That's good. Ultimately, the priorities that we carry should determine the actions that we take.

- *Can you think of a moment when you consciously decided to protect a specific priority?*
- *Have you spent time recently thinking about what matters most to you and what matters least?*
- *Are you satisfied that your priorities are determining your actions? If not, what could you change?*

'Vision and priorities are most likely to get you where you want to go'

OLYMPIAN AND FORMER marathon record-holder Bill Rodgers said, 'Always take the long-term view and train and race smart, with a bit of caution.' It's hard to be cautious and keep that long-term view.

The danger we face is in prioritising the things that seem to matter most in the short term, but that might damage us in the long term. So, before we act in haste to protect ourselves from a little short-term pain, it's worth thinking through what we value most in the long run.

It's achieved by staying connected to your long-term vision and staying aligned to your real priorities and values. Like a pair of train tracks, vision and priorities are the most likely to get you to where you want to go.

- *Do you tend to keep a long-term view or find yourself prioritising short-term demands?*
- *How could staying true to the priorities that really matter to you create conflict or pain in the short term?*
- *Are you aware of your two tracks of vision and priorities? Have you got some clarity of where you want to go?*

KEEP GETTING BACK UP

'VE NOTICED THAT schools don't tend to reward resilience. So often, they love to reward the academically gifted and the most athletic. But the error of this is that it teaches young people that gritty effort, and getting back up after repeated failures, isn't what matters, it is natural talent that counts the most. We all know this simply isn't true.

The world is full of talented folk who too often achieve very little. They lack the fight to win through against the battles of life. And time after time I have seen less talented yet highly resilient people triumph.

One of Charles Dickens' characters in *Great Expectations* said that 'suffering has been stronger than all other teaching . . . I have been bent and broken, but – I hope – into a better shape.'

Resilience is built through hard experiences – it just needs exercising and strengthening, and we do that through falling down and repeatedly getting back up. Deep down, we have that 'never give up' quality already inside of us.

- *What was your experience of school? Did it equip you for the challenges of life?*
- *What do you notice about the power of resilience in enabling people to reach their goals?*
- *Do you feel spent by a bruising encounter in life? What would it look like for you to 'never give up' in this situation?*

'Strength is shown by getting up every time we fail'

RESILIENCE HAS ITS origins in the Latin verb 'to leap'. The ability to jump up when life pushes you down is the difference between success and failure. So long as you can keep getting back up, you're still in the fight.

Floyd Patterson was boxing heavyweight champion of the world twice between 1956 and 1962. In his obituary in the *Washington Post*, Patterson is quoted as saying, 'They said I was the fighter who got knocked down the most. But I also got up the most.'

Life can be full of disappointments and setbacks. It's bruising, and many aren't trained or prepared for it. I now look at the struggles of life as a training ground. I know that every obstacle is an opportunity to grow my resilience. Strength is not shown in never failing, but by getting up every time we fail.

- *In what way is the message of Floyd Patterson inspiring and countercultural to what you were taught about succeeding in life?*

- *How could you see failures and obstacles as training rather than draining?*

- *How would it feel to start to embrace hardships rather than run from them?*

DAY 163

DAMMING
GRIEF

THE BIGGEST DAM in the world, based on water storage, is the Kariba Dam, whose reservoir capacity is 185 billion cubic metres of water, spanning the mighty Zambezi in Africa. Like many superdams, however, it has damaged the river life far beyond its walls. Dams hold back sediment as well as water, and the removal of sediment from coastal habitats is like removing its food – so they self-destruct.

When our grief gets dammed up, it doesn't make it go away. It makes it go rotten. Suppressing sad feelings changes the emotional landscape ahead of us: rather than finding new joy in life, we can find the future disinteresting, barren and bleak.

Many of us struggle with unresolved grief and may need help to get the journey of grief moving again. When my father died suddenly, it was a life-changing shock for me at a young age, and it took a long time to heal. It still hurts. I needed to keep talking, occasionally crying, and never denying that sense of loss. There is no way around grief, the only way is through it.

- *Do you come from a family or culture where emotions are not welcomed?*

- *Have you felt the need to be overly positive or neutral about your grief experience?*

- *What would you need to let the waters of grief (and their sediment) start moving?*

'Let grief be part of your journey and the waters will flow again'

OLYMPIC CHAMPION ERIC LIDDELL spent the final years of his life in Weihsien Internment Camp in China. He died of a brain tumour just five months before liberation. 'Life is full of hard experiences, bitter disappointments, unexpected losses, grim tragedies,' he said. 'Circumstances may appear to wreck our lives, but God is not helpless among the ruins.'

In a world in which we have so much control, I found grief to be totally humbling. Elisabeth Kübler-Ross's cycle of grief starts with 'denial' and 'anger'. Those emotions have their place and need to be felt and acknowledged – not dammed up. They are meant to flow through to the next stages: depression, bargaining and, then, acceptance.

Grief isn't something you can control. But, as the journey progresses, there is a rebuilding among the ruins: a new hope and a deep sense of gratitude for all of the precious times you have shared.

Don't rush it: let grief be part of your journey and your subconscious will lead through to newer, fresher, happier pastures. The waters will flow again and the river will nourish and renew your soul. Your own 'Zambezi' is always ready to heal.

- *Have you felt hopeless about the future because of loss or grief?*
- *When you think about the future, what are you looking forward to beyond this stage of your grief journey?*
- *What is giving you hope in the circumstances of your life?*

THE ART OF
PACKING LIGHT

P ACKING LIGHT IS essential to any successful journey – both in adventure and in life. But it's surprisingly hard to do.

There's the 'good' kit we need and then there's all the stuff that's better left behind, but has a habit of getting into our bags anyway. The extra clothes or spare gear always seems so important. But it's not. And in turn it tends to make the journey harder and less fun. A little bit of reserve is good, but too much is simply cumbersome.

On the other hand, 'bad' kit can be tough to identify. Some things we have been carrying for so long, we can't imagine living without them. It might be helpful to write down a list of some of the things that you have been burdened by. Can you let it go? Imagine what a loving friend might say about it.

- *Have you struggled to let things from the past go?*
- *Do you feel yourself taking too much responsibility for the people around you?*
- *What would it feel like to lighten the load?*

'We can all benefit from inspecting our luggage from time to time'

WE ALL HAVE the superfluous baggage of life: negative habits and patterns and beliefs that we have picked up through disappointing experiences, tough times and relationship let-downs. We may know that they are weighing us down, but they seem to sneak into our hearts anyway. Ultimately these heavy weights can divert us from the happiness and confidence that we are longing for.

We can all benefit from inspecting our luggage from time to time with a neutral eye, or even asking a friend for an honest opinion. Are there unhelpful habits and stories that you tell yourself that add nothing and weigh you down? Can you let them go?

King David in the Bible knew all about troubles, yet he found a simple solution: 'Cast your cares on the Lord'. It's simple but great advice if you want to travel light and be effective.

- *Are there specific experiences or emotions that play on your mind?*
- *What would a kind friend say about what you are burdened by?*
- *Could you cast down the load today?*

SACRIFICE CHANGES EVERYTHING

IN FEBRUARY 1942, Singapore fell to the invading Japanese army. A group of Scottish soldiers was taken into captivity. Conditions were so brutal, and their captors so cruel, that all camaraderie between the soldiers broke down. In an account from Prisoner of War Ernest Gordon, a commander in the Scottish infantry, a work party was returning to camp. At the first checkpoint, the shovels were counted and one was found to be missing. The officer in charge demanded the missing shovel be produced. No one came forward. The officer raged. Still nothing. He threatened to shoot them all if the culprit didn't confess. Calmly, one soldier stepped forward. 'I did it,' he said. The officer beat him to death with the butt of his rifle.

At the next checkpoint, when the shovels were counted again, the full number was found present. The previous guard had miscounted. The story spread like wildfire among the prisoners. That soldier's extraordinary act of sacrifice changed everything. Attitudes altered overnight. The prisoners stopped their in-fighting and instead began caring for one another, sharing their meagre resources, helping each other endure the horrific situation.

True heroism changes us all for the better. Small or big, it doesn't matter. Every kind sacrifice has a ripple effect.

- *To what extent do you think sacrifice is valued or celebrated in society today?*
- *Can you think of a moment when someone else's sacrifice had a profound impact on you?*

'Sacrifice flies in the face of the idea that our own needs, opportunities and rights are paramount'

SACRIFICE IS THE greatest starting point for building a strong team – whether a family, marriage, company or sports team. If we start by honouring one another and forgoing our individual interests, we can become something far greater than the sum of our individual parts.

In a highly competitive world, self-sacrifice stands out. Canadian sailor Lawrence Lemieux was in second place in a race during the 1988 Seoul Olympics, when he saw two sailors in trouble: Joseph Chan was too injured to climb back into his boat, and Siew Shaw Her was being swept away in the waves. Lemieux abandoned his Olympic dream, rescued both men and then resumed, finishing 22nd. The Olympic Committee president said, 'By your sportsmanship, self-sacrifice and courage, you embody all that is right with the Olympic ideal.'

Sacrifice flies in the face of the idea that our own needs, opportunities and rights are paramount. Instead it says, 'I am willing to forgo my own best interests for the sake of something or someone else.' Self-sacrifice can change culture for the better and has the power to reorder our lives around what really matters.

- *Can you see ways in which you are sacrificing for others or others are sacrificing for you?*
- *In which areas do you struggle most to sacrifice? Why do you think this is?*

MAKE
YOUR BED

ANYONE WHO ENTERS the military finds out pretty quickly that making your bed isn't an optional chore. Indeed, this simple daily task was made famous in a speech by US admiral William McRaven, who said making your bed in the morning can be the best way to set yourself up for success.

When we decide to begin every day by achieving one thing well, it can have a profound effect on the rest of our day. This happens for several reasons. Practically, it sets the pattern for how we approach other tasks ahead of us. It gives us a sense of achievement early on – however small – and it sets the tone for the rest of the day.

Doing the small stuff well can also bring with it a sense of calm order. When we feel organised, we feel more secure and have more confidence when it comes to tackling bigger challenges.

- *How could you set yourself up for success at the start of your day?*
- *What small changes could you make to your routine that would leave you feeling calm, ordered and ready to achieve other things?*

'It's about taking care of the little things in life'

ALL OF US get frustrated or stuck in our attempts to make progress with the big stuff in our lives. But by choosing to achieve simple things when you first get up, you are giving yourself a strong platform for the day. You may not have reached the summit of your mountain, but you can feel proud of the fact that you are starting strong and with purpose.

In other words, it's about taking care of the little things in life. If we can manage those well, we improve our chances of going for the bigger things and achieving them. Admiral McRaven writes, 'Remember . . . start each day with a task completed. Find someone to help you through life. Respect everyone. Know that life is not fair and that you will fail often. But if you take some risks, step up when times are toughest, face down the bullies, lift up the downtrodden, and never, ever give up – if you do these things, then you can change your life for the better . . . and maybe the world!'

- *How might achieving some simple tasks at the start of the day impact your mindset?*
- *How could breaking down tasks into small achievable steps impact your sense of achievement?*
- *What inspires you about Admiral McRaven's challenge, and what can you put into practice today?*

DAY 171

IT'S THE LITTLE THINGS
THAT FEED LIFE

ONE OF THE most spectacular places on earth is the Great Barrier Reef off the east coast of Australia. It's the world's largest coral reef system. It's visible from space, and represents the world's biggest single structure made by living organisms.

The reef structure is built by billions of tiny coral polyps, and supports the lives of many millions of other creatures. Taken alone, each individual microscopic organism doesn't amount to very much. But together these tiny creatures have created one of the most prolific habitats on the planet.

It's easy to think that contentment comes from the big things in life like your career or achievements. But it is really the little things that make life most beautiful. It is so often the unseen, fleeting moments that bring the most happiness and joy. A child's hug, a moment of uncontrollable laughter with a friend, a sunset, or some birds flying low overhead.

- *Do you find yourself relying on reaching the 'big things' to feel happiness and fulfilment in life?*
- *What can you do to appreciate the 'little things' that you may have missed?*
- *If you were going to describe your life so far, what are the most notable 'small moments' that knit your story together?*

'Never overlook
the little things'

A PHILOSOPHY PROFESSOR showed his class an empty jar. He filled it with a few big rocks and asked the class if it was full. They said yes. Then he poured in some gravel. He asked the class if it was full. They said yes. But then he further filled the jar with sand and water.

It's easy to think that our lives are made complete by 'big things': a career, a relationship, children. Not everyone will find those things, but even for people who do, life is so much more than just having three big rocks in the jar. What makes life wonderful, and connects the big rocks, is the small stuff. Never overlook the little things: hugs, laughter, smiles, cups of tea in the sun with a loved one.

We tend to celebrate what we see as big and significant. When diving on the Great Barrier Reef, it's easy to get distracted by a big shark or the brightest fish. But the real wonder comes from those tiny coral polyps pulsating and sparkling with life and beauty.

- *What are the 'big rocks' in your jar, and which, if any, do you hope to add?*
- *How intentional are you about what fills the rest of the space? What could fit in that you haven't considered yet?*
- *Which smaller things, attitudes, actions, behaviours or opportunities do you want to see more of?*

DAY 173

KEEP GENEROSITY
FLOWING

R UNNING WATER IS nearly always a sign of life and health within an environment. Stagnant water, on the other hand, promotes diseases and can be deadly. Water is water, but how it moves can be the difference between life and death.

My mum taught me one of the greatest lessons I ever learned about generosity. Money is like a river, she said, then explained that if we block up a river and dam it, the water goes stagnant.

In the same way, if we cling too tightly to money then, like a dammed river, our lives will fester. But if we keep the stream moving, keep giving stuff and money away wherever we can, then the river keeps running and our lives stay healthy.

- *What have you noticed about generous people?*
- *What prevents your flow of generosity to others?*
- *How does being generous change how you feel about life?*

'The best way to grow in generosity is to create a habit'

LIFE HAS PROVED Mum right. Her beliefs about generosity are also borne out in science. Soyoung Q. Park is a scientist at the Zurich Neuroscience Centre. She said, 'Our study provides behavioural and neural evidence that supports the link between generosity and happiness.' Her work also showed that the benefits of generosity weren't affected by the amount we give.

Generosity is not dependent on a person's wealth, it is dependent on a person's attitude. The best way to grow in generosity is to create a habit. If we wait until we believe we can afford to be generous we might have the means but we won't have the mentality.

This seems to work not just for money but for anything of value which we might possess. Any skill, any gift, any time, any love, any generosity of spirit. Whatever it is, when we give it away, we find the river soon fills again: generosity is a gift both to the recipient and to the giver.

- *What would a habit of generosity look like in your life?*
- *How has your own generosity impacted other people and how has it impacted you?*
- *How can you cultivate your generosity to include your skills and time as well as finance?*

EXPRESSING EMOTIONAL PAIN

THIS DAY CONTAINS CONTENT RELATING TO SELF-HARM

MANY CHILDREN WERE told 'sticks and stones may break my bones but words will never hurt me'. Despite the good intentions, in terms of mental fitness, it's an entirely inaccurate statement. Physical wounds are painful, but they generally heal. Emotional wounds are harder to identify and the pain much harder to express.

It can take us a whole lot of time and upset to realise that we are hurting emotionally. Some people can feel so overwhelmed they just feel numb. If people feel like this they may struggle with cycles of self-harm, in part to express, or distract themselves from, the emotional pain or to punish themselves for a perceived fault. Self-harming has many different causes and carries a lot of stigma and misunderstanding.

Expressing emotional pain by talking is important, but if a person struggling with self-harm is faced with stigma, it can be especially hard to open up. Self-harm is neither attention-seeking nor fashionable. It is not limited to a specific gender, age or ethnicity. When we witness it in those we love, it can be heart-breaking. We can help others by acknowledging that self-harm often begins as a way of trying to manage emotional pain, even if it is not ultimately constructive. Then we can begin to offer a compassionate response.

- *What have you noticed about the importance of expressing emotional pain?*
- *When have you found it hard to articulate emotional pain?*
- *What assumptions have you made about self-harm?*

'When life gets painful, write it down'

TWENTY-YEAR-OLD TRYGGVE GRAN was a tough Norwegian ski expert, part of the Terra Nova expedition of 1912, seeking to recover the bodies of Captain Scott and his team from the Antarctic. Gran, like so many hardened explorers, knew the importance of expressing his emotional pain through writing a journal. On the discovery of Scott's body, he wrote, 'I will never forget it so long as I live – a horrible nightmare could not have shown more horror than this.'

Captain Scott's own final entry read, 'We shall stick it out to the end, but we are getting weaker, of course, and the end cannot be far. It seems a pity, but I do not think I can write more.'

A friend of mine uses the phrase 'write yourself clear'. When life gets painful, write it down. It helps us express what we really feel – and it is free, private and accessible to us all. So be as honest and vulnerable as you want to be. Each word or scribble can replace despair with hope. If you begin to 'write it out', you will feel relief, and will also get clarity on whether you need further support.

- *What strikes you about explorers' use of a journal to manage their emotional pain?*
- *Have you tried keeping a journal as a way of exploring your feelings in the past?*
- *Are there any obstacles to you beginning a journalling habit today?*

MATCHING YOUR STRIDES

THERE'S A PLACE in South America called the Meeting of Waters. It's where the Amazon River and the Rio Negro run side by side in the same channel. One is dark and clear; the other sandy and opaque. What creates the unique phenomenon is a difference of both speed and temperature between the two rivers. As the speeds and temperatures begin to match up so the waters begin to blend. I've found the forming of new friendships to be something like this.

Over the years, I've met some incredible people, each of them beautiful and precious in their own unique way. Even so, good connections can take time to build. First impressions rarely do a person the credit they deserve.

The key, in my experience, is how long we are willing to walk alongside each other. The author Albert Camus wrote, 'Don't walk in front of me – I may not follow. Don't walk behind me – I may not lead. Walk beside me. Just be my friend.'

- *Which friendships have taken a long time to build and what do you value about them?*
- *What have you noticed about 'first impressions' versus a person's true character?*
- *What does it look like for you to walk alongside someone in friendship?*

'Friendships are formed when we learn to match our strides'

PROFESSOR ROBIN DUNBAR said, 'Friendship is the single most important thing affecting our psychological health and wellbeing, as well as our physical health and wellbeing.'

It's characterised as much by our differences as it is by our similarities. Psychological research also supports the idea that differences make for stronger friendships over the long term. Opposites tend to connect people.

Some of us are naturally warmer; some cooler. Some people are naturally gregarious – they love meeting new people. Others are quiet, a little mysterious; they take a while to open up. It's all good. It's how we are. Just like the Amazon and Rio Negro; friendships are formed when we learn to match our strides with humility and curiosity, while being ourselves and letting others be themselves too.

- *Do you have a tendency to rush friendships or expect people to be like you?*
- *What would it look like to match your strides with someone who is different to you?*
- *What would curiosity and humility look like in practice when it comes to friendships?*

FEELINGS JUST ARE. ACCEPT THEM

A UNIVERSITY OF GLASGOW study suggests that there are just four basic emotions from which every other emotion flows. These are Fear/Surprise, Happiness, Anger/Disgust and Sadness. It's good to remind ourselves that every one of them is normal.

Emotions tell us something about ourselves; they are a reaction to what we are experiencing. Some of us may have a disposition towards certain emotions such as impatience. Others towards completely different ones, maybe excitement. That's what makes each of us unique.

Trouble comes when we start thinking that some feelings are good and some are unacceptable. But feelings aren't good or bad, they just are. Even Jesus, a global symbol of peace and love, got angry. Emotions are indicators of what's going on in our lives – a bit like a thermometer. If we take the temperature in a swimming pool, it might be hotter or colder than we'd like, but it's certainly not the thermometer's fault.

- *Have you come from a family where certain emotions are not expressed?*
- *Do you try to suppress so-called negative emotions and shut them down?*
- *How could you take a more neutral view of your emotions?*

'When we accept our feelings, this empowers us to listen to what they are telling us'

EMOTIONS ARE AN indicator that something is going on in our lives, something that may need our attention. Author Gretchen Rubin wrote, 'Negative emotions like loneliness, envy, and guilt have an important role to play in a happy life; they're big, flashing signs that something needs to change.' It's important that we don't miss the message because we feel uncomfortable about experiencing a particular emotion.

For instance, many of us instinctually think it's wrong to get irritated or to cry. Or that it is weak to feel sad or low. Or crazy to feel like dancing or to get the giggles. But when we judge our feelings, we risk doing two things: missing what provoked them in the first place, and pushing them down inside us, especially if we don't 'like' them. Psychologists call this 'denial' – and denying our feelings doesn't do us much good, even though we all do it now and then.

In contrast, when we accept our feelings at face value, this empowers us to use them and to listen to what they are telling us.

- *What might your more uncomfortable emotions be trying to tell you?*
- *Could you sit with a difficult feeling for a bit before taking some action that might lead you into a different headspace?*
- *How might you become more accepting and even welcoming of your emotions?*
- *What is the message that your uncomfortable emotion may be offering you?*

FEAR NEVER RELENTS

BRAVE PEOPLE ARE all around us. It's just that some people's mountains are schools, or doctors' surgeries or high-street stores. Wherever there is a mountain to climb, there will be fear. The question is how to overcome it.

One thing I've learned about fear is that it never relents. It never says: 'I guess you've had enough now. It's time to ease off.' It's more like a shrinking elastic band: if you felt afraid in the supermarket it will push you towards the corner shop and then onto home delivery.

We all feel better when we first escape fear, but it has an annoying habit of slowly re-emerging in the place that we initially felt safe.

Avoidance tends just to delay the inevitable resurgence of fear in our lives. Helen Keller, the disability rights activist, wrote, 'Avoiding danger is no safer in the long run than outright exposure. The fearful are caught as often as the bold.'

- *Have you noticed the way fear progressively diminishes your freedoms?*
- *Has avoidance of fearful situations worked as a strategy for recovery?*

'Courage is not the absence of fear but the tolerance of it'

GUIDING PEOPLE IN the wild has given me the privilege of seeing people both confront and overcome their fears. Everyone's afraid of different things and has different challenges to face. Nelson Mandela said, 'The brave man is not he who does not feel afraid, but he who conquers that fear.'

Escaping from fear is self-defeating; fear is within us. But so is courage. Doing something every day that stretches our 'fear circle' will give us a richer, freer life. By this I mean deliberately stepping into a setting that provokes our fear, and then staying there long enough for the fear to subside on its own. And it will.

Remember, courage is not the absence of fear but the tolerance of it. The only way to beat it is to face it. And then it so often shrinks at our feet.

- *Could you stretch the fear circle and re-engage with something that made you feel afraid?*
- *How could you describe yourself as brave in the face of your specific fears?*
- *What would it look like for you to tolerate fear in the week ahead?*

MINING FOR GOLD

MICHELANGELO FAMOUSLY SAID of his statues, 'The sculpture is already complete within the marble block, before I start my work. I just have to chisel away the superfluous material.'

A results-oriented education can seem to be about cramming as much information as possible into our heads. We focus on recalling facts and don't give enough attention to character and attitude. That's an error.

The word 'education' comes from the Latin *ducare* – to lead – with the prefix 'e-' meaning 'out of'. The sense is of leading out of us what is already there. The tragedy of recall-oriented education is that it fosters inequalities in society – if you're naturally clever or sporty you appear to 'win'. But, I have found those natural qualities count for very little, compared to a focused mindset and a winning attitude.

A traditional education is a solid place to start but test scores never truly define us. Nothing can measure your gifts or the unique contribution you can make. There are rich seams of gold within each one of us. Know the power of the character within you, and choose the attitudes that will help you thrive.

- *Have you overestimated the significance of exam grades as a measure of your worth?*
- *Is something brilliantly unique within you, waiting to be drawn to the surface?*
- *How can you help call out the 'gold' in the people around you?*

'Every situation, especially the tough ones, can help sharpen us'

VIRGIN BOSS AND billionaire Sir Richard Branson left school at sixteen with no qualifications. On leaving, his headmaster suggested that he would either end up in prison or become a millionaire.

What set Richard Branson on track for success was a willingness to fail and the belief that the relevant learning was available to him if he looked. He says, 'Education doesn't just take place in stuffy classrooms and university buildings, it can happen everywhere, every day to every person.'

Of course, wealth is not a measure of success, but it can show realised skill and opportunity. Michael Ellsberg, author of *The Education of Millionaires*, argues that the success of people like Branson is built upon 'self-education in practical intelligence and skills, acquired outside of the bounds of traditional educational institutions'.

Whatever your experience at school, establish yourself as a lifelong learner. Every situation, especially the tough ones, can help sharpen us. Every obstacle is a chance to adapt and problem solve.

- *What inspires you about the journey of Richard Branson and the Virgin Group?*
- *Have you limited your ambition because things didn't go well for you in traditional education?*
- *What would it take to be empowered for life not just for school?*

BEING CREATIVE IS WHO WE ARE

EACH OF US has a spark of creativity within us. Some people have known this from an early age, and have found outlets to express themselves ever since. Others, for lots of reasons, have never discovered a way to express their creativity. Or worse, we've written ourselves off as being essentially uncreative. The truth is that everyone is creative. It's just a question of finding the right outlet.

In a busy world, being creative has never been more important. Getting lost in a creative activity, known as 'getting in the flow', actually changes our brain function for the better; quieting the 'inner critic' and making us more satisfied, calm and focused.

Mihaly Csikszentmihalyi, a pioneer in positive psychology, describes flow as, 'Being completely involved in an activity for its own sake. The ego falls away. Time flies. Every action, movement and thought follows inevitably from the previous one, like playing jazz. Your whole being is involved, and you're using your skills to the utmost'.

- *Have you written yourself off as uncreative?*
- *When are you closest to an experience of flow, and what do you notice about your state of mind at that time?*
- *How could you increase or extend your experience of flow? What might you try?*

'You don't need
to be the best'

FORGET WHO WAS good at art or music at school. True creativity is about doing what you enjoy and maybe building on what you are already doing naturally. There are infinite possibilities, from making a kite to graffiti art and everything in between. Remember, this is not for others, it's for you. It's not a competition and you don't need to be the best; you just need to enjoy getting lost in the activity.

The hardest thing about creativity is getting started. It can be difficult to know what you might enjoy and tempting just to stick with what you already know. But, there are no rules on how many different things you can experience. Lots of creative activities offer free taster sessions and you could explore several different things before taking anything further.

The great thing about creativity is that it is a mindset as much as it is an activity: once you start there is no stopping your potential. Maya Angelou writes, 'You can't use up creativity, the more you use, the more you have.'

- *What quirky, fun interests could you explore without making an early commitment on which one to take further?*
- *Have you noticed how getting into a creative mindset tends to lead to more and more creative opportunities?*
- *If you gave yourself permission to dream and there were no limits on your opportunity, what would you spend your time on?*

BROKEN DEFENCES

THE MAGINOT LINE was a massive line of fortifications, obstacles and weapons installations, built by the French in the 1930s as a deterrent against the growing threat of invasion. It ran the entire length of the France–Germany border and was, to all intents and purposes, impervious to attack. But in the end it proved to be an illusion; France surrendered in under a month.

Many of us, consciously or unconsciously, build complex systems of defence, usually against feelings that we find uncomfortable. The trouble is that, like the Maginot Line, there is always a way around. Feelings have a habit of squeezing through gaps or reappearing in other guises, maybe as anger or indifference.

I have learnt the power of simply naming difficult emotions rather than trying to block them. It is a kind of 'mindfulness practice' that welcomes each feeling in with curiosity. To explore it, probe it, ask questions of it.

Every emotion, especially the uncomfortable ones, can teach us something important. Don't be scared of them.

- *Have you found yourself to be quite intolerant of painful feelings, or defensive against anything that might provoke them?*
- *Have you noticed that they have a habit of showing up anyway, or being expressed in less helpful ways?*
- *What would it look like for you to name difficult emotions with curiosity rather than attempt to defend against them?*

'Walls that protect our hearts also become the walls that isolate us'

ON 10 NOVEMBER 1989, ten thousand East Germans streamed through the Berlin Wall in what would be the first step in the reunification of the country. The ninety-six-mile guarded wall had physically divided the capital since 1961 and 101 people had died trying to cross it.

Many of us will have had difficult experiences with people in the past, maybe through bullying or a betrayal of trust. It's natural not to want to get hurt again, and so we build defensive walls. The trouble is that walls to protect our hearts also become the walls that isolate us. Letting people 'back in' moves us from expectation to reality. Of course, we may be disappointed again . . . but, alternatively, we may not.

C. S. Lewis wrote in *The Four Loves*, 'There is no safe investment. To love at all is to be vulnerable.' The risk of love is potential pain, but without risk there is no reward. And love is always worth it. But go gently, one brick at a time.

- *Have you had bad experiences in the past that have led you to want to keep people out?*
- *How have these experiences formed your expectations for how people will act in the future?*
- *What might it look like for you to break down some walls and risk seeing what might or might not happen, that will in turn enrich your life?*

SET YOUR BOUNDARIES AND ACCEPT YOUR LOSSES

ONE OF THE deadliest disasters on Mount Everest in recent times was in 1996. When going for the final summit push, the rule was clear: if you can't make it by 2 p.m., you must turn around or risk running out of oxygen, time and energy.

On 10 May several climbers were moving too slowly in the sub-zero temperatures and rarefied air of high altitude. They decided to push beyond the cut-off time and go for the summit anyway. After all, they were so close.

When they made the call to go for the summit, they were impacted by the 'bias of sunk costs': they had come so far, climbed so high, expended so much energy, they couldn't just turn around. They reached the summit at 4 p.m. A blizzard came in and eight never made it off the mountain.

- *Are you at risk of breaking good boundaries because of the investment you have made in something?*
- *Is the feeling of 'being so close' to a desired outcome keeping you in the wrong situation?*
- *What is a reasonable 'cut-off time' for you to accept that an ambition may not be realised?*

'Take a moment to get an objective view'

THE BUMPER STICKER reads: 'Don't cling to a mistake just because you spend a long time making it.'

It is easy to lose our objectivity in life, especially when we are fighting battles or when we have invested ourselves in something heavily. We can think, 'I have come so far, spent so much, trained so hard . . .' But none of those things determine whether what we are doing is still right for us now.

If you find yourself unable to alter course or stop because you have invested so much in the past, take a moment to get an objective view. The boundaries and limits you set yourself are there to serve you and to preserve you. Use them.

- *Are you attached to a decision you have made despite knowing that it is not a good one?*

- *Are you in danger of losing more because you cannot accept losing what you have invested so far?*

- *What would it look like for you to be more accepting of mistakes and failures?*

THE MYSTERY OF WATER

GENERATIONS OF MY family have made our homes close to the sea. From the restlessness of the North Wales coast, to the calmer waters around the Isle of Wight, water has been part of our story.

The power of water inspires me, from the wild North Atlantic or raging South American jungle rivers. As anthropologist Loren Eiseley wrote, 'If there is magic on this planet it is contained in water.'

Physical survival is dependent on accessibility to water, but I have also experienced water as much more than a resource. It has often been a place of escape.

William Wordsworth said, 'A lake carries you into recesses of feeling otherwise impenetrable.' Whether it is swimming in the sea, lying beside a lake or walking along a river, I have found many moments of healing and connection by water.

You might not be a sailor or a cold water swimmer, but we can all benefit from time by water. Experiment: maybe go and get your feet wet along the beach, or gently swill the water in a pond. Healing will come to you, if you allow it.

- *What is your emotional response to water? How does being by, or in, water make you feel?*
- *How could a sense of the value of water impact the way you interact with it every day?*

'Get in and find the way water works best for you'

FOR THOUSANDS OF years water has been a source of wellbeing. The Romans brought their version of ritualised bathing to Britain in the first century AD. The temple on the site of the hot spring in Bath was there to honour Sulis Minerva; a sort of composite of the goddess of healing water and the goddess of wisdom. The message was clear: 'there is wisdom in getting into these healing waters'.

Anna Deacon described her recovery from burnout through sea swimming: 'Everyone was coming to the water with something: grief, depression, loneliness, pain. I quickly fell in love with the swimming community, how inclusive, wild and free they seemed on the outside, and how they held each other up to cope with the challenges they had on the inside.'

One of the dangers of modern life is that we edit the 'mystery' out. Nobody can really explain why water has such an important role in healing. But what is important is the experience. It's about getting in and finding the way water works best for you.

For me, it is swimming in the sea, sitting in ice, walking by a lake. Try some of these. Let the water wash over your pain.

- *What strikes you about the significance of bathing culture in history?*
- *Do you resonate with Anna's experience of swimming?*
- *How might you immerse yourself in water, for relaxation, meditation or sheer enjoyment?*

AIM AT NOTHING, HIT NOTHING

SETTING GOALS, BOTH big and small, work and personal, short and long term, has been so key for me over the years. Even if we have to change and sometimes extend as we go along, that's all part of it.

Just like the DZ (Drop Zone) keeps parachutists heading in the right direction, so goals keep us focused and heading towards a target.

It's not only about achieving the goals, it's as much about living with purpose and direction. Both of which in turn help us to have good mental health. Because when we aim at nothing, we hit nothing. And that's never good for our sense of wellbeing and value.

It's normal sometimes to avoid setting goals. We all want to protect ourselves from the disappointment or deflation of not reaching our targets. But remember: we shouldn't let our sense of identity become wrapped up in what we manage to achieve and what we don't.

- *How has having specific goals helped you in the past?*
- *Have you got a clear sense of purpose and direction in your life at the moment?*

'Having a goal has helped me see a way forward'

C. S. LEWIS WROTE: 'You are never too old to set a new goal or dream a new dream.'

I see setting goals like a gym. They allow us to exercise our 'effort' muscles and to stretch and strive and build that inner resilience. Whether we can lift 5kg or 50kg, whether we reach our goals first time or thirtieth time. It doesn't matter. The process builds our strength.

By not setting goals, we miss out on the positive side of trying and failing. We deny ourselves the motivation that comes through facing a challenge. In the times when I've really been struggling, I've found that having a goal has helped me see a way forward. Even if it is just hour to hour, day to day.

Remember – what matters most is not achievement but progress. Our goals don't have to be enormous, only big enough to stretch us. A little progress each week can be a game changer for growing confidence and a sense of wellbeing. Before long, you can look back and be amazed at how far you have come.

- *Have you become over-focused on achievement without seeing your progress?*
- *How would you define your short-, medium- and long-term goals?*
- *How has your strength or resilience been built through goal setting?*

10,000-MILE RIDE . . .
PATIENCE IS UNDERRATED

A FRIEND CYCLED 10,000 miles home from China. Midway into the first week, and already feeling exhausted, he decided to mark how far he had come. The line he traced stretched barely a centimetre on his map. Perhaps unsurprisingly he became extremely discouraged. It was only then he realised that he was going to need patience as much as persistence to achieve what he set out to do.

There are lots of different qualities necessary to achieve great things; grit, courage, vision . . . but patience is perhaps the most under-appreciated quality. I'm not the most naturally patient person, so I have had to work hard to cultivate it by shifting my focus away from my impatience and onto something I find constructive. You could try the STOP approach: **S**top what you are doing. **T**ake a slow breath. **O**bserve your thoughts and feelings. **P**roceed with a patient mindset.

- *Have you tended to underrate patience as a strength, in comparison to courage or vision, for example?*
- *How would you describe yourself in terms of natural patience?*
- *Are you willing to try developing greater patience through tools like STOP?*

'Patience is an active mindset that empowers you'

PATIENCE IS NOT a quality we tend to associate with high achievement. We might think that people who are going places aren't willing to sit around waiting for something to change in their favour. Rather, they act; they change the circumstances for themselves. But as Bill Gates, the founder of Microsoft says, 'Patience is a key element of success.'

Patience is not simply a passive sort of toleration, it's an active mindset that empowers you to wait positively and be prepared to act when the moment comes. Psychologist Sarah Schnitker's work on patience also shows that it's not only key to achieving your goals, but cultivating patience is good for your mental health and relationships too.

- *What might it look like for you to adopt a patient mindset that prepares you to act?*
- *How might increasing your patience impact your mental health?*
- *Is there a friend or family member that you could talk through your goals for patience with?*

THE BENEFITS
OF SEEING GREEN

ONE OF THE best things my dad ever gave me was a love for the outdoors and the natural world. It has never left me and I've been lucky that so much of my life, personal and professional, has involved being out in nature.

Taking my shoes off and walking barefoot in the grass is still one of life's greatest pleasures. I need to do it more.

When we breathe nature in, when we take time to enjoy it, appreciate it, then nature often rewards us with a sense of peace, wellbeing and connection with the world around us. It's how we are designed. How we have evolved. Through millennia.

This is borne out in science too: exposure to the natural environment has 100 per cent been shown to improve mood, sleep and wellbeing, as well as reducing depression, anxiety and low mood.

One study of 20,000 people, from Exeter University, concluded that, 'Compared to no nature contact, the likelihood of reporting good health or high wellbeing became significantly greater with more than 120 minutes of contact per week.'

- *How long do you spend in nature each week?*
- *Have you considered how your wellbeing could be improved by your experience of nature?*
- *Do you live in an urban environment? What could you do to interact in some form with nature more often?*

'Being proactive about seeking out the "green" has never been more important'

ONE OF THE realities of life in North Wales is the mountain weather; Snowdonia gets 270 wet days a year. (The Scouts brilliantly rename rain as Scouting sunshine!)

You cannot make your encounters with nature conditional on sunshine; you can only condition yourself to whatever nature offers you.

If we are really going to benefit from at least two hours a week in nature, we have to learn to embrace nature when she is kind *and* when she seems tough. This means not being scared to get out there even when others are hiding away. And the irony is: bad weather often brings out something powerful and primal in us. I love that. It reminds us of our roots.

The artist John Ruskin describes it like this: 'Sunshine is delicious, rain is refreshing, wind braces us up, snow is exhilarating; there is really no such thing as bad weather, only different kinds of good weather.'

With so many of us living in increasingly urban environments, being proactive about seeking out the 'green' in life has never been more important. If you want to feel better on the inside, get outside into nature as often as you can. It heals us. From the inside out.

- *Has the weather limited your time in nature?*
- *How could you reframe your feelings about good and bad weather?*
- *What would it look like for you to proactively seek out more time in nature each week?*

MAKING MISTAKES
AND HOW TO RESPOND

WE ALL MAKE mistakes. Human nature is human nature. David, the rough shepherd boy with a slingshot who killed Goliath went on to become the greatest King of Israel. He was a creative genius, writing many of the world's most spiritual songs.

It's easy to think that someone like David would be immune to temptation. But that is wrong. Returning from war, David caught a glimpse of a beautiful woman bathing below his window. He arranged to meet with her in secret while her husband was away fighting in the army. He knew it was wrong, but he carried on anyway.

I have learnt that there is a correlation between self-pity, rewards and mistakes. David had been a celebrated warrior and yet he had not joined his army in battle; perhaps he was wounded or battle weary. Either way, he made the mistake of his life. Self-pity often provokes people to reward themselves: 'I deserve this . . . this will make me feel better'. Rewards for self-pity are nearly always mistakes that we live to regret.

- *Have you tended to believe that you are less likely to make catastrophic mistakes than others? What is behind that view?*
- *Think back to significant moments of regret in your own life. What was the condition of your heart in the run up to what happened?*
- *What have you noticed about the rewards you allow yourself when self-pity creeps in?*

'Admitting mistakes early on saves us from more pain'

HOW WE RESPOND when we make mistakes is arguably more important than the mistake itself. In a court of law, honesty and remorse have a direct impact on sentencing. They are a key indication of a person's understanding and commitment to change.

David's response to his mistake was neither honest nor remorseful. After sleeping with the soldier's wife, he tried to cover up the scandal by arranging for the woman's husband to be sent to the front line where he knew he would be killed. To cover up his bad decisions, he leapt from adultery to murder. David ended up paying a bitter price for his error.

It takes real courage to be honest when we have made a bad decision. Bad choices have consequences, but it is always better to face them head on. Truth has a way of coming out. And admitting mistakes early, hard though it is, invariably saves us from more pain later on.

Nobody is immune from making mistakes. Equally, nobody is beyond forgiveness, as David found out. When we seek forgiveness, our lives become transformed.

- *Do you have a tendency to be defensive about mistakes you have made or are you normally honest upfront?*

- *What have you noticed about people's responses or reactions to genuine honesty and remorse?*

- *Do you live with hard regrets? How does David's story resonate with you?*

DEFUSING BOMBS

THE EOD REGIMENT is the British Army's specialist unit responsible for Explosive Ordnance Disposal. That is, saving others from unexploded bombshells. In February 2021, the 11 EOD Regiment RLC was called upon to 'safely' detonate the largest unexploded World War II bomb ever found. The 2,204-pound (1-tonne) bomb had been buried under a residential area in Exeter for eighty years. Thankfully, the EOD's training and courage saved the day.

In relationships, we often come across 'unexploded ordnance', historic experiences, perhaps, that make us particularly sensitive to certain words or situations. When we let someone close, and certain triggers are pulled, we can find ourselves reacting in explosive ways. Our instinct can be to blow the whole lot sky-high. 'This relationship is over!'; 'I quit!'. But with the right approach, old hurts don't have to create collateral damage.

The EOD is all about precision: shielding the good, while acknowledging a very defined and specific area of threat.

So define the specific threat. No sudden moves. Handle things gently. And call for support if you like. Help is OK.

- *When someone comes near a sensitive area of your life, do you feel tempted to blow the whole thing up?*
- *Could you isolate the problem and call in outside expertise to deal with it?*
- *Might it be possible to make the other person in the relationship an ally in the process?*

'Nobody is delighted to find mines in the sand, but far better to find them ahead of time than to step on them later'

PEOPLE OFTEN THINK that being engaged to be married is going to be a blissful few months, but it is often more turbulent than expected. Suddenly, and often for the first time in the relationship, we find out where the land mines are.

Many of us would rather not talk about the big stuff, whether this be in-laws, children, money or holidays. But it's worth being prepared, discussing them before we find ourselves in a heated moment, where those very subjects become red hot.

I remember doing a marriage preparation course and, on one level, everyone looked like the 'perfect couple'. But it was clear that everyone had stuff to work through and heated conversations to have. Nobody is delighted to find mines in the sand, but far better to find them ahead of time than to step on them later.

Communication is the oxygen of any good relationship. Through the willingness to tackle the very things that might explode later on, you build the trust and confidence to deal with the difficult stuff in life together.

- *Do you have a habit of skirting over the painful issues in your relationships because you want to avoid conflict?*
- *How could communicating your concerns protect you from serious conflicts, rather than provoke them?*
- *How could you trust each other to work together on the challenges rather than keep things buried?*

DEPRESSION
AND KINDNESS

ONE OF THE stigmatising myths I have encountered around mental health is that you have to be 'fixed' before making a difference to others. This is not a helpful perspective for any of us to hold, and puts false limits on people who are suffering from the already distressing features of mental illness.

What I know is that some of the deepest kindnesses I have received have come from people who know depression all too well. In fact, our world is continually being shaped for the better with kindness and compassion by what Henri Nouwen called 'wounded healers': people who have had, or continue to experience, mental illness.

Mother Teresa was an inspiration to the world. A Nobel Peace Prize-winner, she dedicated her life to helping the poor, destitute and sick. Mother Teresa established homes to serve people with HIV/Aids, leprosy and other diseases in 133 different countries. Yet not so many people are aware that, through much of her life, Mother Teresa suffered from depression.

- *Have you suffered from a mental illness and felt the stigma of 'needing to be fixed' before you could help others?*
- *How did that experience exacerbate or extend the feelings that you were already dealing with?*
- *How does the life of people like Mother Teresa inspire you to see your value and purposefulness alongside your mental health issues?*

'We can all make a difference to each other and our world'

MOTHER TERESA SET the bar of kindness and service to others very high, so I'm not suggesting that we can do what she did in her service to so many. (Although, who knows – some of us might.) We are all different and the impact of illness is different for everyone.

This is a challenge to those of us who might make assumptions around mental health that are simply untrue. Small or large, obvious or hidden, we can all make a difference to each other and our world despite (and sometimes because of) the suffering and struggles we are going through. It's a richer kindness because we understand what it feels like to struggle.

Mother Teresa said, 'Not all of us can do great things. But we can do small things with great love.' This is the heart of it. How together we can help each other to stand a little stronger.

Whatever you may be going through today, you have infinite worth, you are truly able to make a difference. Never forget that.

- *Have you made assumptions around mental illness that have stigmatised other people? How could you look at your value (or others' value) differently?*
- *Can you think of a person who you know has a struggle with mental illness but has made a really positive impact upon you or others?*
- *What small thing can you do 'with great love' today?*

HOW TO REBUILD FROM NOTHING

WALT DISNEY WAS born in 1901, the fourth son in a family filled with conflict. In 1920, he formed a company called Laugh-O-Gram, making animated fairy tales, but it went bankrupt. Walt tried his hand at acting in LA, but failed. Then he set up another animation company, but the producer stole his team of animators and the rights to his first successful animation.

He created Mickey Mouse in 1928, but Disney didn't become really successful until 1938 with the release of *Snow White*. Today, the company has a value of around $100 billion.

Failure is only the end if we let it be. If we simply refuse, there is no limit to how many times we can rebuild on broken foundations. Success is often simply holding on longer than anyone else.

- *What surprises you about Walt Disney's journey?*
- *Are there times in your life when you have allowed failure to be the end?*
- *What do you feel is the key difference between a successful idea and a successful attitude?*

'Never give up
on your fight'

IN 1988, AT the age of eight, Dina Nayeri fled religious persecution in Iran with her mother and brother, leaving their old lives behind them. Their subsequent ordeal to reach a safe haven is full of desperate and demoralising moments. Yet it is a story of astonishing resilience and courage.

After years living in refugee hostels, they were finally given asylum status in Oklahoma. Dina went on to win scholarships to Princeton and Harvard, and has since become a powerful voice for refugees seeking asylum in the West, as well as a hugely successful novelist and journalist. Her fight has become a source of hope for many people facing similar battles in their own lives.

Some fights change an outcome, other fights change us. We might not always get exactly what we have been working for, but the struggles will make us tougher. Never give up on your fight.

- *What do you find most inspiring about Dina's story?*
- *Can you recall a moment when, despite not getting the outcome you hoped for, it was still worth the fight?*
- *Is there anything you can do to ease the burden of refugees who have lost everything and are looking to rebuild their lives?*

BUILD
A BOND

BRUNO LEBEDA WAS trekking up the back of a mountain in the Alps, one of his dogs bounding through the snow by his side, when he stopped for a drink. The dog seemed unusually alert and, when he tried to move on, it sat between his legs, refusing to let him continue. Having learned to pay attention to his dogs, he shrugged and turned back the way he'd come. Minutes later, a loud crumping sound behind him caused him to turn to see a huge avalanche swallowing up the slope where he had been. The dog had saved his life.

It's easy to believe nurture is one-sided; we care for plants or pets or people. But they often care for us too – it's definitely a two-way street. I love my dogs. They are good for my heart, mind and soul. A report in the *British Medical Journal* said 'support from pets may mirror some of the elements of human relationships known to contribute to health'. At a time when loneliness is having such a negative impact on people, a pet may make a big difference.

A caring bond changes people for the better.

- *Are you nurturing something outside of yourself?*
- *Do you see 'looking after' something or someone as an extra chore or burden?*
- *If so, how could you change your perspective so you see the benefits to you as well?*

'We are better off together'

DOGS ARE ONE of the British SAS and Special Forces' great assets, used for clearing dangerous areas, detecting enemy forces and full-on offensive assaults. The attack dogs are impressive, intimidating – and incredibly brave. Both dog and handler. And that bond is special.

In 2011, Australian SAS were patrolling central Afghanistan, unaware of a Taliban ambush. Kuga, a Belgian Malinois dog, was sent to scout ahead. Sensing a threat, Kuga dived into a creek and swam towards the enemy. Taking AK-45 gunfire on his approach, he made the opposite bank then attacked the gunman. But he took five rounds in the fight. Despite his injuries, Kuga swam back to his SAS handler where he got immediate first aid.

Kuga received the Dickin Medal for outstanding bravery. Strengths and need are at the heart of any strong bond: Kuga needed his handler as much as his handler needed him.

If we display only strength, nobody can offer us anything. If we display only need, nobody can offer us enough. Show both and we can both help and be helped. Ultimately, a bond is an unspoken acknowledgement that we are better off together.

- *Have you shown only strength or need in relationships in the past?*
- *What would it look like for you to acknowledge how others are helping you, as much as you are helping them?*

RESIST THE GROUP EFFECT

'DON'T DO IT, Bear. Jungle rivers in flood kill.' That was the solitary voice of Woody, our former SAS safety consultant. On the other side of this conversation in the pouring rain was a director who was 'chasing the shot' and a tired crew who were ready for the end of the day.

There are many pressures on us to 'go with the flow'; sometimes it feels easier just to 'jump in' and get whatever it is over with. But just because the flow is heading one way doesn't mean it's the right way. In fact, negative peer pressure can have a seriously damaging impact on our lives. That day I jumped, and nearly paid the ultimate price. It was a mistake.

It can be hard to resist the pressures of our peers, colleagues or a group. To go against the flow requires courage, but it is always better to stand up for what we believe in, no matter how powerful the consensus of opinion might be.

The best way to deal with peer pressure is to practise saying no. It's not as hard as we fear and people always respect it. Even if they don't show it.

- *Are you being carried in a direction you don't want to go?*
- *What does it look like for you to go against the flow?*

'We make decisions in a group that we wouldn't make on our own'

WE ALL WANT to belong. Peer pressure is created by 'groupthink'. It's when the importance of being in the group outweighs our willingness to do what we know is right. Groupthink generally increases compliance and decreases our objectivity. We end up making decisions in the group that we wouldn't make on our own.

Overcoming peer pressure can be tough. I have learnt three key principles that have helped me: First, get good at saying 'no' and mean it. If people know that you stand your ground, they will respect your disagreement.

Second, build a diverse team. If everyone in your group sounds and looks the same, the uniformity makes you more likely to feel peer pressure and make bad decisions.

Finally, if you're under pressure in the moment, split the group, talk to people alone. Ask them what they really think and you are likely to get a more honest answer.

Over all of this you have to listen to your gut. It usually knows what your head hasn't worked out yet.

- *Are you at risk of 'groupthink' because you want to be included?*
- *Are your teams or groups uniform? How could you embrace diverse opinions?*
- *How do you feel about saying 'no' and how could you practise it?*

ARMY OF VOLUNTEERS

I N JUNE 2018, a youth soccer team and their coach entered the cave system of Tham Luang Nang Non in northern Thailand. Shortly afterwards, heavy rainfall flooded the caves, trapping them inside. A massive international rescue effort launched, involving thousands of rescue workers, divers, police officers and soldiers. Time was running out.

Two British amateur divers knew that they had some experience which just might help. John Volanthen and Richard Stanton volunteered their services. On 2 July – more than a week after the children were cut off – John and Richard found a way through the maze of flooded caves to the now desperate young people.

When it comes to helping others, it is tempting to leave it to the professionals. Yet a society that only accepts professionalised care is not only at risk of losing compassion but also of losing out on an army of highly skilled volunteers.

The care of others is the duty of all humankind. Never feel unqualified to offer what you have. You have more to give than you might imagine.

- *When others are in need, do you feel the pressure to leave it to the professionals? What's the risk of this approach?*
- *What could you offer someone who might need your care today?*

'We can all play our part
in a bigger network'

IN THE UK, seven million people play a vital role in actively caring for members of their family. That's one in ten people. These are the unseen heroes of our society; volunteers who rarely get the acknowledgement for the incredible work they do every day.

Almost 800,000 of those carers are teenagers, or children as young as five years old. It is believed 27 per cent of young carers miss out on school and one in three develop mental health issues themselves. For these young people, caring isn't a decision that they make to serve society. It's an obligation that they face because of their family circumstances.

Caring is costly and carers also need to be supported. It is why I admire organisations like Carers Trust and The Children's Society, even the Scouts, among many others, for raising awareness of young carers and the incredible work they do for local communities.

Often the greatest support we can offer is to people who are in a caring role themselves. Every carer needs care.

- *Are you a carer? Are people around you (at school, university or beyond) aware of your responsibilities?*
- *Were you aware of the number of carers and young carers out there? What could you do to support them?*
- *If you are a carer, do you tend to underestimate your need for support? Who could you talk to about being better resourced for your role?*

TWO STEPS FORWARD, ONE STEP BACK

I HAVE BROKEN QUITE a few bones over the years. It's painful, but particularly with my nose and shoulder, recovery followed a relatively predictable pathway. When it comes to emotional wounds, healing can waver a lot more: you can think that you have got through something only to find it suddenly aching badly.

We might have a good day, even a good week, but then find ourselves struggling at the bottom of the valley again. This can be really discouraging if we don't expect it.

They say time heals all wounds – but often things get worse before they get better. After losing my father, I learnt that healing couldn't be measured by good days and bad days, or even good weeks and bad weeks, but by the general trends within months and years.

- *Have you found old emotional wounds have a tendency to resurface?*
- *Had you expected a more straightforward recovery journey?*
- *How has this impacted the way in which you have felt about your own resilience?*

'In the toughest moments,
we are prepared'

THIS TWO-STEPS-FORWARD-ONE-STEP-BACK EXPERIENCE is exactly how mountaineers tackle the highest mountains in the world. In order to summit Everest, I had to climb it the equivalent of four times. Each time, the climber must reach higher and higher camps up the mountain and then return to base camp as they acclimatise to the increasing altitude. It's brutal and demoralising, but it's the only way to reach the top.

Just like a mountain, when we learn to anticipate an up-and-down journey, then in the toughest moments, we are prepared. Reliving old wounds doesn't mean that you are not healing, it means that you are simply experiencing the unpredictable process of emotional recovery.

- *Do you assume you should 'be over this by now'?*
- *Could you take a broader view of your recovery and see it in terms of months and years?*
- *What might a kind friend say about how far you have come?*

DAY 215

THE IMPORTANCE
OF CELEBRATION

VICTORY IN EUROPE, after nearly six years of war and millions dead, came on 8 May 1945. Streets across the country became a dancefloor as joy rang out.

Celebration *is* good for us, it makes us feel united and energised for the future. If we celebrate, then we are more likely to take risks, tackle new challenges, innovate and feel less stressed. We all need more celebration. Put it down to building mental fitness!

But often it never seems like the right time. So, we delay. VE Day wasn't the end of the war. But Churchill addressed the crowds, saying, 'We may allow ourselves a brief period of rejoicing; but let us not forget for a moment the toil and efforts that lie ahead.'

VE Day showed the necessity of celebration as much as the naturalness of it. It changed the energy of a nation for all the hard work still to be done.

I have learnt that, like all good things, celebrations require a level of discipline to achieve. Perhaps more so than other tasks, because they somehow seem not so vital. But they are.

- *How do you feel about the VE Day celebrations being an incomplete celebration, given that the war hadn't ended yet?*
- *Why do you think they changed the mood of the nation?*
- *Could you think about celebration as an important discipline?*

'We spend so much time trying to fix the difficult stuff in life that celebrations often get missed'

GARY CHAPMAN OBSERVED that we each have different ways to express and receive love within close relationships. Defined as 'The Five Love Languages', they are: giving gifts; words of affirmation; acts of service; quality time; and physical touch.

Celebrations encompass all five. They are in themselves an act of service. We give gifts and spend quality time together. We express affection with words of affirmation and physical touch. Celebrating is a complete expression of love.

Psychologist Shelly Gable showed that, faced with a partner's success, responding in a positive and celebratory way 'was the strongest predictor of current and future relationship satisfaction'.

We spend so much time trying to fix the difficult stuff in life that celebrations often get missed. And sometimes, what we believe warrants a celebration is too high a benchmark.

Celebrations are a crucial, joyful expression of love. You don't need to spend a lot of money; fish and chips can feel like a banquet if you bring the right energy. Just plan things in advance and bring the joy.

- *Have you found that celebrations have become less frequent in your relationships and friendships than you would like?*
- *Does the level of success required in order to celebrate need to be lowered, so you can party with loved ones a little more often?*

UNLOAD YOUR ROPE

ROPE CARE IS one responsibility that every climber takes super-seriously. At the end of the day, your life depends on it. Climbing ropes slow a falling climber by absorbing energy without creating an abrupt shock. Ropes that are left under load for too long lose their springiness, but ropes that are allowed to ease or relax, even though they may be well-used, regain much of their performance.

As humans, we are like that too. If we are left under load for too long, we also lose our springiness. Any shocks or additional burdens quickly feel bruising. I can sense this nowadays – when my ability to flex and absorb energy is being compromised because I am under load for too long.

We may be able to hold the emotional equivalent of a falling climber for a short time, but we aren't designed to walk around holding that sort of load on our own for very long.

- *Have you been under constant load for a really long time?*
- *How has that affected your springiness? Has your experience of anger or flexibility changed?*
- *When did you last feel the pressure come off? What would it be like to feel that again?*

'If we want to offer our best, we have to take the pressure off'

RETAINING OUR STRENGTH requires discipline, on occasion, to choose to unload or unwind, even if it is for just a few hours in a day. Charles Spurgeon wrote, 'Rest time is not a waste of time. It is an economy to gather fresh strength. In the long run, we shall do more by sometimes doing less.'

There may be seasons when we have little or no choice but to be in survival mode. But more often it's just an accumulation of loads that we never unburden, that then build up.

It's as much about humility as it is simply being smart – recognising that we are not as strong as we might hope. And accepting that if we want to offer our family and friends our best, then from time to time we have to take the pressure off enough to regain our emotional flexibility.

- *Do you feel pressure always to 'be strong'? How does this affect your ability to choose to rest?*
- *What burdens have slowly built up over time? If you were going to look at them critically, what could you let go of?*
- *What would a 'pressure break' look like in your day? Is there a way for you to make it happen?*

BE THE MOST ENTHUSIASTIC PERSON YOU KNOW

MY FATHER TAUGHT me that if you can be the most enthusiastic person you know, you won't go far wrong: pessimism and enthusiasm are polar opposites. One says, 'This will never work' and the other, 'How could this not work!'

Life has proven that this advice holds infinite power. Starting anything requires energy. Enthusiasm is often the critical difference between getting stuck or getting going. It sustains us when things are tough. It encourages people around us when they're struggling. What's more, it's totally infectious.

When we choose enthusiasm enough, it soon becomes a habit. It adds a sparkle of enjoyment to everything we do – whatever that is.

- *How does enthusiasm affect the energy in a room versus pessimism?*
- *Where has a lack of enthusiasm led to you getting stuck in the past?*
- *How have you been impacted by people around you who live their lives with great enthusiasm?*

'Success almost always follows an enthusiastic attitude'

RALPH WALDO EMERSON wrote: 'Nothing great was ever achieved without enthusiasm.' So true. Yet for me, the real joy of enthusiasm is that it isn't linked to ability. You can find something difficult and remain enthusiastic about it. This is one of the values that the Scouts do a brilliant job in building in young people. In life, success almost always follows an enthusiastic attitude. Knowing this can make a critical difference to all our futures.

Our enthusiasm can get muted by the fear that we won't be very good at whatever we are being asked to do. The Scouting promise is to, 'Dyb, dyb, dyb.' It stands for, 'Do Your Best'. (Not, 'Be The Best'.) If we approach everything with that level of commitment and enthusiasm we can always look back with pride.

You may not be the fastest, the fittest, the cleverest or the strongest, but there's nothing to stop you from becoming the most enthusiastic person you know.

- *Could you make being committed and enthusiastic a daily decision?*
- *What would it feel like to focus on 'doing your best' and thinking less about trying to 'be the best'?*
- *How could an enthusiastic approach change your experience of a particular task?*

APPROVAL ADDICTION

THE ROYAL CHARTER weather bomb was the most violent storm to hit the Irish Sea in the nineteenth century. Its name derived from the *Royal Charter* ship, which ran aground near our island home on the north-west coast of Wales. It was a new type of clipper, both with sails and steam engines, used on the commercial route from Liverpool to Melbourne. The company 'guaranteed' passage to the other side of the world in no more than sixty days. This guarantee proved fatal.

During its final leg into Liverpool in October 1859, the captain could have taken shelter in the Welsh port of Holyhead as the storm blew through. But fearing the company would disapprove if he missed the sixty-day deadline, the captain made the fateful decision to press on, and 450 lives were tragically lost.

'Approval addicts' compromise their better judgement for what they believe other people want. Professor John D. Kelly says 'recovery begins when we relinquish our belief that our value derives from the approval of others'. This takes time, but our true value should always be separated from our performance. Once we understand this, the allure of others' approval begins to wane.

- *Do you feel the approval of other people holds too much power over you?*
- *Are you able to push back when you feel your better judgement is being compromised?*
- *Have you found your intrinsic value?*

'Sometimes the most honest conversations are the hardest'

CIUDAD REAL INTERNATIONAL Airport, in Spain, opened at a cost of over €1 billion in 2008 and closed again in 2012. It was built on an inactive volcano field and in a special protection area for birds. It was also too close to Madrid Airport, and too far away from Madrid city. Someone hadn't had the courage to flag all this early on, and the cost of that error was astronomical.

Dr Bryan Robinson says, 'When you're afraid to speak up, disagree, say no, think outside the box or stick your neck out in a creative way, you could be unwittingly sabotaging your career.' Trying to please others is a trap of short-term pleasure and long-term pain. Ultimately, it can make us ineffective and untrustworthy.

Sometimes the most honest conversations are the hardest. Saying no can be a great sign of strength. It's about breeding transparency and being straightforward and straight talking. People generally appreciate those qualities in life.

- *Have you noticed how a 'yes culture' can have a really negative impact on productivity?*
- *What would it look like for you to live out of your gifts and skills rather than from your need for approval?*
- *When will you know that you feel secure enough to stop trying to please others?*

SHARPEN YOUR SENSES

BATS NAVIGATE AND find their prey using echolocation. They emit ultrasound waves that bounce off objects in their environment, which then return to the bats' ears, which are finely tuned to recognise their own calls.

Bats aren't blind, but they do rely on sound for the sort of information that most animals get with their eyes. But new evidence is revealing how bats have a very complex understanding of what they are encountering around them.

What we see or hear dictates so much of how we interpret what is going on in life. But often there is another level of perception that can help us 'see' beyond what is obvious and immediate. We are capable of that too. I have to check myself sometimes to ask 'what is really going on here?' Using our gut instinct is about gaining a more in-depth sense of what is going on in our circumstances – not just how something looks or sounds, but also how it feels.

I have learnt to trust my gut instinct more and more. It has been right more times than not. Trust it.

- *Do you tend to rely on one or two primary senses?*
- *Can you recall a moment when you got a strong gut instinct about something that proved to be right?*
- *How could you learn to depend upon and strengthen your gut instinct?*

'It's possible to bring a whole new level of perception to our personal interactions'

BRITAIN'S GREATEST SECRET weapon for air defence during the Battle of Britain was radar. This was still relatively new, but it meant the RAF could anticipate where the enemy bombers would be heading. In effect, radar was a level of perception beyond anything ever used in warfare until that point.

It's possible to bring a whole new level of perception to our personal interactions too. Communication experts talk about three levels of listening:

Level 1 listening is when we are focused on what we want to say next; Level 2 listening is when we are focused on what the other person is saying; Level 3 listening is when we are focused on what they really mean.

Level 3 listening is a powerful tool to unlock conflict, deepen intimacy or express compassion. It observes tone and body language and has a radar out for what isn't being said. It takes commitment to listen well, but the rewards can be huge.

- *Have you found yourself thinking about your next response while listening to others?*
- *Can you recall a time when someone used Level 3 listening with you? How did it make you feel?*
- *Would you like to listen in a more powerful and rewarding way? What are your next steps?*

ISOLATING OURSELVES FOR SHAME

THERE ARE TWO main reasons that people tend to isolate themselves: they believe that the world is not good enough for them, or they believe that they are not good enough for the world.

In my experience, we are often more inclined to believe the latter. While guilt is an 'I did wrong' feeling, shame is an 'I am wrong' feeling.

Over the years I have met a few beautiful-yet-frightened souls who have hidden themselves away in the most remote and hostile places: from deserted islands to festering swamps. The draw for them has been the fact that nobody else would encounter them there. But many of us live our everyday lives in a similar way. Hiding, for fear of being exposed as not being 'good enough'.

- *Can you identify feelings of shame in your life? Particularly not being good enough for others?*
- *How have feelings of shame made you respond? Do you have a tendency to hide your true self?*
- *Despite how powerful shame feels, what would a kind friend say about you? Would you believe them?*

'Vulnerability is good and creates connection'

WE ALL EXPERIENCE a degree of embarrassment and shame about things we've done. Guilt about the real mistakes we have made often leads us into feelings of shame about who we are. There is also often a sense of being a fraud, or believing that if people really knew us they would reject us. We can begin to believe that we aren't good enough, full stop.

We may not go as far as a swamp, but it's still possible to isolate ourselves in the humdrum of urban living – we just hide in plain sight.

The antidote to shame is never isolation, it's connection. According to shame researcher Brené Brown, 'Shame cannot survive being spoken, it cannot survive empathy.' If you feel like hiding, find a well-trusted friend and let them know. Invariably they will be touched by your honesty and vulnerability. And oftentimes they will offer up something equally hard to share.

Vulnerability is good and creates connection. And where there is love, acceptance and connection, shame withers and dies.

- *Do you feel the need to hide part of who you are, and are you proficient in hiding in plain sight?*
- *Do you feel unworthy of love? Who could you trust to open up to and receive empathy from?*
- *How could you become more vulnerable about what you are feeling? What is stopping you?*

LIVE LIFE LIKE IT'S YOUR GIFT

WHEN MY FRIEND was a student and engaged, his fiancée won a magazine competition for a luxury honeymoon to the Maldives. There was one catch: meals other than breakfast were not included.

He called the island, but the food was prohibitively expensive for the two students. Undeterred, they put their clothes in one bag and filled the other with Pot Noodles and energy bars. For the whole week they ate as much breakfast as they could and then ignored the luxury restaurants, eating their snacks in their room.

On the final night, he went to check the bill for the few food items that they had purchased. The receptionist looked confused and said that there had been a misunderstanding. There was nothing to pay. They were 'all inclusive' and could eat whatever they wanted from any of the restaurants.

It strikes me that many of us live like we are on a 'bed and breakfast' ticket in life, when actually we could be 'all inclusive'. Maybe we wait for permission to experience something that is already ours.

Live life like it's a gift to you. It is.

- *Do you have a tendency to limit your perspective on what life can look like for you?*
- *Do you tend to wait for others to allow you to participate, rather than stepping forward?*
- *How would it feel for you to 'live life like it's your gift'?*

'Real confidence means simply going for things . . . to give life your best shot'

'FAKE IT TO make it' is a bad strategy for happiness, not because it never works, but rather because it can. And, when it does, it leads us into living a life that isn't true to who we are. That invariably leaves people feeling like a fraud.

Living behind a mask of false confidence leaves the real you doubting yourself. And fake confidence also often isolates you from others. It's like other people can sense what is real and what isn't.

Genuine confidence is often quiet and unshowy, yet resolute. The best way to build such confidence is simply going for things, without concern for the results. To make a decision to give life your best shot, to smile – and maybe fail – but then to go again.

The sort of confidence that changes lives and inspires others understands that the real value is in attempting stuff and being authentic, rather than being dependent upon the results.

Confidence is linked to positive action, by going for things and taking opportunities that come our way in life. It is why confidence is never found. It is built.

- *Have you seen the downsides of a 'fake it to make it' approach?*
- *Do you feel you are living a life that is true to who you are?*
- *What would it feel like for you to build your confidence by trying things and not caring about the outcome?*

THE COLD WATER SECRET

'WE HAVE BECOME alienated from nature. But the cold is capable of bringing us back from what we once had lost.' So says extreme athlete Wim Hof, otherwise known as The Iceman. 'We are built to be happy, strong and healthy. We've got all the tools. But they are not awakened. So, who is going to wake them up?'

In recent years, cold water therapy has been growing in popularity. No wonder, as frequent exposure to cold is linked to a number of health benefits: it speeds up our metabolism, gives us an emotional boost, reduces inflammation and sore muscles, improves quality of sleep, gives us more focus, can combat depression and boosts our immune response.

The cold is uncomfortable. But get the timings right and it is perfectly doable and infinitely beneficial. I have learnt this over many years. Nowadays it's a habit of mine to get into cold water for three minutes, three times a week. It keeps me strong inside and out – as with so much in life, it's outside the comfort zone we find real rewards.

- *Do you shy away from things that are physically uncomfortable?*
- *What might a good first step into cold exposure, or something else that is physically and mentally difficult, look like?*
- *What do you find curious or exciting about the idea of experiencing the cold as a means to greater wellbeing?*

'It's a simple decision to endure a little hardship'

FINNISH SWIMMER JOHANNA NORDBLAD already held a world record when she had a bike accident leaving her with an extreme leg injury and chronic pain. Johanna's doctor suggested cold water therapy. Not only did it transform her experience of pain, she would go on to set a woman's world record of 103 metres for an under-ice swim in a bathing costume.

Johanna said, 'The first time I put my leg in 4°C water I only managed to keep it in for a minute, but the relief was immediate. Finally, it didn't hurt any more.'

So much of nature is ice cold, and to feel that all around me for a few minutes somehow feels primal and empowering. It's a simple decision to endure a little hardship. At first, everything in your being wants to get out. But afterwards, with those primal endorphins pumping, it can be amazing.

If you want to try it, do your research, be safe, start small, expect some discomfort, then go for it. The 'pain' is simply your blood rapidly leaving your skin and it's fine. It passes, leaving you feeling invincible. Don't believe me? Try it.

- *What inspires you about Johanna Nordblad's story?*
- *Could physical recovery, pain control or mental wellbeing motivate you to try cold water therapy?*
- *What steps would you need to take to overcome your natural aversion to the discomfort of cold water?*

BREAKING AND BUILDING A HABIT

WE ARE ALL creatures of habit, and those habits develop over time. These established patterns underpin so much of our destiny. We typically make habits through the three 'R's:

'Reminders' are triggers to the necessity of something. It could be an action, feeling or thought that prompts us. Like seeing the light switch as you exit a room.

'Routines' are the action part of the cycle. They are what we actually 'do' when we are 'reminded'. Like the habit of turning the switch off.

'Rewards' are the positive feeling or benefit you get from fulfilling the routine. Like knowing you have saved energy by switching off that light.

Because habits become actual physical pathways in our brains, they can be hard to change. As research from University College London makes clear, it isn't possible to form a habit for *not* doing something. You have to *replace* it with something better, something positive.

- *What positive habits have you incorporated into your day, and what difference do they make to you?*

- *Are there any habits that you would like to change? (Or any addictions that you might need further help to address?)*

- *How could you apply 'reminders, routines and rewards' to increase your chances of making a new habit stick?*

'If we want to form new habits, it's best to start small and feel like we are winning'

OUR HABITS DICTATE so much of how our lives look. It's a case of sow and reap. If we smoke, we will probably damage our health. If we habitually smile when we greet someone, our lives tend to brighten up.

I have learnt that if we want to form new habits, it's best to start small and feel like we are winning. Health psychology lecturer Benjamin Gardner says, 'Behaviour change achievements, however small, can increase self-efficacy, which can in turn stimulate pursuit of further changes.' Basically, if you are doing well, then it becomes simpler to keep doing well.

If you're hoping to change your habit of staying up too late watching TV, rather than moving from midnight to 9 p.m., try creating a new ambition of 11.30 p.m. You're much more likely to achieve your goal and then make further gains.

You may add in reward habits, like a cup of tea while reading a great book during those extra thirty minutes. It's all about increasing your sense of control and affirming your progress. Remember: always forward, even when we slip backwards. Keep going. See the long-term gains, not the short-term losses.

- *How could making smaller steps help you make bigger changes?*
- *Might an 'always forward' approach help you gain a bit more control over a troublesome habit?*

CHANGING COURSE

I T TAKES ABOUT twenty minutes for a fully loaded supertanker to stop when travelling at normal speed, so most supertankers turn off their engines about fifteen miles away from their dock. Even when changing course, the turning diameter is about 1.2 miles.

Changing direction in life can also feel frustratingly slow, especially when we are excited or apprehensive. To hold fast to the vision requires belief – to see beyond what is actually in front of us.

I have learnt that, like the tanker, we need to persist with change if we are going to finish successfully. We must anticipate the time that worthwhile things often take.

When I look back on my attempt on Everest – a major change of direction in my life – I faced three major obstacles: the hardest was self-belief. Did I actually have what it would take? Second: could I get together the necessary resources? Finally – timing – when would it happen? How long could I hold my nerve through count-less days and nights of climbing, with their endless false summits?

Persevering through obstacles can feel nerve-wracking, but you have to believe in the change if you are going to make the change.

- *Can you remember giving up on a change because it seemed to take too long to be realised?*
- *What obstacles do you face to making change happen?*
- *How can you hold fast to your vision for change?*

'Hold on to your vision, beyond what you see around you'

MARY JANE SEACOLE had a vision to change the course of her life. She was a British-Jamaican nurse and businesswoman, moved by the stories of suffering coming from the Crimean War.

Seacole, who was very experienced and well regarded, attempted to join the nursing contingent to assist in the horrific, unsanitary field hospitals, but was rejected multiple times, including by the War Office and the Crimean Fund. She wrote in her biography, 'Was it possible that American prejudices against colour had some root here?'

Yet despite every rejection and obstacle, Mary Jane Seacole refused to give up. She travelled to Crimea on her own resources and went on to become one of the most celebrated nurses in military history, renowned for her intense compassion, courage and care.

Holding on to a vision for change takes courage, persistence and belief. When opposition or detractors come, and they will, it can be all too tempting to give up. But good changes are always contested.

Hold on to your vision, beyond what you see around you, and in time it will be realised.

- *What inspires you about Mary Jane Seacole's story?*
- *Have you faced opposition or prejudices that have limited your vision for change?*
- *What vision for change do you need to hold on to in the face of discouragement today?*

LISTEN WELL

NELSON MANDELA SAID he learned to listen well by watching his father lead meetings: he would inquire, listen intently and never offer his comments until everyone else had spoken. 'I learned to have the patience to listen when people put forward their views, even if I think those views are wrong. You can't reach a just decision in a dispute unless you listen to both sides.'

So much of the discord in life is a product of misunderstandings that come from poor listening. When we interrupt, we lose much more than we gain. In business, a rushed approach costs time and money. In personal relationships, the cost is even greater – love, trust and respect.

Arguments are rarely ever won; the best outcomes are always listened-out. We have to train ourselves to listen well. I like the 'reflective listening' model for its simple power to tune me in to what someone is saying: Listen to the message. Look for the meaning. Then reflect the meaning and emotion back as you understood it. Confirm with the speaker you have understood correctly.

Subconsciously this invariably creates rapport. We all have a deep-rooted need to be properly heard, and fully understood.

- *Do you find it hard to listen well? Do you tend to zone out or jump in?*
- *What do you believe about the power of listening well?*
- *What steps could you take to improve your listening skills?*

'Great listeners give space for people to articulate what they really mean'

MY PARENTS OFTEN told me I had two ears and one mouth for a good reason. It was good advice growing up. Maybe it's useful advice even now.

What I notice most about communication today is how much of it can end up simply as information transfer. We are so used to speed in life, it can be easy to push people to 'get to the point'. But I always notice when great communicators listen to someone about their life. The pace slows, and they listen on a deeper level. It is never rushed. It can feel 'inefficient' to us because of our habit of listening 'fast'. But great listeners give space for people to articulate what they really mean.

Research in psychology has concluded that only 7 per cent of our communication is made up of the words we use. The rest is tone of voice and body language. How we say what we say means as much as what we say.

Listening well is not only a gateway to meaningful verbal communication, it is communication. Listening says 'you matter' – the starting point for any great relationship.

- *Have you found yourself falling into 'information transfer'-based communication?*
- *What excites you about reclaiming an 'inefficient' approach?*
- *How could you develop your body language as an invested listener? Is there a conversation coming up that you could apply this to?*

BENEFITS OF VOLUNTEERING

THE MOST COMMON question you'll hear in the Scouts is: 'Can I have a volunteer?' Typically the response will be a roomful of hands in the air. Understandably, as we get older, that enthusiasm can begin to wane and we tend to be a little hesitant. There's that niggle of doubt in our heads: 'It depends'; 'I'm exhausted'; 'I don't know how'; 'My schedule is jammed'.

Volunteering tends to be the thing that we might have time for after everything else, but the benefits of volunteering – whatever the task – are well proven. And as Chief Scout, I have seen this time after time – first hand. And it is inspiring.

A UK national survey showed that a massive 77 per cent of volunteers said that volunteering had improved their mental health and wellbeing. It is a great opportunity to gain confidence, break the cycle of isolation, and most importantly, make a difference to the lives of others.

- *What is your honest reaction to the word 'volunteer'? What image does it provoke?*
- *Could other people's experience of volunteering change your perspective?*
- *How could making a difference to the lives of people who have greater needs than your own change how you feel?*

'Start with a cause you feel passionate about . . . ideally with a friend'

WINSTON CHURCHILL SAID, 'You make a living by what you get. You make a life by what you give.'

In my experience, most people want to volunteer, but just don't feel that they have the time or confidence. I get that, but most organisations have a hugely flexible approach to volunteer commitment and will always do their best to make you feel valued and included, as well as helping you fit your volunteering around your schedule. Especially Scouts!

Start with a cause you feel passionate about, or where you can see local need. Then start small. And ideally with a friend. Volunteering is rooted in connection, service and relationships.

- *How do you feel about choosing a volunteer opportunity? What causes come to mind?*
- *What's holding you back? Confidence or time commitments?*
- *What do you feel passionate about? How could that energy help you to take your next steps?*

IF YOU HAVE
FIVE MINUTES

YOU MIGHT THINK a website explaining how English speakers say 'no' unnecessary, but there are hundreds of subtle ways people try to say no politely: 'I would love to, but sadly I haven't got the time'; 'I'm all booked out'; 'Maybe when things quieten down a bit.' I'm sure we've all used a version of these. They sometimes leave me wondering how we decide how much time is 'enough' time.

Most of us learned our time management skills at school, with our day divided into periods of forty to sixty minutes on the basis that this was the established amount of time necessary to achieve something. If I look at the big block events of my day, I realise not all of them really need forty to sixty minutes. We simply fill the time we think makes for a 'good' meeting. I have learnt not only to be curious about how much time is enough but also that the gaps of unallocated time can be an opportunity for fun, relaxation and spontaneity.

- *How have you pre-determined how much time is enough time for certain tasks? Have you ever questioned this belief?*
- *Do you ever wonder if you really need all of the time you have allocated to something – or do you wonder if you are just filling up the space?*
- *How much of an opportunity for growth and fun can you see in the margins of your time schedule?*

'There's so much fun to
be found in the margins'

WRITER ANNE LAMOTT said, 'Almost everything will work again if you unplug it for a few minutes – including you.'

It turns out that five minutes is a perfectly good amount of time to do lots of things. It's easy to coast through endless segments of five minutes waiting for something else to start. If instead, though, we can treat time like a gift rather than a restriction, we can soon turn, 'Sorry, I only have five minutes' into 'I have five whole minutes for something great!'

That's enough time to do five sets of press ups; listen to two great songs; walk 500 metres; send a nice text to your mum; pay a colleague a compliment; write a card to a relation; meditate; do 250 jumping jacks; make a great coffee; draw a sketch; stretch your hamstrings; learn a joke.

I have discovered life doesn't have to be solely about the big blocks of time. There is so much fun to be found in the five-minute margins. Our happiness, creativity and inspiration are so often activated by small but meaningful activities.

- *How might your five-minute margins actually support your work and make your life richer?*
- *What are you going to choose as your first five-minute activity? Could you build several into your working day?*
- *What's the worst mistake we can make when it comes to time?*

DAY 241

YOUR DIGITAL LIFE

NEW TECHNOLOGY HAS been at the heart of so many of my adventures over the years. Likewise, at home, connecting with friendly folk through social media and sharing in the fun stuff that my family and friends are up to is great. But, like anything good, although a little bit might not harm you, too much often will. Research from Ottawa Public Health demonstrated that daily social media use of 'more than 2 hours was associated with poor self-rating of mental health and high levels of psychological distress'.

It helps to check ourselves regularly on this stuff, and I have a few boundaries that work well, like setting my own rules when using my phone. I try never to be on technology for longer than thirty minutes at a time, and I turn my phone off after 9 p.m.

Whatever it is, make sure the tech serves you – it is a tool to make your life better, not suck the joy from your days. If you sense that is happening, maybe it's time to re-establish those ground rules for yourself. You're the boss.

- *How has technology positively changed your life over the last few years?*
- *How does using social media affect your mental health?*
- *Might you need to bring in some new boundaries to help you keep your priorities?*

'Use tech to help you get out there, rather than as an alternative to adventure – adventures rarely happen behind a screen'

WHILE TECHNOLOGY OFTEN gets criticised for how it can steal our time, it is also out there saving lives. In terms of safety devices, a smartphone with GPS is probably the greatest single development in the last twenty years.

In December 2018, Rachel Neil and some friends had finished a day's snorkelling off the coast of Okinawa, Japan. On their return, their boat capsized, throwing all eight passengers overboard. Rachel managed to catch onto her 'grab-bag', containing a smartphone, as she fell in.

Caught in an endless whirlpool, Rachel phoned for help from the water. She said, 'Once we knew that help was coming and that our lives were pretty much in someone else's hands, it got a little scary.' But it was ultimately the technology that saved their lives.

The fact that technology has the potential to massively transform our odds of survival is another reason for us to use tech for good. The key is never to let technology dominate, diminish or restrict us. If it does, dial it back and reassess. Stay in charge.

- *Do you see technology as a tool that can serve you, or has it started to call the shots?*
- *What encourages you about the way smartphones can be used for the good?*
- *How could your device play a part in helping you live a more active and adventurous lifestyle?*

DEBT
AND YOU

CREDIT CARDS, MORTGAGES, business loans, student loans: debt is a reality of life for most people. My parents' generation was quite opposed to borrowing. But these days, few people can live without it.

The CEO of the Money and Mental Health Policy Institute says: 'There is still a huge taboo around being in debt and having other money problems. The result is that people often carry this burden alone, which can cause their financial problems to escalate, and can also leave them feeling overwhelmed or unable to see a way out.'

Like with money in general, debt is neither good nor bad – it's all about how we manage our obligations. If managed well, debt can serve us. But when we become unable to manage it, it can become a heavy emotional and practical burden. So we should approach debt carefully and cautiously.

There is much professional support available to help you plan and avoid the pitfalls of debt, or to help you out of a hole if things have got difficult. Like with so much: you are never alone. So don't let debt be a burden you carry alone.

- *How do your attitudes towards borrowing and debt compare to the generation before?*
- *How does being in debt make you feel? Would you be likely to hide any problems?*
- *Do you need help with managing a debt issue? Who will you share your burden with?*

'Nobody should have to live their life under the constant threat that bad debts generate, whoever is at fault'

THE GREATEST DANGER with debt is that it can easily result in people feeling trapped and hopeless. This can impact people's mood and decision-making, all of which can further impact their baseline debts. Nobody should have to live their life under the constant threat that bad debts generate, whoever is at fault. Sometimes bad stuff simply happens: we lose our job, and in a heartbeat we are on the back foot.

Tragically, there are offers of 'help' out there that are a trap to exploit people further who are already in debt. But there are some great charities offering free, practical help, like Christians Against Poverty, National Debtline and StepChange.

For those not struggling, be aware of ways we can support friends or family who may be dealing with debt. Helping others in their time of need, which we all go through at one point or another, is a beautiful thing and a great privilege. Be generous to others – even just with a non-judging, listening ear; it builds trust and strengthens relationships. And some things matter more than money.

- *Have you felt trapped or helpless because of debt?*
- *If you are struggling right now, what steps can you take to receive help? Have you explored the charities mentioned above?*
- *Are you in a position to help someone who is struggling with debt? What support or advice could you offer?*

PICK YOUR BATTLES

HAMBURGER HILL LAY on a remote mountain ridge in central Vietnam. In May 1967, US Command ordered its capture, launching an assault, on foot, uphill, against the heavily fortified People's Army of Vietnam forces.

Repeated attacks were repelled and bad weather also hindered operations. Finally, after massive casualties, US forces took the hill, only to abandon it within two weeks, deeming it of 'no military value'. It's a powerful example of a trap that is all too easy for us to fall into.

Our determination to win, our commitment to an objective, can override our better judgement. We try to win an argument, but end up losing a friend. Fight for a promotion, but lose our reputation. Even reach a summit, but risk someone else's life.

What I have learnt is the importance of keeping your head in times of crisis, and challenging the story you are telling yourself.

Ultimately, if you have achieved your goal but have compromised your relationships or your heart, it was never worth it.

- *Have you found yourself being so committed to your goal that you have sacrificed something that you never intended to?*
- *Has the virtue of being 'committed to your goal' left you inflexible to adapt and change course as may be necessary?*
- *How might you hold yourself accountable for what you know to be right, rather than just your achievements?*

'I have had to shift the goal posts to reach a difficult goal'

THE 1996 EVEREST disaster was a tragedy that shocked the climbing community, not least because Scott Fischer and Rob Hall, two of the world's most experienced mountain guides, lost their lives.

While there were many contributing factors, one key judgement call stood out. Rob Hall guided his client Doug Hansen to the summit at 4 p.m. despite being the author of the original 'rule' that if you haven't reached the top by 2 p.m. you should begin your descent.

Professor Christopher Keys, in his exploration of those events asks, 'Why would a group continue to pursue a goal despite mounting evidence that it could not be attained?' The answer may lie in what Keys calls 'goalodicy', the belief that a goal is attainable despite all the evidence.

Keeping perspective sometimes means adapting a plan, or even accepting 'failure'. Making this call when committed to a goal is tough, but often wise. I have had to shift the goal posts to reach a difficult goal. That's all part of it.

- *Can you recall a time you ignored a boundary you had set in advance? What made you compromise?*
- *Can you relate to the idea of 'goalodicy'? What is the difference between this and just dreaming big?*
- *If you are pursuing a goal, when might accepting temporary failure be wise?*

THE RECOVERY SECRET

THERE ARE THREE core life systems: Productivity, Security and Recovery. The first two tend to be what we can clearly see in others, but the third is often unseen, both in the body and in society. We tend to notice when people achieve, build and produce, or when they fight, run and shout. But we don't always see them sleep, rehydrate, eat or heal.

Yet, as humans, we model what we see. It's easy to notice the action, but it's just as important to know that behind the scenes of many successes is often a solid foundation of good recovery principles. Looking after yourself and pacing yourself for the long haul. How well you focus on recovery tends to set the conditions for the success or failure of an endeavour.

The 'recovery secret' is the bedrock of successful performance. Elite recovery coach Nick Littlehales has coached some of the biggest names in sport. He said, 'I think in modern top-level sport, we accept that certain things are vital to performance; nutrition, hydration, stretching, mental wellbeing. But to me, human recovery – sleep – is fundamental and is something that feeds into all of those things, and much more besides.'

I believe that these principles are just as vital in life as they are in sport.

- *Have you tended to think more about your productivity than your recovery?*
- *What have you noticed about your performance when you have neglected your sleep or self-care?*

'Make recovery a part of your daily and weekly pattern'

STEVEN CALLAHAN SURVIVED for seventy-six days in a life-raft after his sailing boat, *Napoleon Solo*, sank in the Atlantic. Steven's body and mind were ravaged by the unrelenting pressure of nature and the absence of recovery. His body was emaciated and covered in sores, his muscles were wasted, he was beyond exhausted. And when he was finally rescued by a passing fishing boat, he was close to death. It took Steven six weeks just to be strong enough to walk again.

In normal life it's easy to think that we can ignore or even abuse our body and its need for recovery. We try to 'just get on with it'. But experiences like Steven's are a visceral reminder that our bodies and minds are precious and need daily care to stay in top condition. Recovery might not feel very glamorous or productive, but that doesn't mean that we shouldn't recognise the fundamental role it plays.

Making recovery a committed part of your daily and weekly pattern is simply to acknowledge that we all need time and care to recover, if we are going to perform at our best. Nobody is immune to these needs and investing in recovery every day has a real and tangible effect on your health, wellbeing and performance.

- *How does poor sleep impact your performance and mood, and what could you do to improve it?*
- *What would you like to change in your approach to recovery – sleep, nutrition, hydration, stretching, mental wellbeing or something else?*

MAKE TIME
TO DO NOTHING

THE FRENCH PHILOSOPHER Blaise Pascal famously said, 'All of humanity's problems stem from man's inability to sit quietly in a room alone.'

Technology has become the architect of our social interactions but the demolition man of our solitary experiences. Research has shown that the average user now spends seven hours online every day. Much of this has replaced the time that we might previously have been quietly 'doing nothing'. As a natural introvert, I tend to limit my interactions if I am going to be properly recharged for life. It is this pattern of engagement and withdrawal that keeps many of us going.

Overactivity online leaves us at risk of being content consumers rather than life generators.

'Freewheeling' time is different. It is about letting our minds range freely, without constraint or direction. It's the space we need to be creative and let ideas and dreams develop.

If we never leave time simply to be, to breathe, to observe, to sit quietly, then it is harder to be creative and to be content. Those elusive qualities won't be rushed and won't be forced upon us.

- *Do you think of inaction or 'boredom' as a bad thing?*
- *What do you notice about life when your time is constantly filled with something?*
- *Are you able to sit quietly in a room alone? What happens when you do?*

'Sometimes doing nothing yields much greater creativity and productivity in the long run'

PEOPLE TALK ABOUT the 'New York minute' – as if time moves faster there. In the big cities of the world, like Hong Kong, Shanghai or London, it can become a badge of honour to tell each other how busy we are. But a culture that insists we try to cram a million things into our day is not good for us in the long term. Life doesn't *have* to be like that and wasn't designed that way.

I now really try to allow space for 'doing nothing'. Of course, 'doing nothing' really isn't nothing, it's just that we tend not to value activities that don't appear to have a defined purpose. Sometimes the best things only come when we stop and listen.

So allow yourself to slow down. Relax. Breathe. Doing nothing, sitting in coffee shops, walking alone in nature, reading books or meditating are some of the best 'return on investment' activities we can do. This is a key part of taking care of your mental fitness – and it yields much greater creativity and productivity in the long run.

- *Does it seem counterintuitive that making 'doing nothing' a goal could actually increase your productivity?*
- *Where does the need to be busy all the time come from?*
- *How could you value your 'nothing activities' more than you currently do?*

AGAINST ALL ODDS

NEXT TIME YOU look up at the moon, think how improbable it would have seemed for anyone, only a few decades ago, to imagine that a human being could journey there and back. The 'odds against it' would have seemed astronomical, so to speak.

And yet, on 20 July 1969, at 8.17 p.m. UTC, Apollo Lunar Module *Eagle* touched down on the moon. Six hours and thirty-nine minutes later, Neil Armstrong became the first person to step onto its surface. 'One small step for man, one giant leap for mankind.' The whole Apollo space programme demonstrated that what would have seemed an impossibility to most people who'd ever lived was, in fact, achievable.

Because if we never try in life, we will never know. Just because people haven't done something before doesn't mean it cannot be done, or that it shouldn't be *you* to do it. Often what holds us back is the idea that 'the odds are stacked against us'. But remember: odds aren't facts. They are just opinions dressed up in numbers.

If history has taught us anything, it's that the optimism of action has a funny habit of overcoming the pessimism of 'the odds'.

- *Is there something in your life that you're put off from doing because you feel the odds are stacked against you?*
- *What have you got to lose if you give it a try?*

'Being prepared to give something a go is the start of infinite potential'

FEW PEOPLE REMEMBER the name of the gold medallist of the large hill ski jumping event at the 1988 Winter Olympics in Calgary. But most people remember the name of the man who came in 55th place. Michael 'Eddie' Edwards – better known as Eddie the Eagle.

Eddie was someone who didn't stop to question the odds, or the obstacles ranged against him. He was simply willing to give it a go. After all, what was the worst that could happen?

Self-funded and strapped for cash, overweight and sporting steamed-up glasses under his goggles, in borrowed ski boots, Eddie still realised his dream of representing his country at the Olympics. So what that he came in last in both his events? The world loved him. And the world remembers him. For the very reason that he was willing to try – and he dared it all.

Eddie the Eagle didn't gain a medal. But he gained true fulfillment and pride in his life. Similarly, we don't know what embarking on any endeavour will yield. We may fail. We may succeed. Does it actually matter? Just being prepared to give something a go has a value that is impossible to quantify.

So go for it. Take a chance. Just enjoy the process.

- *What inspires you about Eddie the Eagle's story?*
- *Is there something you are considering trying out? What's holding you back?*

DAY 253

THE POWER OF KINDNESS

KINDNESS AND COMPASSION are now classified as fundamental to living well in the modern age. In truth, they always have been. But now it's official. From relationships and business, to leadership, therapy and medicine, showing kindness is proven to strengthen community.

Empathy is the ability to relate to someone else's feelings. It says, 'I sense you are really hurting right now. I think I understand a little of how you are feeling.' While empathy is really important in life, it is only a half-step to change.

Compassion, or kindness, on the other hand, is the ability to acknowledge someone else's situation and be motivated to help. It says, 'I can feel you are distressed by this situation and I want to help.'

Compassion is the perfect combination of understanding and solution. We all have the power to exercise compassion today, in a way that is beautiful and unique. No matter how small an act, we can make a meaningful difference to others. Little things are never just little things. They can change a life. And that is a true superpower. Try it. It will make you feel amazing.

- *What is your experience of the difference between empathy and compassion?*
- *When were you last impacted by somebody's compassion towards you? How did it make you feel?*

'Tiny acts of compassion have impacts disproportionate to their size'

ACCORDING TO NEW research from Texas A&M University, a single candle flame can be seen by the human eye from 1.6 miles away. Likewise, tiny acts of compassion have impacts disproportionate to their size. Aligning yourself with the struggle of someone else and offering to make a difference to their situation changes them, changes you and changes society.

Think about a moment of compassion that you observed in a public place: maybe someone giving up their seat on the train for a person in need; an act of generosity to somebody with less; a word of encouragement to a parent who looked overwhelmed. How did that tiny light impact your day? Did it provoke copycat compassion in others?

A report in the *Scientific American* reflected that 'kindness itself is contagious, and that it can cascade across people'.

This is something I have seen time and again, from mountain expeditions to pressurised TV shoots: if someone shows kindness at the start, it tends to cascade across the team and set the culture for the whole venture.

Make such actions a choice and goodness will follow.

- *Have you noticed the disproportionate power of compassion?*
- *Have you found a change in your own behaviour after observing another compassionate act?*
- *How could you initiate a compassionate culture shift in a place you have influence today?*

DAY 255

NOT EVERYTHING HAPPENS FOR A REASON

EVERYONE SUFFERS. EVERYONE fails. Everyone loses. Often, we try to distract ourselves from the pain we are feeling by looking for a deeper reason behind what has happened. We rarely find it.

In the depths of our struggle it's not unusual to hear the words: 'Everything happens for a reason.' But a lot of the time, difficult things happen for no reason at all. People get sick, ventures fail, nature acts, disasters happen.

Looking for a reason for every negative experience is a bit like looking through the wrong end of a telescope: we can often feel further away from the pain, and no wiser to the event.

Instead of looking for a reason for suffering, I believe that we can find meaning *in* the suffering. Every disappointment, every struggle can shape us, teach us and form us for life ahead. Not because disaster came for that purpose, but because that disaster gives us a chance to grow, to evolve and get stronger.

Storms do that. They beat us up. But if we can hold on and endure they often also leave us smarter and stronger than before. It's called the refining fire.

- *Have you at times been tempted to believe 'everything happens for a reason'? How has this made you feel?*
- *Which difficult life events have ended up being a secret blessing?*

'Choose your attitude for the better'

VIKTOR FRANKL, THE PSYCHOLOGIST and Holocaust survivor recounts: 'In some ways suffering ceases to be suffering at the moment it finds a meaning. Such is the meaning of a sacrifice.'

Finding a rational explanation for things we have suffered is sometimes impossible. Never more true than in the gravity of what Frankl had faced. Yet he goes on: 'The last of the human freedoms is to choose one's attitudes.' Choosing to find meaning over futility doesn't cancel out our losses but it does leave us changed because of them. And, more importantly, it gives us a way through them.

Finding meaning in life's struggles is the opposite of some sort of cosmic fatalism. It is choosing your attitude and engaging your emotions for the better. It is about slowly piecing life back together in its new shape as the storms come and go.

- *How have the most difficult moments of your life changed you?*
- *What's the difference between fatalism and finding meaning in life's struggles?*
- *Which tough experiences wouldn't you change because of how they have impacted you?*

WORRY THRIVES
BY STAYING GENERIC

O NE THING I'VE noticed about worry is that its influence is often greatest when it stays generic. Mark Twain famously said that he had spent most of his life worrying about things that never happened. We can be overcome by a kind of mood of worry that engulfs us like a fog and leaves us feeling overwhelmed and disorientated: 'what if I fail in my career?'; 'what if my finances collapse?'; 'what if my relationship doesn't work out?'; 'what if my health fails me?'

Can you see how these worries aren't specific enough to do anything about them? The fog of worry lingers with unanswerable 'what ifs'. We become engulfed in the feeling of dread but without any concrete reference points to assess whether our worries genuinely need our attention or not.

Worries are not all the same. It can be helpful to categorise them into two groups: solvable and floating. Solvable worries relate to concrete, time-limited problems. They require your attention and respond to problem-solving techniques. Floating worries, however, relate to a generalised theme, have no time perimeters and cannot be resolved by problem-solving techniques.

- *Have you found yourself becoming overwhelmed by different 'what if' scenarios?*
- *Can you identify the loose themes around which your worries centre (health, finance, relationships, money etc)?*
- *Are you able to identify and separate the floating worries from the issues that really need your attention?*

'Trying to problem-solve floating worries leaves you more likely to keep worrying'

WHEN YOU ARE lost in fog it can be tempting to panic and try to get away. Inevitably, you end up even more disorientated, but now you are exhausted as well. Responding to 'floating worries' by trying to get away from the fear they provoke is much the same. The fact is, the content of your floating worries is far less important than the fact that you are worrying at all.

It can be helpful to think about your general levels of stress and pressure. I have found that the fog of worry generally switches on when I am up against it in other areas. At those points we can easily get tangled up in 'what if' questions that provoke anxiety about whether we will get sick, lose something precious or fail in some other area of life.

Trying to problem-solve (worry about) floating worries does two things: it legitimises the concern you are carrying, however unlikely it is; and, it leaves you exhausted and more likely to keep worrying. Ultimately, floating worries, like fog, lift when we don't give them the attention that they demand.

- *Have you had a tendency to panic and immediately start trying to resolve your floating worries?*

- *Do you notice how these sorts of worries often appear when you are already feeling stressed and exhausted?*

- *What would it look like to sit with your floating worries long enough to see that nothing bad really happens and that they tend to fade away on their own?*

FIGHT OR FLIGHT VS REST AND DIGEST

WHEN IT COMES to survival, the human body is remarkable: it alters its processes in direct response to the situation. The autonomic nervous system has two key branches that balance each other: the fight or flight system (sympathetic nervous system) and the rest and digest system (parasympathetic system).

If you were confronted by a big grizzly bear in the woods, it's the fight or flight system that kicks into play. It operates before you can even consciously think about the situation, flooding your body with adrenaline, withdrawing blood from your extremities to feed your major muscle groups so you can run away quickly, and dilating your pupils so you can see better. It quickens your heartbeat and even increases the capacity of your lungs.

In the urban world there aren't too many bears wandering around, but it's helpful to know that the fight or flight response can be subconsciously activated by stress as well as obvious danger. In its most intense form, when we are over-stressed, we might experience 'panic attacks', and while not dangerous, they can be really worrying.

- *Are you aware of your 'fight or flight' response? What have you noticed in the past?*

- *Has there been a moment in your life when the fight or flight response saved you from direct danger?*

'There is power in knowing these two partnered systems'

THE REST AND DIGEST (parasympathetic) system is the much-needed, natural counterbalance to the fight or flight response – yet we tend to take rest and digest for granted. But, in a stressful world where we are often in mild fight or flight mode, it can be really helpful to do little things that help support recovery.

The rest and digest system increases blood flow to the gut, aids digestion, reduces blood pressure and heart rate. And even protects us from rotting foods or food poisoning. (I have all too often been aware of my digestion in the wild.)

There is power in knowing how these two partnered systems: fight and flight and rest and digest interact. Especially because it is possible to actively stimulate the rest and digest system yourself.

I try to do little things every day to help this, whether it is stretching or lying on the grass in the sun after a meal, or jumping in an ice trough for three minutes in the morning to keep that inner resilience muscle honed! Whatever works for you. Find your own rest and digest toolkit and you will be set to feel better when the pressure is on.

- *Have you noticed how stress can affect your sleep, appetite and digestion?*
- *What are you currently doing that activates your rest and digest system that you maybe weren't even aware of?*
- *What might your own toolkit look like? Could you research the possibilities further and find out what works for you?*

HIDDEN WOUNDS

THE HOT, DAMP conditions of the jungle are perfect for bacteria to thrive in. Before each of our jungle expeditions, we would always check that everyone was wound-free before heading into dense swampland. The one time this failed was in Sumatra, where I 'fast-roped' out of a helicopter and managed to burn my chest, while sliding at speed down the hemp rope. As I plunged into the dank swamp, I could tell the wound was deep as blood started to seep through my shirt.

Hidden wounds, like rope burns or blisters, often layered behind clothing or in sweaty socks and thick boots, are the perfect entry point for infection. Before you know it, your whole foot has swollen up, or worse, septicaemia sets in.

Guilt is an 'I did wrong' feeling, but shame is an 'I am wrong' feeling. Shame is far less defined and acts a bit like bacteria. It tends to go undetected at first, entering through hidden emotional wounds and quickly spreading to other areas of our lives. Shame can leave us feeling like we don't deserve to be heard, that we should mask or deny our real needs.

- *Have you noticed how quickly a feeling of unworthiness or self-consciousness can spread across all areas of your life?*

- *What are your typical responses to feelings of shame? Do you tend to try to hold things together and put on a brave face?*

- *How does a person's empathy and understanding affect how you feel about yourself? Could you share more about how you feel with a trusted friend?*

'Talking is a great first step to being free'

RESEARCH PROFESSOR BRENÉ BROWN says, 'If you put shame in a petri dish, it needs three ingredients to grow exponentially: secrecy, silence and judgement.'

Denying shame the conditions under which it can thrive means bringing things from the darkness into the light. When feelings of shame are shared with someone trusted and looked at objectively and compassionately, they invariably start to lose their grip on us.

Bacteria die in direct sunlight. It is why, as a climber, I spread out my sleeping bag on top of my tent in the morning sun. To share our shame takes courage, but rarely do the experiences of our pasts have the meanings we attach to them.

Talking about the wounds we've taken (or inflicted) with a kind friend or therapist who isn't going to judge us is a great first step to being free of them.

- *Do you carry hidden wounds that make you feel unacceptable or unworthy?*
- *What have you believed about yourself that may not be true? Have secrecy, silence and judgement supported these beliefs?*
- *What might it look like for you to bring some of these experiences into the light?*

COURAGE IS DOING THE DIFFICULT STUFF

T'S EASY TO believe that courage is a sort of personality quota, like being an introvert or being spontaneous. Sadly, this idea has created a chasm between those who we believe are 'courageous people' and everybody else.

Courage comes from the Latin word for 'heart' – *cor*. It's your ability to retain your will, despite experiencing fear. And the truth, that is so often missed, is that everyone can have it.

Courage is a muscle, not a character trait, that each of us can cultivate. The way to do this is gently to begin to do some of the things that we find most difficult. You may need to break bigger challenges down into smaller steps at first.

- *Have you believed that there are 'courageous people' and everybody else?*
- *Can you identify a specific event where you really expressed 'heart' despite fear?*
- *What might it look like for you to cultivate courage in your life?*

'We shouldn't compare our battles with those that others may be facing'

ELEANOR ROOSEVELT ONCE said, 'You must do the thing you think you cannot do.'

Most people run from the scary stuff in their lives. The result is those same monsters, which we fear so much, get ever bigger. But when we face them and choose to tackle them, however timidly at first, the fear lessens and the courage muscle inside us gets that little bit stronger.

Remember – some of us will be wrestling with tasks that others find easy. Some will be struggling with mental health issues that others cannot understand. We shouldn't compare our battles with those that others may be facing. But in whichever situation we find ourselves, visible or invisible, choose to engage and to tackle the very things we find most difficult. That's courage. Pure and simple. And it is there for any of us to claim as our own.

- *Which 'fear monsters' might you need to turn and face?*
- *How might you break overwhelming tasks into smaller, more manageable steps?*
- *What could you say to yourself to build your courage today?*

WHEN BEING RIGHT
IS WRONG

WINNING AN ARGUMENT can often mean losing a whole lot more. Most of us, myself included, prefer winning over losing. Who doesn't? But when it comes to growing healthy relationships – whether in a team or at work or at home – having to be right all the time is not a winning strategy.

I think most of us instinctively know this and yet we can still find ourselves drawn into disagreements that don't really serve anyone.

It's easily done. Especially when we're under pressure. On an expedition, small arguments can ignite about 'better' food, 'better' strategy or 'better' equipment. 'Better' is always the opinion of the person who wants to win the fight. With a partner, disputes flare up about in-laws or money or who said they would do what.

Wherever there is pressure, there is often friction. The fact is, when we belligerently refuse to listen and just insist on being right, often the other person will stop arguing just to keep the peace or else falls back into a posture of silent resentment. It's pretty rare that we actually convince someone to change their mind when we approach conflict like this.

- *Have you found yourself getting drawn into fighting fruitless battles?*
- *How has unrelated pressure increased the likelihood for disagreements?*
- *Do you have a tendency to argue or withdraw?*

'Relationship-building is at the heart of so much'

BEING RIGHT FEELS like it should be a good thing. But, when someone is described as 'always wanting to be right', it's rarely meant as a compliment.

Needing to be right all the time usually comes at the cost of trust and respect. Most of the goals we're striving towards involve some kind of team around us. Marriage, family, school, work. Relationship-building is at the heart of so much. So, if we lose the trust of those around us, how does that serve any objective?

I'm not saying there is never a moment to stand up for what we believe is right; there often is. But we need to cultivate the wisdom to know when we are just trying to win an argument, and when we are really trying to do the right thing.

And when the time comes for needing to stick to a view, the key to keeping it healthy lies in humility, listening and respect.

- *Do you find yourself regretting the arguments that you start?*
- *How could you build relationships over 'winning' the arguments?*
- *How would humility, listening and respect impact a disagreement?*

SOMETHING SWEET CAN MAKE ALL THE DIFFERENCE

MILITARY RATION BOXES almost always contained a chocolate bar. They weren't even full-sized but they boosted morale on many occasions after a gruelling exercise or night in the hills. When the mood dropped or the energy levels wilted, the simple things could be a game-changer.

In a busy and pressurised world, everyone struggles to keep going. Having something 'sweet' in your daily ration box is a self-care step that can really help.

Bear in mind that we live in a world where it is easy to over-indulge. 'Too much of a good thing' leads to complacency and, ultimately, boredom. The result is we take for granted what should be a treat, and the thing itself loses its value to us, and therefore its ability to give us a lift. So, when we reward ourselves, we need to apply a little wisdom in terms of frequency.

Reward effort, celebrate success: small things that make a huge difference in the busyness of life.

- *Have you tended to ignore rewards, or even believe that you don't deserve them?*
- *How might a small reward for your efforts make you feel on a challenging day?*
- *What would you suggest to an exhausted friend who is under pressure?*

'When the mood drops or energy levels wilt, simple things can be a game-changer'

WHEN IT COMES to rewards, it's easy to think too big. The life-coach's acronym (weirdly) is SAS: **S**mall, **A**ffordable, **S**avoured.

Small and affordable treats (in terms of money and time) are things like a good coffee, a walk around the park, five minutes of meditation, or calling a friend at lunch. These are things that most of us can do which makes the day a little brighter.

Savoured means giving the treat your full attention and appreciation. That is what turns something normal into a mood booster, which will break up the stresses and strains of your day and can really make a difference.

Writing a list of small and affordable activities or treats that you could incorporate into your day means that it's easy to make quick decisions for something positive when the moment presents itself.

- *What does it feel like to really savour something so that you feel its value?*
- *How might these small rewards weave easily into your day, and what could you do to prompt yourself to act?*
- *What do you need to change in your mindset when it comes to receiving rewards?*

THE POWER OF COMMITMENT

WORDS CAN EITHER strengthen our resolve or weaken our will. I have experienced the incredible power of encouragement at a few key times in my life, both on mountains and in the military. The right words can empower the right mentality.

There's a moment in the movie *The Empire Strikes Back* when Yoda counsels Luke Skywalker by saying that there's no such thing as trying: the only choice is doing or not doing a task. Sometimes we will succeed and sometimes we will fail, but when we commit to 'do', not to 'try', in my experience things are more likely to go well.

A survivor once said to me, 'tentative has no power'. In other words, when you're all in, you tend to win. You tend to survive where others who are more tentative fall down. This doesn't mean being gung-ho. Far from it. True confidence is always quietly held. But it's important for us to develop that state of mind.

- *What difference has verbally committing to something made to your actions?*
- *Have you noticed the impact of being tentative versus being 'all in'?*
- *What does 'true confidence, quietly held' look like to you?*

DAY 270

'The words we use become the life we live'

WILD PLACES DEMAND that we move from being tentative to being committed. It's both a word and a state of the mind. Our chances of achieving what we have set out to do are largely determined by whether we adopt a 'try' or a 'do' mentality.

I've noticed that people tend to have a 'try mentality' for two reasons: first, they lack confidence in their ability to succeed; second, they are trying (often subconsciously) to foreshadow their impending failure to others. 'I'll try' becomes an exit strategy that protects us from anticipated failure. The words we use become the life we live.

I've learnt that when we commit upfront, even if we lose, we win. There have been countless moments in my life when I have failed to achieve my goal, but I have learnt to care less about the achievement and more about the strengthening that the journey provides.

- *Could you exchange 'I will try' for 'I will do'?*
- *What are you afraid may happen if you commit but fail to achieve your goal?*
- *How could the language of commitment change your state of mind?*

WHERE TO FIND
YOUR CONFIDENCE

N THE EARLY days of filming *Man vs Wild* we were often briefed by indigenous survivalists – experts in the local terrains. Invariably, they were highly skilled. I was always struck by their knowledge. And my lack of it. It was humbling; I felt like a total rookie.

Most of us suffer from impostor syndrome from time to time. Research shows 70–80 per cent of adults feel it at least once in their lives, with 25–30 per cent of high achievers finding it more problematic. It's when the image I project 'out there' feels much more competent than the 'real me' inside.

Over time, my sense of inferiority knocked my confidence. And when confidence goes it can be hard to recover. I soon began to second-guess everything I was doing.

Comparison-making is never a good way of building confidence: it leaves us feeling either inferior or superior to others. True confidence comes when we accept our uniqueness and see our value in being in the game and giving our all.

- *Do you doubt your value when you are in the company of people who seem particularly skilled or gifted?*

- *Do you feel like an impostor waiting to be 'found out' in certain areas of your life? How does that impact how vulnerable you are able to be?*

- *What do you notice about the impact of constantly making comparisons with others versus being more accepting of yourself?*

'It's OK just to be yourself'

IMPOSTOR SYNDROME MAKES us fear being exposed as somehow lacking, and that fear can drive us to work ever harder to hide our perceived weaknesses. We then try to keep our vulnerabilities hidden, which in turn isolates us further.

Actor Tom Hanks reflected, 'No matter what we've done, there comes a point where you think, "How did I get here? When are they going to discover that I am, in fact, a fraud and take everything away from me?"'

My father taught me that it is OK just to be myself, and to confront doubt and fear head on. Never run away. Running always makes stuff worse. The best response to impostor syndrome is not trying to be better, but being more honest. Acknowledge what you lack, be grateful for the uniqueness of who you are, choose a humble, kind and determined attitude, and give your best. The rest will take care of itself.

- *How does knowing that other people around you also feel impostor syndrome make you feel?*
- *What would it feel like to be more honest with yourself and others?*

CRISIS LEADERSHIP

DORIS MILLER WAS the first black American to receive the Navy Cross, the highest decoration for valour in combat after the Medal of Honor. He was also awarded a Purple Heart posthumously.

Miller won his Navy Cross on the battleship *West Virginia* which was torpedoed during the Japanese surprise attack on Pearl Harbor on 7 December 1941.

During the attack, he helped many wounded sailors to safety, and while manning an anti-aircraft gun, for which he had no training, he shot down several enemy planes.

The most surprising thing about Doris Miller was that he was a ship's cook.

Crisis times have a habit of exposing the leader within us. They are no respecter of titles or qualifications, but they do reveal heart.

It's in all of us to come alive in a crisis and to deliver, but you have to back yourself. Don't hesitate – the worst leadership in a crisis is a vacuum. Know that you've got it within you. Trust your gut and go.

- *Have you ever found that a crisis revealed something in you that you hadn't seen before?*
- *What inspires you about Doris Miller's story?*
- *How can you favour speed and adaptation in times of crisis?*

'Crisis times ask us to have the courage to change ourselves'

GEORGE VI HAD not expected to be king. It was only with the abdication of his elder brother that he found himself on the throne.

In a time of war, the nation needed resolute, encouraging and inspirational words from their king. But George VI disliked public speaking intensely and had struggled with a severe stutter since childhood.

Crisis times ask us not only to change our circumstances but also to have the courage to change ourselves. George VI took a step of faith and, at huge personal risk, appointed speech therapist Lionel Logue to coach him.

It worked. On 3 September 1939 he galvanised the nation in a radio broadcast: 'I ask them to stand calm and firm and united in this time of trial. The task will be hard. There may be dark days ahead . . . but we can only do the right as we see the right, and reverently commit our cause to God'.

It was his determination to tackle the difficult, be vulnerable and never give up that allowed him to deliver that critical speech to serve the nation in such a unique way.

- *Do you feel unprepared or unqualified to lead? Can you see how attitude wins over aptitude?*
- *What inspires you about King George's determination to overcome his limitations to serve the nation in crisis?*
- *What do you value most in moments of crisis you have experienced?*

LIFE IS BETTER AROUND A FIRE

CONTROLLING FIRE MAY be humakind's greatest technological achievement. It allowed humans to extend their hunting grounds, improve their diets, protect themselves from predators, create more advanced tools and adapt to harsh environments and climates, providing warmth and light.

Even today, in so many notable survival stories, the ability to create fire has been key to a successful outcome. But it's more than just practical. Something genuinely powerful happens when you gather around a fire with a group of friends on a cold night. A campfire speaks to something deep within us, and is often at the heart of the best of human connection and community.

While computer games or televisions often put us into a solitary zone, minds in neutral, with little inter-connectivity, a fire does the opposite. A fire we sit around. A fire unites us. It's why I call it nature's TV. We can't help but stare into it. It's often all you really need for a memorable night that feels spontaneous, original, a little primal and great fun.

- *Have you thought about the profound impact that fire has had on us over time? How does that ancient connection make you feel?*

- *What experiences have you had of campfires? How long ago did you experience one?*

- *Have you noticed how campfires bring out singing, storytelling and genuine connection?*

'Something genuinely powerful happens when you gather around a fire with a group of friends on a cold night.'

IN GREEK MYTHOLOGY, Prometheus steals fire from the god Zeus and gives it to humans, effectively enabling the growth of civilisation. Since the first 'Olympiad' in 776 BC, a fire was kept burning for the duration of the games to invoke Zeus's favour, despite the theft. The modern Olympics reinstituted the flame.

The games are about competition, but also unity. There is mutual encouragement among competitors. The Olympic flame represents the human spirit of endeavour, knowledge and shared life. The fire is the bond.

It can be tempting to think about using your 'personal' fire for competition. But the ancient Greeks were not in the Games just to win; their efforts were a 'tribute' and the whole community celebrated their efforts as shared achievement. It was supremely effective in building an enlightened civilisation.

Competition doesn't have to be just about personal success, it can be *for* others, a shared story of overcoming adversity and offering our best. Passing on the torch of encouragement to others is part of what keeps us all sharp, happy and alight.

- *What inspires you about the early Greeks' perspective?*
- *Have you seen the fire of confidence increase in you because of the encouragement of other competitors?*
- *How could you pass the torch onto others in your place of work, school or community?*

TIME CAN BE
YOUR FRIEND

'TIME MANAGEMENT' HAS always seemed like a misleading idea to me. Time just does its thing and we can't manage it. We can only manage ourselves.

Encountering different cultures has taught me a lot about time. The Aboriginal concept is not linear like ours, but multidimensional. The more important an event, the closer it is in time. In other words, the most important thing you have experienced is right now.

Time can be like a pond you are swimming through: you can travel up, down or around. You can go fast or slow, or tread water. But you never leave the pond. In Western culture, always rushing on to the next thing and leaving the past behind, there is something here for us to learn.

Efficiency can be good and can help us be productive. But the danger is it can rob life of those moments when we have space to think or dream, or be spontaneous.

- *How focused have you become on 'time management'?*
- *What do you like about the Aboriginal multidimensional sense of time and the way it places events in order of importance rather than chronology?*
- *How could you look at a few moments of 'inefficiency' as an opportunity to think or dream about the things that are most important to you?*

'If we can see time as an ally, we can live in victory'

THE LANGUAGE WE use is a good indication of how we relate to something. Phrases like 'I'm running out of time' or 'I'm up against the clock' indicate that we are passing responsibility for living calmly onto a clock – rather than holding onto it ourselves.

Time is a bit like money. If you never believe enough is enough, you will struggle to find peace. As soon as my mindset goes into 'time poverty mode' – in other words, being overly rushed – I feel my stress levels rising and my enjoyment of life declining. But, when I feel that 'time is on my side', everything becomes more enjoyable.

If we can see time as an ally rather than an enemy, we can live in victory rather than defeat. Author Stephen Covey writes, 'The key is not to prioritise what's on your schedule, but to schedule your priorities.'

I have never met an older person who regretted spending time on the things they care most about, but there are plenty who regret always bowing to the pressures of a schedule that never ends and priorities that bring them little joy.

- *What language do you use to describe your relationship with time?*
- *What do you notice about the times you have enjoyed most – are they hurried times or slower times?*
- *What would it look like for you to live according to your true priorities rather than your pressures?*

HOW TO
SINK A BOAT

SOME OF THE most frightening moments in my life were spent facing giant Arctic waves in the middle of the North Atlantic Ocean. Miraculously, our small rigid inflatable boat stayed upright through a fearsome storm and we eventually made it safely into Iceland after a terrifying 1,200-mile crossing.

In reality, the majority of maritime accidents, and also mountain ones, don't happen because of one catastrophic event, but often they are caused by multiple small, non-fatal events that, when added together, cause a disaster.

We often tend to believe that in life, our emotional struggles can only be justified by major life events like a bereavement or a serious illness. But in reality, a handful of small pressures and challenges over a long period of time tend to wear us out to the point at which we start to struggle or sink.

If more water is coming in than is being bailed out, even if it is just a trickle, then any boat is in trouble. It is that hidden danger of sinking quietly.

- *Have you believed that your emotional struggles aren't really justified because there aren't any obvious challenges in your life?*
- *What could you identify as non-fatal, inconsequential leaks?*

'Pay attention to
the small stuff'

IT MAY BE surprising to learn that, statistically, the majority of boats that sink do so while they are moored or docked; relatively few sink while they are under way. Maybe it is the illusion of security, or boat owners' failure to notice what's going on that is the real danger. Either way, it is often the non-dramatic occurrences that cause the greatest damage.

Paying attention to the small stuff is one of the keys to keeping good health and wellbeing. Most people experience an emotional health crisis because of the volume of small stresses they are facing more than any single event. The key thing is noticing when we are beginning to get overwhelmed and put some simple solutions in place to stay healthy.

'Bail out' steps can be as simple as talking to others, exercising, meditating, praying or keeping a journal. But remember: it's OK not to be OK, even when there isn't anything obviously negative or huge going on in your life. No one should sink quietly. If you are concerned about how you are doing, seek an appointment with your healthcare provider. You've nothing to lose.

- *Have you been paying enough attention to the volume of small stresses in your life?*

- *How overwhelmed have you felt recently and what have you used to cope?*

- *What might a routine of daily 'bailing out' include for you – and might you need further help?*

TAMING YOUR INNER CRITIC

N THE EARLY days filming *Man vs Wild*, one of the toughest battles I had was against my inner critic. Regardless of how capable I felt, doing everything in front of a camera was terrifying.

Over time, I heard its voice get louder: 'you didn't do that right'; 'why did you say it like that?' Or the real big one: 'is this whole thing even working at all?' Left unanswered, the inner critic can hinder everything we do.

Rather than trying to silence it, try to tame your inner critic. Sit it on the table in front of you. Let it have its say. Often it will reveal its absurdity to you all on its own. The key is in seeing the critic as something separate from your own authentic self. That's a powerful change. So long as it can masquerade as the voice of truth in your head, it has power over you. Some people find it helpful to turn the language of the critic from 'I' to 'you'. It is another way of seeing its accusations and judgements as separate from your true self.

- *Do you suffer from a noisy inner critic? Can you see it as something separate from your internal thoughts?*

- *To what extent do you believe the judgements of the inner critic are true?*

- *What steps could you take to move this belief from fact to opinion?*

'Holding on to the hopeful voice within can be life-saving'

JAMES SCOTT, A twenty-three-year-old Australian medical student, had just two chocolate bars left when he got lost in the Himalayas in 1992. He went on to survive for forty-three days in perishing conditions by drinking snowmelt and eating insects. Scott lost a third of his bodyweight. He said, 'My body just ate itself – but I had abundant fresh water through snow, a strong faith and the determination not to let my loved ones grieve.'

To survive in the Himalayas, unsupported, for six weeks is extraordinary. What is striking about Scott's approach was his commitment only to listen to the positive voice within. He never gave up on himself, and didn't allow the inner critic a foothold.

Scott recounted: 'My attitude throughout the ordeal was generally one of hope and optimism. There is nothing extraordinary about me. The lesson I have learnt, simplistic as it might sound, is that no difficulty is impossible to overcome.'

Dr James Scott is now a psychiatrist, helping other people overcome their difficulties. He is an inspiration in how, even in the hardest circumstances, holding on to the hopeful voice within can be life-saving.

- *What inspires you about James Scott's survival attitude?*
- *How could Scott's inner critic have affected his survival if he had allowed it to dominate his mind?*
- *How could nurturing a compassionate inner voice better your life?*

BALANCING YOUR EMOTIONAL BOOKS

WHEN SHARA AND I decided to get married, we went on a marriage preparation course. It proved really helpful. To learn simple things such as budgeting; unless there is more money coming in than there is going out, ultimately we would end up in trouble. I have since realised that this applies not just to money management but also to our relationships and general mental wellbeing.

Every time we have to deal with something difficult or extend ourselves in some way, or maybe we are away too much, it costs us. Of course, one or two small withdrawals is only a small percentage of the total, so we don't experience much pain. But, studies show that only about eight weeks of emotional 'extension' can be enough to lead a person into depression. When our life withdrawals outweigh the deposits, watch out.

Our emotional health is not won and lost over what happens in one day. It's about the small withdrawals slowly mounting up over time.

The way to retain our long-term mental fitness is to balance those outputs with conscious inputs. Just a little positive deposit every day will help keep a healthy balance sheet.

- *Do you tend to ignore or diminish your emotional outputs?*
- *Do your deposits tend to be one big input once in a while? How effective do you find that?*
- *What deposits are you making into your 'emotional health account'?*

'When it comes to our emotional capacity, there are no credit cards'

MY LATE FATHER was old-school anti-credit. He hated debt. He used to say that if you didn't have it, you didn't have it. Obviously today there are many good, and often necessary, reasons to use credit or mortgages, but every debt is always going to have an element of danger to it. At the end of the day, they have to be repaid.

When it comes to our emotional capacity, there are no credit cards. You cannot borrow emotional resources from others. And yet, many of us live as if we have unlimited credit. Often we simply fail to grasp the fact we are able to run out.

Every one of us has psychological needs in the same way that we have physical needs. Of the core psychological needs, 'related-ness' is the one that keeps us going best under pressure. We might not be able to spend other people's emotional resources, but we can receive their emotional support and investment.

Whether it is a mentor, supportive friend, coach or colleague, allow others to invest in you and you will have the capacity to allow for great 'withdrawals' in your life – you will also be able to care well for others.

- *Have you considered your need for greater emotional resourcing?*
- *What specific emotional costs have you been carrying recently?*
- *Who might make an investment in your emotional account? Who might you be able to help?*

NEVER GIVE UP

I N THE SPRING of 2003, Aron Ralston was hiking in the canyons of southern Utah when he dislodged a boulder which pinned his wrist to the canyon wall. Alone, in excruciating pain, miles from any hope of rescue and with barely any provisions, he was trapped there for five days until he was forced to choose: his hand or his life.

In an amazing story of character, courage and resilience, Aron chose to give up his hand but not his life. In order to free himself, he had to break the bones in his own arm and amputate his hand with a woefully blunt penknife. And even then, he still had to escape the canyon and hike back to safety.

Aron embodied what it means to 'never give up': he refused to accept the apparent hopelessness of his situation until he had explored every single means to freedom, even the most radical ones.

- *Do you feel stuck in a situation that feels hopeless?*
- *How could you apply the 'never give up' spirit to your situation?*
- *What are the means to freedom available to you?*

'The bravest decisions risk the greatest losses'

THE HARDEST DECISIONS in life always involve a loss: you have to lose something precious if you want to gain something priceless. Aron Ralston's escape is a very visual example of that: he had to lose his arm to gain his freedom (and his life).

A lifetime of guiding in wild places has shown me how clearly people weigh up the losses when it comes to survival: 'I can't do that' is always followed by an internal or verbalised 'because'. Often, it's the fear of the loss of comfort, loss of dignity, loss of habit, loss of security or, ultimately, the loss of life.

'Because' can become the reasoning behind our missing out on the changes we are longing for or that we need. The bravest decisions risk the greatest losses. But, they also present the greatest gains.

'Never give up' is a mindset that believes, however strong the 'because', you still have a choice.

- *Have you been limited by the fear of losing something you are attached to?*
- *What is your default 'because' and how is it limiting you?*

RITUAL IGNITES CREATIVITY

BEETHOVEN USED TO start his day by counting out exactly sixty coffee beans, which he'd then grind into the perfect drink before sitting down to compose. Ernest Hemingway would rise at dawn without fail, no matter how late he had been out the night before. Benjamin Franklin swore by morning 'air baths' – sitting next to an open window working for several hours naked, whatever the weather.

It's pretty interesting the quirky things that people find work for them to enrich their lives. I like lying in the grass with my legs up against a tree, cuddling the dogs. Magic.

The great thing about rituals is that they create a sort of concrete 'on-ramp' to a more fluid way of living and being. The rituals form a structure around which the air flow of life can freely move. But with no structure the rest can feel just like wind.

Orson Welles said, 'The enemy of art is the absence of limitations'. Perhaps that is what these geniuses were tapping into. Rituals give a platform for freedom of expression, whatever form that takes for us – even if it is simply living the remainder of the day lightly and happily.

- *What surprises you about exceptional creative people who had working rituals?*
- *Who do you know who has a quirky ritual that they just love?*
- *How could regular, little moments unlock bigger things in your life?*

'Our creativity isn't limited to a particular destination. Setting a ritual can help us enter a happier, calmer, more liberated state of mind.'

LEGENDARY DANCE CHOREOGRAPHER Twyla Tharp writes, 'A lot of habitually creative people have preparation rituals linked to the setting in which they choose to start their day. By putting themselves into that environment, they begin their creative day.'

It is no surprise that our environments impact our mindset – we feel a change of headspace in a particular place. For me, it's the wild seas around our North Wales home. But our creativity isn't limited to a particular destination. Setting a ritual can help us enter a happier, calmer, more liberated state of mind.

We can create the conditions for freedom wherever we are. That might be with a preparation ritual or something simpler. I know it sounds simple, but I find walking a great gateway to creativity and healing. Tchaikovksy was determined to walk for two hours every day to help his composing. There is something so freeing about being physically on the move. I guess our minds just join the dots and suddenly the endorphins – and the good ideas – start to flow.

- *Where have you found yourself to feel most free or creative in the past?*
- *How might you create a healing, happy environment in your own home or office?*
- *Have you found a link between creativity and physical movement?*

DAY 289

MOVE
MORE

ARNOLD SCHWARZENEGGER IS in his seventies. He still works out every day because, in his own words, 'It brings me great joy.'

We all know that physical activity has a positive effect on physical and emotional health. But, according to the National Institute for Health and Care Excellence, 'It also has a positive effect on wellbeing and mood, providing a sense of achievement or relaxation and release from daily stress.'

It's easy to think about exercise as something you do for the sake of either achievement or physical prowess: to run a race, participate in a sport, build a six pack, whatever it is. But in truth the most compelling reason for exercise goes far beyond any of those.

I look at exercise like I do sleep and nutrition. We do it to make our quality of life better and to aid our longevity.

- *Have you limited the role of exercise to a particular achievement?*
- *How do you build movement into your daily routine?*
- *Could you look at movement in the same way as you look at sleeping or eating or brushing your teeth?*

'Being physically active is proven to help us stay mentally strong'

MOST OF US lead pretty sedentary lives. We work at jobs that require sitting at a computer for hours. And then, at the end of a long day, 'relaxing' can mean sitting down to watch Netflix. As humans, we inherently seek the path of least resistance, which isn't always the best path for happiness or longevity.

The biggest obstacle to exercise is rarely in our bodies, it's in our minds. The well-known fitness coach Joe Wicks said, 'When you're feeling down or struggling mentally, that's the time to get physical. Move your body, get outside, elevate your heart rate, push yourself outside your comfort zone.'

Getting started is often the hardest part, even when we know the benefits are obvious. But being physically active is proven to help us stay mentally strong. Look at the word emotion, the clue is right there. Motion.

Remember, start small. I do ten minutes of yoga-style stretching every morning. It's light work but it gets me moving, and often leads me into a fuller workout. Find something that is fun for you and do it with a buddy if that helps, but whatever you do, stick with it.

- *What holds you back from exercise, your body or your mind?*
- *What have you done before that you enjoyed and could restart?*
- *How could you build movement into your day in a way that is sustainable?*

A VISION BIGGER THAN US

PROBABLY THE MOST spectacular sight in the city of Barcelona is the Basílica de la Sagrada Família. This beautiful cathedral designed by Antoni Gaudí has been under construction since 1882. To date, over one hundred years later, the cathedral remains unfinished.

Gaudí's architectural vision was not limited to his lifetime, because it was rooted in a vision far greater than he was. It was Gaudí's spiritual vision that drove his creative ambition. Ultimately, he wanted the cathedral to visualise the life of Christ and inspire people for generations beyond his own.

Having vision is central to success in life, but there are dangers there too. It can be easy to become success driven at the expense of others. Or encounter periods of futility and purposelessness when our visions aren't realised. These experiences can make us question if there isn't a bigger story that we are supposed to be part of.

- *Have you found yourself becoming driven to achieve success at the expense of other good things in your life?*

- *How has your sense of self-esteem been impacted by a failure to achieve a personal ambition within an expected time frame?*

- *What would it look like for you to perceive a bigger vision for your life, one that might not even be realised within your lifetime?*

'Part of life's adventure is asking spiritual questions'

I HAVE FOUND that having a vision far greater and more enduring than anything I could dream up is a powerfully rewarding and motivating force for life. Personally, I have discovered that way of life in trying to live as Jesus Christ taught his friends, that rough gang of misfits.

For me, that is about knowing his presence beside me and trying to love other people. To try to walk humbly, and to look up for God's help every day. The prophet Micah in the Bible describes this way of life as, 'To act justly and to love mercy and to walk humbly with your God.'

Part of life's adventure is asking spiritual questions, the answers to which may lead us into a vision that will add purpose and happiness to our lives.

- *Have you spent time exploring the possibility of a deeper purpose and vision to your life?*
- *How could your personal ambitions and spiritual ones connect?*
- *What difference do you think having a spiritual vision could make to your life?*

DAY 293

LIFE REWARDS
THE DOGGED

F I'M CERTAIN of one thing when it comes to success, it is that behind every successful person you'll find a string of failed attempts. Too often someone's success blinds us to their previous failures. But most successful people will have had to walk through a huge number of 'failures' first. It is like the failures are doorways that we have to go through to succeed. No failures, no success.

What this often means is that the real difference between successful and unsuccessful people is the dogged ability to keep going. To keep pushing onwards, giving more when most people simply give up. Winston Churchill said, 'Success is the ability to go from one failure to another, with no loss of enthusiasm.' I call this quality 'grit'.

Statistically, 'grit' is the most accurate predictor of success – not looks, not wealth, not social status. And definitely not talent. But grit.

The world is full of unfulfilled talent. Life rewards the dogged, not the qualified.

- *Have you believed that successful people have not failed first?*
- *How has this made you view your own failures?*
- *How could you celebrate your grit as much as your successes?*

'With each new attempt, you're getting closer'

EVERY LIFE IS full of failure – mine included. But it's not the number of failures that matters, but how we respond to them.

A former sergeant of mine on Special Forces Selection once told me that the only failure is giving up. I have always remembered that. So on that basis, failure isn't really failure until we quit. Instead, it's just a stepping stone towards the good stuff.

Write down something you 'failed' at that meant a lot to you. Is it too late to try again? If not, think about the next steps you need to take. Then try again. Go again. See failures as rites of passage that you must pass through. And with each new attempt, you're always getting closer.

- *What are you saying to yourself about your failures?*
- *How could you look at them with more understanding or compassion?*
- *What does it feel like to treat failure as a 'rite of passage' to success?*

EATING TRUTHS

*THE FOLLOWING TWO DAYS CONTAIN CONTENT
RELATING TO EATING DISORDERS*

EVERY ONE OF us has a unique relationship with food. Some see it solely as fuel; others associate it with emotion. Few people get the balance right.

How, when and how much we consume is such a complex issue. And our eating habits directly affect our mood, health and emotions.

It's tough to see that eating disorders are on the rise, particularly among young people. They are really serious and complex conditions that need expert care.

According to the charity 'Men Get Eating Disorders Too', disorders can be 'a coping mechanism or an expression of underlying emotional stress'.

If you are suffering in this way, know that you are not alone. Food is intrinsic to our physical survival so we are hard-wired to place importance on it. But when that relationship becomes damaging it is important to seek help. All of us must do what we can to work against the stigma that might keep people from getting that help.

We are most at risk in the battles we are fighting alone.

- *Were you aware that both men and women experience eating disorders and that their causes are so diverse?*
- *Is there a trusted friend or even a professional you could open up to about any struggles you might be having about these issues?*

'Food is a core part of our human story . . . but it can go wrong sometimes'

BECAUSE WE ALL have a relationship with food, we probably all have an opinion about eating disorders. They are often misunderstood as being selfish or about vanity, whereas those issues have got nothing to do with the development of the various forms of these illnesses. Nobody sets out to develop an eating disorder; the causes and dynamics are complex.

It's by no means a universal explanation, but 'control' has been explored as an element since the work of pioneering psychiatrist Hilde Bruch. In a pressured world, I empathise with the desire to seek some control, especially with something as tangible as food. But eating disorders are rarely about just one thing; causes can include genetics or personality traits, especially competitiveness, perfectionism and low self-esteem.

Men are increasingly suffering, and younger boys and girls have equal prevalence. Neither do all eating disorders look the same; people with larger bodies suffer too.

Food is a core part of our human story. As with everything human, it has the propensity to go wrong sometimes. The key is getting help and helping others to walk into freedom without judgement.

- *How does understanding a bit more about the complex causes of eating disorders make you feel about people who may be suffering with them?*
- *What assumptions have you made about what eating disorders look like?*

SUCKER FOR NOVELTY

ADVENTURERS TEND TO love new gear and that can make sport shops dangerous places! Everything from climbing ropes to canteens, sleeping bags to sunglasses – it's easy to be convinced that some new piece of kit is higher spec, more durable, stronger or just plain newer than what we have already.

You don't need to be an adventurer to struggle with the appeal of novelty. Our brains are hard-wired to believe that new things offer us an 'advantage': new information that could strengthen our position in a group or give us the edge over a competitor.

The attraction of novelty is another 'cognitive bias' that affects the way we process information and make decisions. Exploring new things initially feels good but there are two key drawbacks. First, the draw of new things can powerfully interrupt our natural concentration and flow. Second, it is built on a false assumption that because something is new it is naturally better than what we already have.

- *Do you often find yourself distracted or interrupted by the appeal of something new?*
- *How strongly have you been convinced that new is better?*
- *When were you last disappointed in something new which transpired to be less good than what you already had?*

'Take a moment to think about the most precious things in your life'

PROFESSOR SHERRY TURKLE is the founding director of the MIT Initiative on Technology and Self. Her groundbreaking work has explored our changing relationship with new technology and our bias to believe that what is bright and shiny is likely to be better. She says, 'Not every advance is progress. Not every new thing is better for us humanly.'

It's so easy to confuse something that is 'bright and shiny' with something that is valuable. But take a moment to think about the most precious things in your life. The likelihood is that they aren't new. Old friends, long-term relationships, aged pets, even adventure gear that you know is tried and tested. New does not automatically mean better.

Of course, there are moments when a new thing is wonderful, such as when we are surprised by a gift or are actually choosing something for what it is, rather than just because it's new. As Shakespeare tells us in *The Merchant of Venice*, 'All that glitters is not gold'.

- *How could you actively value the good old things in your life today? Who might you need to reach out to?*
- *What could you do to weaken the bias of novelty in your life? What might a more realistic view be?*
- *How will you respond when the good old things in your life are in danger of being displaced by the new, bright and shiny?*

DAY 299

DOOM
SCROLLING

THE DIGITAL REVOLUTION has seen our lives change faster than at any time in human history. The Internet was only born on 1 January 1983. Yet today, research suggests that we are overwhelmed by the equivalent of 34 gigabytes of information each day.

Many of us struggle to process the volume of information and the emotion it provokes. Historically, we'd expect to bear our own emotional burdens, plus perhaps those of our immediate family, friends and local community. Today, we become emotionally impacted by trauma or tragedy far beyond that scope.

Research from the University of California suggests that 'media coverage following disasters and mass violence events may have a more complex, unintended, injurious impact'. Our capacity to deal with this emotional overload inevitably has its limits. When people have nowhere to direct their response, they can be left feeling powerless, anxious and often exhausted.

It isn't 'uncompassionate' to limit our exposure to traumatising content. It can be wise. Maybe once you get the facts, it is ok to cease absorbing more of a disaster. That's not to say don't give and act in some practical way, if you feel compelled, but you don't have to stay locked into content that distresses you.

- *What might it look like to create some boundaries around how much traumatic content you expose yourself to?*
- *How does traumatic content tend to impact you?*
- *Do you feel guilty if you don't pay attention to the news?*

'In an increasingly connected world, exposure to compassion-provoking material is a daily experience'

COMPASSION COMES FROM the Latin word *compati* which means 'to suffer with', and it is one of the most unique and powerful signs of our humanity. But it is also a precious and limited resource. Compassion is not something that we can, or should, store away for a 'worst case' emergency. It is designed to be shown and shared regularly. But it is also a precious and fragile resource. As charity founder Chris Marlow says in his book *Doing Good is Simple*, compassion fatigue is a real thing: 'Emotions, so strong at first, can easily shift into apathy. The subsequent guilt is para-lysing; it can prevent us from ever doing anything and freeze us into inaction.'

An ABC model can help us stay soft-hearted towards suffering: **A**wareness of the feelings and demands you are carrying. **B**alance of your inputs and outputs, allowing you to take care of yourself. And **C**onnection to others, linked to your ability to ask for help.

Your compassion is a precious resource. Taking care of yourself when under emotional demand will ensure it keeps flowing freely and beautifully.

- *Are you conscious of a time when you began to feel numb or overwhelmed in the face of suffering?*
- *How do you feel about the idea of being 'resourced for compassion'?*
- *How could the ABC model form a simple prompt to ensure you do OK in emotionally demanding circumstances?*

LET OTHERS SHINE

MARK TWAIN WROTE, 'One compliment can keep me going for a whole month.' It's powerful to be encouraged. How much greater to be someone who can keep others going for a whole month!

There are three key forms of encouragement: 'Active encouragement' is the direct actions and words we give out to help others. 'Self-encouragement' is the good stuff we read, focus on and tell ourselves, to keep positive and motivated. But 'passive encouragement' is more subtle: sometimes it's our restraint that allows other people to feel their best.

We have all met people who, after we've recounted some anecdote, go on to tell an even funnier story in which everything is bigger and more dramatic. Restraint is when we acknowledge that, while we may have a bigger and better story, we are not going to share it. Restraint says more about your character than any story you could tell about yourself. It is a valuable gift that allows others to shine.

So, try to resist trumping others, and let those people have their moment. Delight in other people's stories, achievements and dreams. Only let yours be dragged out of you.

- *Do you find it difficult to step back and allow others to shine?*
- *What do you find endearing about someone who is slow to reveal their achievements?*

'You don't have to be a professional to help enable the success of the people around you'

JOHN FAIRLEY. AIMEE BOORMAN. Dwayne Jarrett. Three names that you don't immediately recognise. Jonny Wilkinson. Simone Biles. Usain Bolt. Three names that you probably do.

The first three names coached each of these star athletes respectively at the start of their careers. A great coach takes great pleasure in another's success. They don't need (or even want) to be the one in the limelight, in order to find their value. You can only imagine the satisfaction John Fairley must have felt to see the young Jonny Wilkinson, whom he coached at Farnham Rugby Club, becoming Rugby World Champion in 2003.

Coaching is about encouraging the best out of others, empowering them to be more than they thought they could be. In many ways, coaching is the ultimate expression of active and passive encouragement. And of love.

You don't have to be a professional to help enable the success of the people around you. It's about having the humility to see where people's gifts lie, then offering gentle encouragement – or restraint – so they can take those abilities to the next level.

True champions always make their life, their purpose, about others.

- *Look around you. Who could you encourage, empower or inspire today?*
- *How could you employ a gentle coaching mindset with the people in your world?*
- *How does the success of others make you feel?*

REDEMPTION STORIES

I N A THROWAWAY world, where everything seems replaceable, it's easy to forget about the precious value of the original. There's always 'better' stuff about to be released and shiny alternatives can get delivered in hours. The originals get thrown out and forgotten.

The same can happen with ourselves, if we lose a sense of how precious we are, unable to move past those things that have proven disappointing. But there is something that can transform our history into our destiny: the gift of redemption.

'Redemption' comes from the Latin verb *redimere*, meaning to 'buy back for a price'. Redemption stories are often complicated. But they are founded on the principle that there is a 'way back'. Redemption refines and transforms what was broken so that it is new again – in fact, even more precious. It can liberate us to be the best that we can be, not the best that we were.

Whatever we have experienced, however much we've been damaged, we have no replacement. On the contrary, those parts of ourselves that seem worthless are often the most fertile places for renewal.

- *Have you become stuck in a world of disappointment, unable to move forward?*
- *What do you know needs redemption in your life? How might that journey from darkness to light begin?*
- *Could broken parts of your history be redeemed, to offer you your destiny?*

'There is a "way back" for what is damaged and broken . . . nobody is beyond repair'

IT WAS IN the desert sands of North Africa that I filmed my first ever TV series called *Escape to the Legion*, where I went through simulated basic training. It was designed to give a taste of what Legion life is really like – behind the mystique. It was one of the hardest four weeks of my life.

The Foreign Legion was founded in 1831 and soon became a place where all kinds of criminals, misfits and lost souls could find a home and make a fresh start. As a mercenary regiment that exists to this day, it is as tough a band of warriors as there has ever been. But it is the Legion's heart for redemption that I have always loved the most. New recruits join with a 'declared identity' so that everyone has the potential for a new beginning.

Their training is some of the toughest in the world. For every recruit who can endure it, they become forged into a hardened warrior, with renewed values for a life of service.

Whatever their past, people can start afresh in the Legion. As every legionnaire knows: redemption can turn obstacles into opportunities. Nobody is beyond repair.

- *Could obstacles in your life become opportunities for growth?*
- *What things have defined your 'identity' in the past? What could define you in the future?*
- *What strengths and virtues do you want to live by?*

THE PITFALLS OF PERFECTIONISM

'PERFECTIONISM IS THE voice of the oppressor, the enemy of the people.' So writes author Anne Lamott.

We think of perfectionism as a trait that gives us an edge over people who are less detail-oriented, even though we nod our head to its mildly negative conseqences. It's the old interview question: what would you say are your faults? 'Oh, I'm a bit of a perfectionist.' Sigh.

The reality is that perfectionism can be a massive hindrance to our happiness. It can lead to depression, anxiety, procrastination and an unwillingness to try anything that might risk failure.

But to achieve anything worthwhile we must learn to fail. This mindset has been key to me through so much: fail repeatedly, and keep failing until I find a way to succeed.

Perfectionism says: 'you have to get this right or else'; wisdom says, 'you won't always get this right, but try, enjoy the process, even the setbacks, go again, see what happens . . .'

Letting go of our fear of ever looking 'unsuccessful' is a key step for anyone who wants to grow, succeed and be happy.

- *Have you thought of perfectionism as a harmless, possibly advantageous trait?*
- *What do you notice about perfectionism's ability to hinder risk-taking and forbid failure?*
- *How could you adopt a more real and flexible attitude towards failure and growth?*

'Perfectionism is not a path to happiness or enlightenment'

PERFECTIONISM IS A bit like snow. It's a single word that can mean lots of different things. (Eskimos really do have fifty words for snow!) What perfectionism is not is simply achieving our goals. Because even then, perfectionism still says: 'you could have done it better or in less time'. Perfectionists tend to avoid rest and are rarely satisfied – and that's not a path to happiness or enlightenment.

Struggle, rest, try, fail, go again. Never give up. Adapt. Persist. Fall down. Laugh. Assess. Keep going. This is the path to a rich life. This sort of mental fitness takes time to build but it is so worth it. Freedom from perfectionism always is.

Psychologists have developed the Perfectionism Scale which identifies three core types of perfectionists: 1. Self-Oriented Perfectionism, in which we negatively appraise our own performance; 2. Other-Oriented Perfectionism, where we judge others harshly and unrealistically; and, finally 3. Socially Oriented Perfectionism, in which we believe society is judging us and we must achieve social approval.

All of these limit us. They might have different faces, but it is the same critical and restricting voice.

- *What does perfectionism mean to you?*
- *Which of the three styles of perfectionism do you most resonate with and why?*
- *Do you approve of yourself enough to accept and celebrate success as well as the effort of failure?*

SAY
YES!

A FEW YEARS AGO I travelled to Nepal with an expedition that was attempting to fly a paramotor – basically a paraglider with an engine strapped to your back – over the summit of Everest. This meant building a machine that could ascend to over 29,000 feet (8,840 metres). Everyone we spoke to about it said: a) we were crazy to attempt it due to the winds and altitude; and, b) it was technically impossible to design such a powerful engine that we would be able to carry on our backs.

But then again they hadn't met my great buddy and engineer, Gilo Cardozo.

Gilo is a born enthusiast, and a man who loves to say 'yes' when others say 'no'. The truth is, his role in our Everest mission was technically incredibly difficult. And I am in no doubt the only reason the project eventually succeeded was because, no matter the obstacle, no matter the technical 'problem', Gilo always said, 'We can do this.' And he always found a solution.

- *How do other people's perspectives on your dreams affect your approach to them?*
- *Who do you know that carries a positive 'yes' attitude, even when things look impossible?*
- *Which ambitions have you shelved because they seemed out of reach? Has anything shifted?*

'Having the courage to say yes opens up the possibility of adventure'

VIRGIN ENTREPRENEUR RICHARD BRANSON dropped out of school at sixteen. His headmaster said he would either end up in prison or become a millionaire. Richard said, 'If somebody offers you an amazing opportunity but you are not sure you can do it, say yes – then learn how to do it later!'

We all need a 'Gilo' living inside our head who is ready to answer the naysayers with a confident 'yes'. Perhaps the biggest naysayers are the 'doubters' inside ourselves. It could be a fear of failure, or a sense of impostor syndrome, inexperience, extreme shyness, poor self-esteem or even the fear of 'just doing it'.

Saying 'no' means that, more often than not, nothing will change in our lives. But having the courage and conviction to say 'yes' when others around us are saying 'no' opens up the possibility of adventure and living life in all its fullness.

- *What would it feel like to say 'yes' knowing that you still need to learn how to do something?*
- *What is holding you back from embracing new opportunities? Is it an external or internal challenge?*
- *How would it feel to say yes, knowing that you might fail, but you might not? Could it be worth the risk?*

THE POWER
OF GRATITUDE

HAVE YOU EVER noticed how it's almost impossible to be both grateful and miserable at the same time? It is why gratitude is one of the surest roads out of the deep valleys of depression and despair that there is.

Gratitude is one of life's great mysteries.

The mistake we often make is that we fixate on the things we don't have, rather than appreciating the many things that we do. For all the many problems in life, there are always simple things for which we can say: 'I'm grateful for that.'

Roy T. Bennett wrote, 'Be grateful for what you already have while you pursue your goals. If you aren't grateful for what you already have, what makes you think you would be happy with more?'

Even the most unappealing meal can be something to be grateful for when food is scarce. Take it from a man who has eaten some horrors in times gone by! And a hug from a friend when we are down can be true gold.

- *How has gratitude impacted your mood?*
- *Have you believed that having something different would make you feel more grateful?*
- *What could you notice and be thankful for today?*

'Be grateful for the simple stuff'

CULTIVATING AN ATTITUDE of gratitude isn't always easy but, like all things when we do it regularly and consistently, we get better at seeing the good around us. When we start living with eyes and hearts full of thankfulness then the world always feels a better place.

So maybe make a list of the positive things or people that you do have in your life. Write them down if you like – I do when times are dark, and it always helps me.

When dark thoughts close in, look outwards, and see the small blessings that all too often we forget about. Be grateful for the simple stuff: things like clean water, a roof above us, a friend, even fresh air . . . the very things that so many in this world lack. Because a sense of perspective and a grateful heart are two golden secrets to being happy.

- *How could you practise gratitude as a daily activity?*
- *What might you have taken for granted in the past which you could be grateful for in the future?*
- *What might help you to renew your perspective on your circumstances?*

METAMOTIVATION

PSYCHOLOGISTS SAY WE are driven by a pyramid of basic needs. The lower levels are all about survival: hunger, thirst and procreation, for instance. The top levels are 'higher' callings, called, by one psychologist, 'metamotivations'.

There have been moments in the wild when I have thought if I could just have a drink of cold water I will never want anything ever again. Finally taking those first few gulps is always intensely satisfying, but it's a feeling that doesn't last. 'Deficiency needs' are loud when they aren't met, but quiet when they are. 'Being needs', however, have a motivation that last well beyond the immediate moment. These include justice, goodness, meaning-fulness and wholeness.

I am constantly blown away by so many unsung, everyday heroes who operate with true 'metamotivation', despite often having pressing deficiency needs themselves. How is it that those who tend to give most freely are often those who are most content with materially very little? If we can be generous when we still have our own needs, we develop a habit of positive living that is much more likely to endure, even when we have plenty.

- *Are you facing significant 'deficiency needs'? Are you able to get support?*
- *What motivations in your life last beyond being immediately satisfied?*
- *If you were going to describe your top three metamotivations, what would they be?*

'Find out what values are at the top of your pyramid and make them your priority'

JON BENNION-PEDLEY WAS a millionaire living a lavish lifestyle when his life was dramatically turned upside down. Following a serious car accident, he started living out of his 'metamotivations' and ended up giving away a fortune to serve people in need in Africa.

So often in life, when we nearly lose it all, we appreciate how much we actually have.

The lesson is not to wait until all of our other needs have been sufficiently met before we start to give. C. S. Lewis suggested that 'the only safe rule is to give more than we can spare. If our kind deeds do not pinch or hamper us, I should say they are too small'. Living an enlightened life starts from the heart. And the rule of the universe says: the more we give, the more we will always receive.

Do what moves your heart to action. We all have something to give, even if it's just our time. Find out what values are at the top of your pyramid and make them your priority.

- *Have you noticed how hard it is to know when your needs have been sufficiently met?*
- *Can you think of an example of someone who lives out of their metamotivations?*
- *How might you live more in line with those bigger aspirations for the benefit of others?*

A GREATER POWER

I AM STUMBLING, GOING from my knees to my feet, then back to my knees. The world is a white blur. It was within moments of leaving the summit of Everest that the real level of exhaustion set in. It's hard to describe how much energy is required at that point, just to keep moving. My oxygen had run out and I was hanging on by a thread.

Stay alert, Bear. Keep it together just a little longer. Never Give Up. NGU.

I keep repeating this to myself. Over and over. Mumbling words. Asking for help. From without and within. For strength to keep going, from a power greater than me.

It's not so often that we come to the end of ourselves. It's humbling but it's also the place life can truly begin. When we can no longer be self-reliant, we get a real sense of what's false and what's real.

Eventually, I slump down on the ground next to the cache of spare oxygen, sucking it down in gulps. NGU.

- *Have you ever reached the very end of yourself, physically, mentally or spiritually? What did you find there?*
- *Beyond the earthly, have you ever asked for strength and comfort from a power greater than you?*
- *If you have sensed something greater than you in a desperate moment, could you ask for that presence to stay in the brighter moments too?*

'When our ability to cope is at its limit, people have often encountered the Divine'

ERNEST SHACKLETON SUCCESSFULLY undertook one of the greatest rescue missions in history. Having witnessed his ship *The Endurance* terrifyingly crushed by polar ice in the Antarctic, Shackleton and a handful of men sailed 800 miles to South Georgia in a small open boat.

Clinging to the outer edges of life, they then had to cross the vast, uncharted, snow-capped mountains to reach a small whaling station, where they could raise the alarm and have the remaining crew rescued.

Shackleton later wrote in his book *South*: 'I know that during that long and racking march of thirty-six hours over the unnamed mountains and glaciers of South Georgia it seemed to me often that we were four, not three. I said nothing to my companions on the point, but afterwards Worsley said to me, "Boss, I had a curious feeling on the march that there was another person with us."'

When our ability to cope is at its limit, people have often encountered the Divine. Just because we cannot see something doesn't mean it's not there. I guess that's what faith ultimately is. A trust in the unseen. It has always been a quiet strength to me. That fourth man, holding my rope.

- *What inspires you about Shackleton's rescue of his crew?*
- *How would you keep going if you felt your ability to cope was at its limit?*
- *Have you ever sensed that divine presence, that 'fourth man'?*

SACRIFICE IS NECESSARY

WHEN I WAS a child we had these clear colouring pencils with eight different coloured leads in them. To use the colour you wanted you had to pull out the lead you were using and push it into the top of the pencil, then the next colour would appear at the writing end. It taught me two important lessons. First, you have finite capacity. Second, to get what you need, you have to push something else to the back of the queue.

It's fun for a moment to think that we have the capacity to do everything, or kid ourselves into believing that we can give everything equal attention. But the reality of life is that to achieve anything new, sacrifice is necessary. The best sort of sacrifice is not begrudgingly given, but actively chosen before we begin. It is asking ourselves two questions: 'what am I going to have to give up if I choose this?', and; 'what or who will lose my attention if I choose this?'

- *Have you had a tendency to say 'yes' without thinking about your capacity?*
- *How comfortable are you with the idea of pushing demands 'to the back of the queue'?*
- *What would it look like to actively choose sacrifice?*

'Every good thing in my life has required sacrifice'

WHEN WE THINK about sacrifice we tend to emphasise what has to be given up, rather than what has to be gained. But what makes sacrifice different from straightforward loss, is that sacrifice is always 'loss for a purpose'. Author Napoleon Hill wrote, 'Great achievement is usually born of great sacrifice, and is never the result of selfishness.'

Looking back, every good thing in my life has required some sort of sacrifice. Sacrifice is the gateway to achievement, but also to every good relationship. Giving something up for the sake of something else is tough, but the power comes in the choosing. When we sacrifice, we are simply redistributing our finite capacity to the things that really matter to us.

- *How does accepting that you have finite capacity affect your willingness to let go of things?*
- *If you prioritised the demands in your life, are you matching them to your sacrifices or to the things that are most important to you?*
- *How could you actively choose to sacrifice things for the sake of better relationships and friendships?*

DAY 317

GIVE UP COMPARING
YOURSELF

THE SUN HAS a circumference exactly 400 times greater than the moon, but it is also 400 times further away. So they may appear to be exactly the same size in the sky, but in real terms there is no comparison.

If we are constantly making comparisons between ourselves and others, we may believe we are comparing 'like for like', but we have no way of understanding other people's experiences, gifts or their journey to this moment. And we have no idea what burdens they may be struggling with to which we are blind.

The temptation is always to compare upwards: to people who are 'doing better', 'achieving more' or are 'wealthier'. But this invariably leaves us feeling jealous and dissatisfied. As Theodore Roosevelt said: 'Comparison is the thief of joy.'

Comparison is different from competition. Having a competitive spirit at times, and when wisely directed, is a great thing. But, we have to check ourselves. Comparison-making has a habit of creeping into every area of our lives and it always turns the milk sour.

- *Do you tend to believe you are comparing yourself on a 'level playing field'? What may you be missing?*

- *How do you find comparison-making impacts your mood and ability to be generous to others?*

- *What would it feel like to swap the negative comparisons for a positive 'competitive' spirit?*

'If we constantly try to "keep up" with others, we are running their race, not ours'

YOU MIGHT NOT realise how competitive some US bass fishing tournaments can become. During the 2005 Red River Bassmaster Central Open, one of the fishermen, days before the competition, tethered live bass to stumps around the lake. And, sure enough, when the competition started, he rapidly filled his boat with the fish.

Unbeknown to him, another competitor had accidentally snagged one of the lines before the competition and raised the alarm. They secretly marked the tethered fish and when they appeared at the weigh-in, the game was up.

I have learnt that there is always a lot more going on under the surface in people's lives than we imagine. Social media might capture beautiful snapshots of aspirational lifestyles, but how much of it is real, and how much is manipulated?

Success can never really be measured by 'cheating' our way to a better result. True success is about who we become on our journey through life. If we constantly try to 'keep up' with others, we are running their race, not ours. We lose our unique power and purpose.

- *How does comparison-making impact your satisfaction with your life, relationships or situation?*
- *Have you wondered if the comparisons you are making may be false because of what is going on 'under the water'?*
- *What would becoming 'successful' in life look like to you?*

DAY 319

AS THE ARTIST INTENDED

MICHELANGELO'S DAVID MAY be the most famous statue in the world. But if you were to climb a ladder and see it directly side-on you would notice that David's head, hands and arms are all out of proportion with his torso and legs. But Michelangelo didn't make a mistake; he knew David would be viewed from below. And today, it's often regarded as the most perfect and beautiful sculpture in the world.

I have found that life makes so much more sense when I start the day kneeling. I can see the beauty of the created world from a different perspective, and feel empowered for the day ahead. It's about recognising my humility and understanding I can't only rely on my own resources.

Spending a little time each day quietly letting a sense of peace and love wash over us gives us a window into the artist's perspective. That's prayer, I guess. And like with the statue of David, it is only when we kneel down that we begin also to get a fresh perspective on our own true worth.

- *Can you think of a time when a change of perspective completely altered your view of something?*
- *Are you happy with your view of the people around you? Do you tend to see the good or the faults in them?*
- *How does the idea of seeing things and people from a different perspective make you feel?*

'If you want to see what's really there, you have to relax and stop trying to see it your way'

MAGIC EYE POSTERS are a throwback to my nineties school years and were firmly fixed on many a bedroom wall. The images were apparently a mass of random coloured lines and shapes, and yet, viewed the right way, they revealed a hidden 3D image.

Sometimes you could be stood in front of one of these images with a few buddies and they would be saying, 'Wow look at that awesome dolphin jumping.' And all you could see were coloured, wavy lines.

I learnt something from Magic Eye posters – if you want to see what's really there, you have to relax and stop trying to see it your way. It was as if it was somehow harder for the image to appear if you already had an idea of what to expect.

I have found the same is true for people and life. When we relax and stop trying to push our own agenda, or our own expectations of how situations or conversations should be, then we start seeing a wonderful uniqueness in it all, which is never predictable or disappointing.

- *Do you tend to look at people with hard expectations?*
- *Can you think of a time when you had preconceived ideas that were proved to be completely wrong?*
- *What would it take for you to relax and let people show you more of their real selves over time?*

THE POWER OF AN HONEST APOLOGY

WE ALL MAKE mistakes. But it's what we do next that counts.

A sure-fire way to make a mistake worse is to deny it and then refuse to apologise. Both responses are all-too common in life – especially public life – and they are both weak. An honest, heart-felt apology is a sign of genuine strength and integrity. Beyond that, a sincere apology has the power to give both parties a pathway to peace.

When we have done something wrong, it's natural to become defensive. Mistakes can be embarrassing and sometimes humiliating. In an attempt to minimise that, we can quickly move into 'excuse mode'.

Excuse mode has three guises. If your mistake is like a sinking ship, the first guise would be denying the ship is sinking at all. Second would be minimising the importance that it's happening. Finally, it would be blaming everyone else.

Excuses may feel valid but they are the opposite of a good apology. A good apology has three simple parts. It is unqualified: 'I'm truly sorry'; it takes clear responsibility: 'This is my fault'; and finally, it offers restitution: 'Can I do anything to make things right?'

- *Can you think of an experience when you deserved an apology but got 'excuse mode'?*
- *Which part of a 'good apology' do you most value?*
- *Is there an immediate situation where you could practise this for yourself?*

'We take full responsibility and we make no excuses'

AFTER A DEVASTATING defeat in the National Hockey League, Toronto Maple Leafs' Chairman did something extraordinary. He wrote a personal and open letter to all the fans including the lines: 'we have fallen short of everyone's expectations, and for that we are sorry. We take full responsibility for how this team performs on the ice, and we make no excuses'.

We don't often see powerful leaders own and take true responsibility for their failures. But when we do, it is magnetic and appealing. Research shows that the single most significant part of an apology for the recipient is 'taking responsibility'. As Benjamin Franklin wrote: 'Never ruin an apology with an excuse.'

People who believe in their ability to change are more likely to take responsibility when they do something wrong. To them, an apology is a prompt to do better, as well as to make things right as best they can.

Good apologies are always more than words, they are actions. So develop the power to apologise without excuses, to own the mistake and offer reconciliation.

When this is done properly, it is the ultimate show of courage and character.

- *Can you think of a time when someone took responsibility without passing the blame?*
- *Do you believe you can change and grow following your past mistakes?*
- *Are there ways you can live out an apology through change behaviour more than words?*

DECISION-MAKING IS A MUSCLE WE CAN STRENGTHEN

THERE IS A wild stretch of water called the Menai Strait near our small island home in North Wales. On a beautiful day it can look as calm as a pond, but under the surface the tides can run as fast as four metres per second. If you are crossing the Strait in a boat you are making a hundred tiny decisions every minute, adjusting your course, power and anticipating the next steps.

It's an exercise in 360-degree boat handling. It can be exhilarating and exhausting – but in essence it's about trusting your instinct, using your experience, being prepared and then just going for it.

One of the great things about wild places is that they force us to make lots of small decisions quickly. And when we have enough exposure to these sorts of situations then people's confidence in their decision-making ability rises sharply.

- *How is your decision-making muscle?*
- *Have you defaulted into excessive information gathering or opinion canvassing before making a decision?*
- *When did you last make lots of small, instinctive decisions? How did it feel?*

'Your chances of making a good decision are determined by your experience'

I DON'T BELIEVE that people are born good or bad decision makers. Rather, decision-making is like a muscle; the more we use it, the stronger it becomes. The more we practise, the faster we can connect the three 'I's for a good decision: Intention (what you want); Information (what you know); and Instinct (what you feel).

Life is constantly changing and those changes demand our response. Becoming more decisive makes the demands of life not just less stressful but more enjoyable.

Your chances of making a good or a bad decision are usually determined by your experience. Like any skill, the more practice you put in, the less you leave to chance. As Dale Carnegie wrote: 'Inaction breeds doubt and fear. Action breeds confidence and courage.'

Start small. Make small decisions every day. Get that inner muscle working. Then, when the big junction points come along, you're more likely to make a decision you're happy to live with.

- *Which of the three 'I's (Intention, Information, Instinct) have you relied on the most?*
- *How could you trust your instincts more?*
- *What could you do to 'practise' making quick decisions well?*

DAY 325

WHAT TO DO WHEN YOU GET STUCK

UICKSAND IS ONE of the trickier hazards in the wild. The danger, if you stray into it, is not that you're going to go under, like in the movies. But rather that you'll get stuck and stay stuck. After that, depending on where you are, you could rapidly suffer from sunstroke, hypothermia or dehydration. Or you simply run out of energy, fighting against the gloop.

The key to surviving is first to stay calm, then gently ease a limb onto the surface, spread your weight, then wriggle your way back the way you came. Never fight the sticky, clingy sand. The more you battle, the more it will pull you in and hold you fast.

When we face an unexpected problem that brings us to a stop, the natural response is to panic. And all too often, we can end up making things worse: minor disagreements become major fallings out; a financial challenge becomes a debt mountain; simple misunderstandings become major issues of mistrust.

Sometimes doing nothing initially is best. Stay calm; assess the situation; then plan your escape.

- *Have you run into patches of 'quicksand' in life? How did you respond?*
- *Looking back at crisis times, do you sometimes wish that you had taken more time over what to do next?*
- *How might you fight that urge to react quickly?*

'I have learnt the importance of taking my time'

EMILE LERAY WAS driving across the Sahara in 1993 when a rock broke the car's chassis. He had no means of communicating his position and was miles from civilisation. 'I put myself in survival mode,' Leray said. 'I could not have gone back on foot – it was too far.'

The worst thing you can do in such a situation is leave your supplies in a fit of panic, hoping that things will somehow magically work out better on foot. Instead, Leray, an experienced electrician, deconstructed his Citroën 2CV and rebuilt it as a motorbike. It took twelve days and left him with just half a litre of water. He then rode his improvised motorbike out of the desert, before being picked up by the police.

Adrenaline is the 'rushing' neurochemical: it makes us faster, but not necessarily smarter.

I have learnt the importance of taking my time when responding to challenges. It may be just a few minutes, or it may be a few days. The key thing is to make sure you are committing to the smartest course of action, not 'any' course of action.

- *Have you felt the temptation to rush into a response to challenges?*
- *How could you take a more considered approach, even when the instinct to escape is strong?*

READY TO ADAPT

A FEW YEARS BACK, while filming on a makeshift raft in the middle of the Pacific, I was cooling off by jumping in the water every hour. One time, I landed on top of a twelve-foot tiger shark that had been ghosting under my raft. It was intense, but within a second or so I had clawed my way back onto my raft.

A leap into the unknown is always a risk, but we often underestimate our ability to adapt. As we used to say in the military: Improvise, Adapt, Overcome.

Every decision comes with the risk that we might encounter an unpleasant surprise, but that is not a reason to avoid the opportunity in the first place. Most of the things we fear most either never happen, or almost certainly not in the way that we fear.

In my experience, being 'safe' is a trap – and often the safest place is in the thick of the action. It is inaction that we should fear most. That's not to say be reckless, but become good at assessing risks, then making a decision to go for the things that are worth it.

- *Does anticipating risks tend to end your willingness to step into new opportunities?*
- *Do you believe the worst will probably happen?*
- *How could confidence in your ability to adapt to the surprises of change impact your confidence to take the next step?*

'The mission succeeded in revealing the resilience and ingenuity of people under pressure'

'OKAY, HOUSTON, WE'VE had a problem here.' Astronaut John L. Swigert Jr said those terrifying words 205,000 miles from earth.

The Apollo 13 space mission was to be only the third moon landing in history. But an oxygen tank on the spaceship Odyssey blew up, destroying all of the other oxygen tanks on which the craft's power depended. The crew were now stranded in space.

The crew, with the guidance of Mission Control, set about solving a litany of apparently insurmountable problems. They used gravity to power their small craft around the moon and back towards earth. They had to survive on a tiny amount of water, limited oxygen and live in sub-zero temperatures for days. But eventually they splashed down to safety in the Pacific Ocean.

The Apollo 13 mission failed in its ambition to land on the moon, but succeeded in revealing the resilience and ingenuity of people under pressure.

You have that resilience and ingenuity too. Don't decline your 'moon shot' just because you fear what might go wrong.

- *What do you notice in the Apollo 13 story that could apply to your own ability to deal with the unknown?*
- *What part might teammates, friends, family or colleagues play in supporting you through unknown surprises?*

KNOWING YOUR OPTIMUM PRESSURE

SOME OF US react badly to extended periods of high pressure, while others thrive on it. Just knowing that shows that each of us probably has a different 'optimum' operating pressure. Think about it in terms of bikes: road-racing bike tyres generally tolerate a lot more pressure than, say, those of a mountain bike. Both need pressure to function, but the range is calibrated differently. Too little and the wheels just won't turn; too much and the tyre bursts.

Knowing your 'optimum' working pressure can be really helpful both for managing your workload and your sense of wellbeing. Too little load can actually cause stress – we may find ourselves struggling with motivation, lethargy, distraction or worry. Overload can equally cause burnout if it is sustained.

- *How have periods with too little pressure impacted your mood?*

- *What about times when you have felt hugely over-pressurised?*

- *How would you describe the optimum pressure for you to feel both energised and challenged?*

'Each of us has a different "optimum" operating pressure'

WHEN A GOOD tyre is treated well, it can carry us a long way. Part of good maintenance is checking the tyre pressure every so often (internal conditions) and also adapting the pressure to the type of road surface (external conditions). Matching your resources to your demands is how we can try to keep the pressure within a reasonable range.

Of course, nobody can control every stress or demand that life makes of them. Even if we could, life isn't about that. It's about remembering the level of pressure that we thrive at. There will be many things that we cannot change and times when we are over or under our ideal. But I've found that knowing what that ideal is gives us something clear to aim for. We then have the opportunity to calibrate the things that we can control to the best pressure for us to thrive under.

- *How closely do you think your internal and external pressures are aligned at the moment?*
- *Can you be flexible when the pressure rises or falls past what you are comfortable with?*
- *What does it take for you to get back towards your target pressure?*

STRUGGLE IS STRENGTH

T HE STRADIVARIUS VIOLIN, notably one of the finest musical instruments in the world, is shaped from wood sourced in the Risoud Forest, Switzerland.

Yet the Stradivarius doesn't get cut from the large, full-branched spruce trees in the forest, only from the thin trees that have been struggling in the shade of their larger counterparts. As these trees battle to reach the light, they put out fewer branches, which means fewer knots, less sap and less moisture in the wood.

It is the tree's perceived weakness that actually creates the perfect wood for an incredible resonance and sound. While other spruces are being turned into kitchen floorboards, these 'struggling' trees are being crafted for greater things. The 1721 Lady Blunt Stradivarius violin was last sold for just shy of £10 million.

When you are struggling for air at work or school, or battling to be heard alongside louder voices, when you are needing to run just to keep pace . . . don't give up. You are being shaped for great things.

It's in the struggle that you will find your strengths, and in the fight that you gain your edge.

- *Have you found it tempting to write yourself off because of the apparent gifts of others?*
- *What have you noticed about people who have had to battle for their success?*

'When we struggle, we get strong'

JOSEPH PILATES WAS born in 1883 in Mönchengladbach, Germany. He was a struggling child who suffered from asthma, rickets and rheumatic fever. But Joseph was determined to overcome his physical struggles through strength training – something that was far less mainstream than it is today.

By 1912, he was already a competent skier, diver, gymnast and boxer, and ended up teaching self-defence classes in England. When war broke out, he was confined to a camp for German nationals where he continued to develop his exercise techniques. Transferred to work in a hospital on the Isle of Wight, he attached springs to patients' beds so they could use resistance training to regain their strength. 'Pilates' was born.

Joseph Pilates would go on to establish his strengthening programme in the USA, and today it is practised by over twelve million people worldwide. All this from a boy who was struggling with weakness and illness.

When we struggle, we get strong. We can see resistance as a curse, or we can see it as a gift. You decide. When life weighs you down, do ten reps.

* *What inspires you about Joseph Pilates' story?*
* *When he gained strength for himself, what do you notice he did with it?*
* *How could you use specific struggles in your life to gain new strength?*

GROWTH FROM TOUGH TIMES

'WHAT IF IT were all a gift?' asks motivational speaker Tony Robbins. 'What if . . . all the pain, the joy, the tears, the heartaches . . . was all a gift. All for you'.

It's easy to think about life as a gift when things are going well, but a lot harder when things go wrong. Yet it's often those times that give us the most.

It's incredible how often trauma survivors say they would decline an imagined opportunity to change their experience. Aron Ralston cut off his own arm to free himself from being pinned by a huge boulder. 'Today, I look at it as a miracle. I wouldn't tinker with a bit of it,' he says.

Boat-wreck survivor Rob Nelson and his girlfriend nearly drowned in the Hawaiian surf, yet he recounts, 'Life isn't about what you lose from your mistakes, but what you gain from them. I've gained so much from this experience, both spiritually, and mentally.'

Everything we've experienced so far makes us who we are today. Life's battles are where we build wisdom and resilience.

If we can be grateful for the tough moments behind us, we can also better face the tough moments ahead.

- *Looking back, do you regret that things didn't work out well?*
- *How have tough moments shaped who you are?*
- *Would you be where you are in life without having experienced specific struggles?*

'It's hard to benefit from the tough moments in life if we are always wishing that they hadn't happened'

COMING TO A place of peace and acceptance over what has happened to us is the first difficult step to growth.

My life could have taken a very different course had I not suffered my parachute accident while serving as a soldier. It's tempting to wonder, 'if only I had done this or that in time' or 'what if I hadn't volunteered to jump that day?' Those thoughts lead only to regret and more questions. But asking 'how have I grown as a result?' or 'would I have done all those other things in my life, without that accident?' Such questions widen our vision.

It's hard to benefit from the tough moments in life if we are always wishing that they hadn't happened. Regret and remorse can play a part in correcting our course, and repairing the damage when we've got things wrong. But they aren't helpful for the long haul.

Accepting our journey through life takes courage, not judgement. Seeing the positive ways in which difficult experiences have shaped us can help, maybe eventually leading to a place where we can look at them with gratitude rather than regret.

- *Have you found yourself wrestling with regret and remorse over past decisions?*
- *What would it be like to look back on your experiences with gratitude not judgement?*
- *What hidden blessings have you experienced from difficult events?*

STORM TO PERFORM

I F LIFE HAS taught me one thing it is this: don't be afraid of the storm. The rewards of building a great team are huge but it doesn't happen just by recruiting great people. Teams are only ever forged when they have come under pressure, and that means that every performing team will have their moments of conflict, disagreement and challenge. Don't be afraid of this. Psychologist Bruce Tuckman describes this progression in teams as Forming – Storming – Norming – Performing.

Often the friction is worse when a team is relatively newly formed. People have different ways of thinking, working and expressing themselves. A lot of the time, these don't match up.

A natural reaction is to think the team is not working. But Tuckman's model demonstrates that we will only reach the abundant 'performing stage' if we walk through the storms together first.

The most life-rich places on the planet are often the stormiest. The Amazon rainforest receives four metres (twelve feet) of rainfall a year. Torrential rainstorms are necessary to create the abundance of life in that ecosystem.

- *Are you uncomfortable or fearful of the conflict or disagreement around you?*
- *What fruit have you seen as a direct result of a period of conflict or disagreement in a team you have been part of?*

'Those storms become the very heart of our strength'

ONCE, WHILE FILMING in Red Rock Country, Utah, our crew was going for a shot that involved negotiating my way down some pretty punchy rapids over many hidden obstacles. Mess things up and you're in trouble. But in comparison to some of our previous narrow escapes, this one went like clockwork.

Our team had moved into the 'performing phase' after a stormy and conflicting time around a similar obstacle in the Sumatra jungle some months earlier. The bonds of trust and understanding had cemented, and the end result made for a totally different experience.

We can be too quick to shy away from conflict, especially if we have a naturally peacemaking mentality. But conflict is inevitable when gifted people work together. Closing the storms down often means that disagreements fester beneath the surface.

Coming through 'stormy' moments forces us to think smarter, make changes and strengthen our trust for one another. You just have to make sure you operate clearly, transparently, sensitively and respectfully. Always listen more than we talk. Do this, and those storms become the very heart of our strength.

- *How could you enable a storming phase without conflict becoming damaging or hurtful? What qualities matter when in the storm?*

- *How could you sit in the discomfort of conflict without feeling the need to fix or resolve the issues prematurely?*

GETTING
PRODUCTIVE

ARK TWAIN SAID, 'If it's your job to eat a frog, it's best to do it first thing in the morning. And if it's your job to eat two frogs, it's best to eat the biggest frog first.'

Productivity and priority are closely linked. If I get the order of things wrong, which I often do, my productivity for a whole day can massively drop. But if I get my priorities right, it feels great and I achieve more.

I've got a Scout buddy who knows how to deal with putting off the big tasks. He learnt his lesson the day he was offered a place on a once-in-a-lifetime trip to Fiji – the catch being it was leaving in two days and he had a backlog of work.

That trip drove him to tackling two weeks' work in two days. He got up early, dealt with the biggest tasks first and worked until completion. He was done with time to spare and soon on the plane. Perhaps most importantly, he had learnt the value of mapping his priorities, starting with the biggest tasks, then getting started and keeping going.

Today, when I want to hit a goal, I tell the family: 'I'm off to Fiji'.

- *Could you spend more time ordering and prioritising your day? Could this make a difference?*
- *Do you think procrastination could be stifling your productivity?*

'Simple system.
Solid results.'

PRODUCTIVITY IS ABOUT prioritising – that means knowing what's most important. There's nothing worse than being busy all day, then realising you haven't got much closer to your goal.

Inventor of the lightbulb, Thomas Edison, said, 'Being busy does not always mean real work. The object of all work is production or accomplishment . . . Seeming to do is not doing.'

As a 'doing' kind of person I've learned to value the 'system, planning' part. I use an Action Priority Matrix: 'Importance' runs up the vertical axis and 'Effort' runs across the horizontal axis. Then I simply plot out my day's tasks.

Low importance, low effort tasks are fillers; stuff you can get done in dead time between tasks. High effort, low importance stuff can be pushed to the end, if at all.

What matters is the stuff at the top. 'Easy wins' are high importance, low effort. I get as many of them as possible done first. Then there are high importance, high effort things – these are what I really need to prioritise. I give them time and consistent effort.

Simple system. Solid results. And everything feels more achievable when you work to a plan like this.

- *Do you struggle to set the right priorities so you can be productive?*
- *Could the Action Priority Matrix help you prioritise your day?*

DAY 339

CELEBRATE THE SMALL WINS

I LEARNT A LONG time ago that if you hold back your celebrations only for the really 'big ticket' events in life, you rarely end up celebrating. And as we get older we can all too easily find ourselves needing more and more impressive events to justify celebrating – until eventually we end up living life without ever really marking anything.

Celebrations carry so many benefits to our wellbeing; increasing optimism, connections, positive self-care, enhanced resilience and stress reduction. I have also seen what a difference 'celebrators' make to teams I have been part of, both military and civilian.

People naturally love to have an excuse to have some fun and let their hair down. These benefits shouldn't be reserved for a couple of occasions in a year – they are the sort of things we need to experience regularly.

- *When was the last time you celebrated something small?*
- *Do you tend to hold off celebrating the small things in the hope that something bigger is coming?*
- *What emotional benefits have you noticed when people celebrate?*

'The key is noticing and celebrating small wins every day'

JÜRGEN KLOPP, MANAGER of Liverpool Football Club, says, 'Life is too short not to celebrate nice moments.' He's right. We can become preoccupied with minimising the negatives in life. But amplifying the positive moments, however small, can be more beneficial.

So, rather than waiting or hoping for something big, I've learnt to pepper my life with as many 'micro-celebrations' as I can. It's almost a family joke: how I want to celebrate the tiniest of things. But try it. Maybe raise a toast to a good day, secretly punch the air to an assignment completed, or write yourself, or a loved one, a short note saying: 'Well done!'

These might just be small moments but to celebrate them is good for us. You don't need balloons and banners for these sorts of celebrations. You don't even need to tell anyone else (although it's always most fun to celebrate with other people). The key is noticing and celebrating small wins every day. It lifts our spirits. Do this and you will quickly feel the benefits of this kind of positivity – and before you know it, that enthusiasm will radiate out to others.

So today, take some time to celebrate some of the small wins.

- *How would it feel to start having some 'micro-celebrations' every day?*
- *What impact could this sort of 'positive noticing' have on your mood?*
- *Who could you bring on board to create a culture of celebration in your family or workplace?*

EVERY DESERT HAS AN END

T HERE'S A DESERT in the west of China called the Taklamakan. The name means 'once you go in, you never come out' in the Uighur language. And yet, over the centuries, caravans along the Silk Road did come through that vast wilderness and emerge safely on the other side. But it can be so tempting to think that when we are in a desert we'll never escape it.

Most of us have been in a 'desert' place at some point in our lives. When life has felt lonely and barren and hard, when we feel weak and barely able to go on. We look around us and all we can see is a hostile environment stretching to the horizon. It feels like it will never end.

Depression and low feelings can often seem like that. Or tough periods at work, or when we're going through the breakdown of an important relationship. But if we can find the strength within us just to keep going one more day, eventually we'll see that every desert comes to an end.

- *Have you found yourself in a desert place?*
- *How has the sense of permanency affected your mood?*
- *What would it look like to keep going on the basis that 'every desert comes to an end'?*

'You can do anything
for another ten seconds'

WHENEVER I'VE STRUGGLED with feelings of lowness, failure or fatigue, I've often found encouragement in reminding myself that this time, too, shall pass. Just holding on to that hope can be enough to keep us going. As an ultra-marathon adventure buddy once told me: 'You can do anything for another ten seconds.'

For others struggling with low feelings, they might need the support of a friend or counsellor. It's also important that people who have been feeling like this for a long time seek guidance from a medical professional. Sometimes physical and mental health issues are a core part of these struggles and they may require medical or psychological help.

Either way, it's OK. Whatever it takes. Tough times are simply part of life, part of being human. Don't beat yourself up about being in a battle period. But keep going and doing the positive actions to keep you moving forward – and it, too, shall pass.

- *Have you tended to blame yourself for being in a tough season?*
- *What might be a more compassionate way of looking at your circumstances?*
- *What does 'keep going' look like to you? Might you need to ask for help?*

DAY 343

WHERE YOU FIND
YOUR HOPE

N OLD MAN told me once, 'Choose wisely where you find your hope, as it will shape your life and future.'

Where we look to for our hope and strength is one of the most significant decisions any of us makes. Hope is about where we place our hearts – it is a resource that is drawn from beyond our current circumstance. Archbishop Desmond Tutu wrote, 'Hope is being able to see that there is light despite all of the darkness.'

Where we find our hope determines many of the key decisions we make about our lives. Hope has the power to set our direction and drive our efforts, but not all hopes are equal.

It's easy to find hope in things that are temporary, disappointing or dissatisfying. Wealth, success, status or achievements might fit that bill. They can be transient and unsatisfying. Like sand foundations.

- *What difference does having hope have on your sense of wellbeing? How does it feel when your hope is shaken?*

- *Have you experienced disappointment when you have looked for hope in achievements?*

- *Who inspires you to be hopeful because of their general outlook or ability to overcome adversity?*

'Hope has the power to set our direction and drive our efforts'

BEING DISAPPOINTED BY something we had placed our hope in is a painful experience. It can make us feel hopeless or even cynical. We can start to question if anything we invest ourselves in will prove to be worthwhile. Actor Jim Carrey said, 'I think everybody should get rich and famous and do everything they ever dreamed of so they can see that it's not the answer.'

Placing my hope in a power greater than me has been a key decision of my life. This hope is not dependent upon my achievements, performance or what I can gather for myself. It is not lost when I make mistakes or fail to realise dreams. It goes far beyond all of that stuff.

Faith is hard to describe sometimes. A bit like describing ice cream or swimming. But when we know our need for forgiveness and we receive overwhelming love and the light of heaven inside, it frees us and strengthens us. That's the message of Christ. It's a hope that can't be shaken.

- *What have you found out about hope from your experience of fulfilled and unfulfilled ambitions? What do you think about Jim Carrey's experience?*

- *How might a hope beyond your personal control, influence or circumstance offer you strength and freedom?*

- *What inspires you about people who have an enduring hope despite experiencing deep suffering and struggle in their personal circumstances?*

AMBITION POWER

BEING CALLED 'AMBITIOUS' is often a coded criticism for being pushy or self-serving. Young people are particularly impacted by a negative reading of ambition, which in turn can limit their dreams, efforts and achievements. But I love how the Scouting movement has helped young people reignite a positive view of ambition, showing how it is key to connecting their enthusiasm to a vision.

For me, ambition goes hand in hand with our biggest dreams. We need to dream in order to expand our thinking beyond the boundaries in our lives. Positive ambition is about making those dreams a reality, not about being ungrateful for what we have, or forgetting who we are. It is about seeing beyond our current limitations.

If we have positive ambition, which can be summed up by courage, kindness and a never-give-up spirit, we then have a real shot at realising our wildest dreams.

- *What have you believed about the notion of ambition or being an ambitious person?*
- *Do you feel 'limited' in what you can achieve in life? What would it take to redefine your boundaries?*
- *What would it look like for you to embrace positive ambition? What would you aim for if there were no limits in your life?*

'Be courageous and resilient in the face of obstacles. You only get one life.'

MATT STUTZMAN IS a silver-medal-winning Paralympian archer. He has no arms. He cradles his bow between his toes and uses his jaw to draw and release his arrows with devastating accuracy – and he holds the Guinness World Record for the longest accurate shot of just under 1,000 feet.

Matt was determined to break the world record. It took ingenuity and hard work to make it a reality. Just like his long shot, we have to aim high if we are going to hit an ambitious target.

People can be quick to point out the ways in which we are being unrealistic. There is no shortage of naysayers to belittle our goals. I call them the 'dream-stealers'. Avoid them; ignore them. You're better than that.

Sometimes our own insecurities might stall our progress. That's normal. Doubts are a sign of our humanity, but they need not be a roadblock to our progress.

If ambition determines the angle of aim, grit is the bowstring that makes the arrow fly. So keep aiming high. Be courageous and resilient in the face of obstacles. You only get one life. Go for it, and never give up.

- *What inspires you about Matt Stutzman's story? What obstacles do you imagine he had to overcome to make his ambition a reality?*
- *Have you been disheartened by people's response to your ambitions? Has it affected your self-belief?*

DON'T CONFORM

A T TIMES WE all feel the pressure to fit in. It echoes into the heart of human survival: belonging to a tribe meant access to shelter, food, warmth and community while exclusion was almost certainly a death sentence. These ancient instincts are alive in us today, even though the risk of unbelonging is far less clear. They prompt us to look and behave in a way that might make us get included, often at the expense of who we really are.

The pressure to conform to the norms of a group can be particularly strong when we are moving into a new workplace, school or college. I certainly felt that draw when I moved schools but also I knew that my character wasn't totally conventional and that I liked many alternative things like climbing over football. It took me a while to find the confidence to follow my own path and to worry less about conforming but finally, at about the age of fifteen, I decided to run in my own lane.

American President John F. Kennedy said, 'Conformity is the jailer of freedom and the enemy of growth.' Not conforming can be costly, but I believe it's worth it if it means that you can be free to be yourself.

- *Have you felt the instinct to conform to the norms of a group in order that you might fit in?*
- *What do you admire about people in your life who have chosen not to conform?*
- *What would it look like for you to 'run in your own lane'?*

'It's easy to overcompensate by conforming to the norms of a group'

PIONEERING RESEARCH BY psychologists Roy Baumeister and Mark Leary has shown that the need to 'belong' is a fundamental human need, not dissimilar to our physical needs. Belonging isn't a bad thing but it's helpful to know that this powerful drive is at work in our lives, influencing our decisions and behaviour.

The research suggests that we carry an internal 'belonging monitor' (sociometer) that constantly estimates how accepted or rejected we might be in a group. The trouble is that we aren't always objective, and the readings we take can be skewed. This means that it is easy to overcompensate by conforming to the norms of a group and hiding even more of what makes us unique and happy.

It takes courage to risk standing out from the crowd, especially when instinct says the opposite. St Paul wrote about this in a letter to persecuted Christians in Rome: 'Do not conform to the pattern of this world, but be transformed by the renewing of your mind.'

I have often drawn strength from this truth. It's given me the courage at key times to be myself. And that route is the path to happiness.

- *Have you felt the drive to conform for the sake of belonging, even if it means hiding what makes you unique?*
- *Do you often sense people's disapproval rather than their acceptance? How do you compensate for this feeling?*
- *What might it feel like to belong to God, beyond the conformity of the crowd?*

SHARPEN
YOUR AXE

THERE IS AN old story about two woodsmen who had a tree-felling contest. The younger man worked at a furious pace without rest all day and managed to fell twenty-five trees. The older woodsman appeared to work much slower, but at the end of the day, he had felled thirty-five trees. When the younger man asked him how he did it, the old woodsman replied that every hour he would sit down for ten minutes, sharpen his axe and take a break.

King Solomon wrote, 'Using a dull ax requires great strength, so sharpen the blade. That's the value of wisdom; it helps you succeed.' When it comes to smart survival, I learned the hard way; it's easy to mistake activity for efficiency. But the smart survivalist takes the time to stop and think and plan how to be most effective and efficient.

In life, it's easy to believe you are being productive, when in fact you are just being busy.

- *Do you find it easy to rush in and get started with things without planning how to be most effective?*
- *What is the difference between you being busy and being productive?*
- *Are there any circumstances you can think of that would have benefited from a different approach?*

'Resist the urge to "just get started" before you map out a plan'

ABRAHAM LINCOLN SAID, 'If I only had an hour to chop down a tree, I'd spend the first 45 minutes sharpening my axe.' Enthusiasm is a great quality, but if it's really going to come into its own, it needs to be matched with efficiency. Being keen is good; being keen and wise is great.

We soon find that using a blunt tool to do a difficult job is both exhausting and demoralising. It can be hard to stop sometimes – it's acknowledging that something hasn't gone right. But it's rare to regret taking a moment to adjust our approach or to rest or adapt, even if it costs us a little time in the short term.

Two things have helped me: resisting the urge to 'just get started' before I have mapped out a plan, and listening to the wisdom of more experienced 'woodsmen/women' who have gone before me.

Working smart always trumps being fast over the long term.

- *When did you last feel demoralised by a task? What had you believed about it before you started?*
- *Once you get started do you find it hard to adapt or amend your approach? What is stopping you?*
- *Who can you look to for wisdom on how to join your enthusiasm with strategic efficiency?*

EXPERIENCE SOMETHING NEW, SOMEWHERE NEW

HUMANS ARE CREATURES of habit. As much as 85 per cent of what you thought about yesterday you will think about today. This means that one of the challenges of getting older is that we stick with the same old things, and can lack the new experiences that challenge and sharpen our minds and our moods.

Our brains are in a constant process of degeneration and renewal. Studies show that the level of stimulation we experience can have a real impact on that renewal process, affecting our memory, mood, confidence and responsiveness.

'Roaming entropy' is the principle that our brain's ongoing development (neuroplasticity) is linked to experiencing new challenges in new environments. In other words, doing new and diverse and challenging things is what keeps our minds and spirits and bodies fresh.

Choosing to be curious in life, embracing those new challenges and environments is a win-win. If you don't like them, it was still good for your mind; and if you do like them . . . well, you've found a fun, new hobby.

- *How many new and challenging experiences or environments have you encountered recently?*
- *How firmly fixed are you on your 'likes and dislikes'? What could help you to explore something different?*

'Stick in that uncomfortable place if you are determined to succeed'

THE FEAR OF looking foolish is one of the key blockages to people learning new skills and trying new challenges. But managing the frustration of learning something new is a vital emotional skill, for both young people and adults. Frustration stimulates both our imagination and our senses in a way that can be powerful and productive. The process of problem-solving strengthens those neural pathways.

It's pretty simple to practise feeling frustrated – all we need to do is learn something new. Paint a picture, or write a postcard using calligraphy, or try kite-surfing, or whatever appeals to you. Maybe plan to attempt one new skill once a fortnight. When we become more tolerant of frustration, we are more likely to expand that 'roaming entropy'. And that's good for us.

People who are perfectionists will experience correspondingly higher levels of frustration. That's OK. Just be prepared to stick in that uncomfortable place of frustration for longer than you might anticipate, especially if you are determined to succeed. Remember our brain is a muscle. We train it by embracing new things that frustrate and challenge us. That's what mental training is.

- *Does the fear of looking foolish keep you from trying something new?*
- *How could you learn to tolerate frustration for long enough to find the new activity enjoyable?*

THOUGHTS AREN'T FACTS

WE HAVE A lot of unique thoughts each day; approximately 6,000 according to research from Queens University in Canada (although some suggest that the number could be ten times that). The vast majority of our thoughts don't materialise into anything more than a fleeting shade of an idea, but some intrusive thoughts can 'feel' more troubling, especially if they're connected to threat in some way.

During periods of stress it can become hard not to get alarmed by these sorts of thoughts. They can feel frightening and overwhelming, quickly stealing our peace and getting us stuck in a kind of loop. The way to freedom is not to start overvaluing them. They may look like smoke, but that doesn't mean there is necessarily a fire to put out.

Remember that thoughts are not facts, even ones with lots of emotion attached.

- *Have you tended to become troubled or anxious about your thoughts?*

- *Have you noticed how your anxiety about those thoughts, or attempts to push them away, seem to make them appear more frequently?*

- *How do the emotions related to a thought make it more or less powerful?*

'99 per cent are false signals, posing no threat at all'

IN THE MILITARY, counter-measures can be deployed against radar surveillance systems to confuse the picture: things like chaff, corner deflectors or decoys that aren't aircraft at all. They create false signals that fill the radar screen, 99 per cent of which pose no threat at all.

In a similar way, I find that troubling thoughts are usually FEAR: **F**alse **E**vidence **A**ppearing **R**eal. When we scan our mind to anxiously seek out threats, we tend to find them whether they are real or not. The issue with these sorts of thoughts is not the thought itself, but the fact that we are scanning for danger in the first place.

Choosing to be less bothered about them is a powerful step towards peace because it interrupts our tendency to go straight into reactive mode. Take a breath and allow the thought to be there until it fades on its own. And it will.

- *Are you scanning your thoughts for potential threats or observing them with neutral curiosity?*
- *What's your natural response to a threatening thought: observing or reactive mode?*
- *How would it feel to observe a troubling thought with neutral curiosity until it fades, rather than trying to reassure yourself or work out what it means?*

BUILD
A LEGACY

XAVIER HERNÁNDEZ CREUS is one of the greatest midfielders of all time, and was integral to Spain's victory in three successive major championships, including the World Cup 2010. Despite his successes, when talking about football and his trophies he said, 'There's something greater . . . a legacy'.

Legacy is the vapour trail behind the fighter jet. It is what is left behind us, the signal that we once passed this way magnificently. Maya Angelou wrote, 'If you're going to live, leave a legacy. Make a mark on the world that can't be erased.'

The real value of legacy is the positive imprint of our lives on others: the way we treat people, things we've created, loved and fought for. But it's often struck me how little we think about our legacy until later in life. By then, most of the impact we could have had has already happened. It's a bit like checking our compass when we can already see the summit.

To spend a little more time reflecting on our legacy earlier in our journey is smart. And it makes us much less inclined to feel regret in later life.

- *Do you find it difficult to think about the mark you might have left on the world after you are gone?*
- *What kind of legacy do you aspire to leave behind?*
- *How might you change the way you live today in order to start building that legacy for the future?*

'Legacy is not about the distribution of wealth, it's about the distribution of self'

AFTER WORKING FOR twenty years in the UK, social worker Robert Glover took on the goal of attempting to reform orphanage care in Shanghai. He had long held a desire to try this – an almost insurmountable mission.

In the nineties, orphanages in China were operating beyond their capacity. Robert determined that the solution was to place orphans in the care of fully vetted local families. Fostering was entirely new in China. So new they had to create a word for it in Mandarin.

The programme was a huge success. Children benefitted; families formed networks of support; and the pressure on the orphanages eased. To date, Robert and his organisation, Care for Children, have overseen the successful placement of over one million children.

We cannot imagine how a legacy will end, only how it will begin. Legacy is not always about scale or giving of wealth; it's about the giving of self – and it often starts in our hearts, with the smallest of deeds.

- *Have you vision for a legacy way of living?*
- *We often think about a wealth legacy, but how can you leave your mark through your gifts and actions?*
- *If you could make life better for one person today, what would you do?*

REPETITION WINS

EACH YEAR IN London, there is an epic rowing battle between some of the best athletes in the world. Each individual rower will have completed close to half a million strokes just in preparation to compete in 'The Boat Race'. Over the six hundred strokes of the actual race, these athletes will discover which of the teams has perfected that stroke. Repetition breeds mastery.

In his book *Outliers*, Malcolm Gladwell popularised the '10,000 hour rule' – that it takes 10,000 hours of intensive practice to achieve mastery of a complex skill. While the number isn't an exact measure, it's a helpful indication of the persistence necessary to take any of us from novice to expert.

Passion and perseverance are both necessary. Without passion, you won't want to repeat the same thing day in, day out. But you also need grit to keep persisting through the discouraging times that will inevitably come.

So often we reach an 'invisible ceiling', where we appear to reach our limit of improvement. That can be frustrating. But those that can keep persisting – no matter how slow their progress – are those that tend to win.

Like water that cuts through rock, it's not about strength, but about time.

- *What skills would you like to master?*
- *Are you able to enjoy the journey as much as the destination?*

'We need the spirit of a champion to keep going'

AGE THIRTY-THREE, SANDRA SÁNCHEZ was told she was too old for professional Karate, despite the thousands of hours she had trained in the sport, since the age of four.

She writes: 'People I respected told me I was good, but not good enough to win nationals or a world championship.'

Sánchez would not give up though, and sought out world-renowned trainer Sensei Jesús Del Moral. Despite initially declining, he eventually took her on with a punishing training schedule. 'Winners train on January 1st, losers stay in bed,' says Del Moral.

Sánchez trained in the Kata discipline for six hours a day and won Olympic gold in Tokyo aged nearly forty, making her Spain's oldest ever Olympian. She is also a two times World Champion and seven times European Champion.

We need the spirit of a champion to keep going, even when we're told we might never make it. The truth is that we can determine so much of our destiny with a winning attitude. And such an attitude is within our grasp if we choose it.

- *What inspires you about Sandra Sánchez's attitude to her sport?*
- *How do you respond to the sense that something is out of your reach or even impossible?*
- *What is powerful about the discipline of repetition? How could you harness that benefit in your own life?*

PADDLE YOUR OWN CANOE

WHEN SOMETHING GOES wrong in life, how often do we expect or hope someone else will come along and fix it for us? And when that doesn't happen, how often do we become bitter and resentful?

Don't get me wrong. For many, the need for help is real and necessary, whether they're struggling in a cycle of violence, poverty or poor physical or mental health. I'm not talking about those instances, but rather the times when we expect someone else to do all the hard work in our place, whether it's our boss, teacher, government, partner or friend. Waiting for those 'someone elses' to save the day.

One of the most valuable lessons of survival training is self-reliance. The realisation that no one is coming to the rescue. That it's down to us to sort things out. There's a simplicity, a self-awareness, a power to that. Barack Obama wrote, 'The best way to not feel hopeless is to get up and do something. Don't wait for good things to happen to you.'

- *Have you tended to wait for other people to change your circumstances?*

- *What could you choose to do for yourself this week that might change things?*

'You can create a positive future'

NANDO PARRADO WAS stranded in the High Andes for sixty days before he accepted that rescue wasn't coming. His decision to take action included scaling a 17,000-metre peak and a nine-day journey. Ultimately it saved him, and fifteen other air crash victims.

Rather than waiting or hoping for rescue, look at where you are now. Then look at where you want to be. What links those two points? It is action. Consistent, positive, daily action. Action when it's raining; action when we feel weak; action when all about us is crumbling; action when all is dark.

And remember, when it comes to our mental health, asking for help *is taking action.*

So get out your paddle, take a deep breath, smile and get going. Movement is power. Do something towards your future. You can make it. You can create a positive future.

- *How far are you away from where you want to be?*
- *What action can you now take to start the journey towards that point?*
- *Do you need to take action by simply asking for help?*

CULTURE OF KINDNESS

CORRIE TEN BOOM was a watchmaker in Holland when war broke out in 1939. In May 1942, the first Jewish woman knocked on her door asking for help. Corrie and her sister spent the next two years hiding Jews from Nazi persecution, before they themselves were arrested and sent to a concentration camp.

There, the sisters created an extraordinary culture of kindness in a truly dark place. Corrie had a bottle of vitamins with her – a vital and scarce resource under the circumstances. Rather than keeping them for herself, every morning she would distribute a vitamin to each woman.

Against all the odds, Corrie survived. But her sister never made it out alive. After the war, Corrie's kindness continued and she set up a rehabilitation centre for anyone who needed care. Her life was a testament to the power of kindness to create ripples that last for generations.

It is easy to be kind when we have plenty. What I find so beautiful about Corrie was her ability to show kindness to others even in the face of desperation, hate and death. That sort of kindness doesn't just change lives, it changes cultures.

- *What inspires you about Corrie ten Boom's story?*
- *Have you found that kindness or generosity are harder when you are under pressure yourself?*
- *Do you believe that showing kindness can change people's hearts?*

'We don't know what the consequences of a single act of kindness will be for another person'

VICTOR HUGO'S POWERFUL novel *Les Misérables* flows from one single act of kindness: Jean Valjean, a man brutalised by years in prison, accepts a night under the roof of a local bishop. Unable to resist the temptation, he steals the bishop's silver and runs away. When Valjean is caught and dragged back, the bishop tells the police that the silver was a gift and Valjean is released.

This single act of kindness transforms the trajectory of Valjean's life. He eventually becomes mayor of his town, and was ultimately willing to lay down his life for others.

We don't know what the consequences of a single act of kindness will be for another person, only that with each act of kindness we have the power to change the world for the better. To change other people's lives for the better. And also to change ourselves.

Kindness is often thought of as a term of gentleness. And in many ways it is. But true kindness is really the ultimate symbol of strength and courage.

- *Can you think of a moment when somebody's kindness towards you had a far bigger impact on you than they might have imagined?*
- *Can you see how showing kindness can be the ultimate test of strength?*
- *What would it look like to exercise kindness through one or two random acts each day?*

DAY 363

EXPOSE YOURSELF
TO THE LIGHT

THE BRITISH ARE never far away from a weather-related complaint. But for some people, changes in the seasons are no laughing matter as the amount of light they are exposed to can have genuine effects on their mental health.

We are all impacted by the cold and dark to an extent. Biologically your skin produces vitamin D from cholesterol when exposed to sunlight, which helps combat depression and other mental health conditions. So a lack of light can leave us vulnerable to low mood.

Seasonal Affective Disorder (SAD) affects up to 3 per cent of people in the UK and nearly 7 per cent in the US. Most people show symptoms for the first time in their twenties or thirties. The main symptom is depression in a seasonal pattern, alongside general lethargy, poor concentration, sleep disturbance and low function.

Exposing our skin to light is a great habit to develop. So get outside! Roll up your sleeves and let the light reach your skin, whatever the weather. It is one of my fundamental pillars for good strong physical and mental health: to be outside as much as I can.

- *Do you experience low feelings when the weather is dark and the days are short?*
- *What small changes can you make to expose yourself to more light, whatever the weather?*
- *Might you need to speak to your healthcare provider about your experience of low mood or depression?*

'Get outside! Roll up your sleeves and let the light reach your skin'.

VICTOR HUGO, AUTHOR of *Les Misérables* wrote, 'Winter is on my head but eternal spring is in my heart.' Our emotional health can be a fragile thing, with times when we are more vulnerable because of our physical circumstances.

Dark months can weigh heavily on our mental health, and that can easily steal the spring in our hearts. Winter weather impacts our willingness to socialise with others, and social contact is a key component of mental wellbeing. This is why winter conditions can have a disproportionately negative impact on elderly people or people who have health and mobility needs.

Within our capacity, keeping a 'spring in our hearts' requires a commitment to keep our connection to the outdoors alive – even when the elements oppose us. Alfred Wainwright, in his classic 1973 book *Coast to Coast*, said, 'There's no such thing as bad weather, only unsuitable clothing.' Instead of letting the darkness steal your light and the cold steal your friends, put on your coat, grab a torch and rekindle the spring in your heart.

- *Have you noticed that the darkness or weather has impacted your ability to socialise with others?*
- *What have you believed about the weather or darkness that has become a stumbling block?*
- *Could you (safely) change your outlook and make the winter a period that is equally sociable? What groups or clubs could you join?*

DIAMONDS UNDER PRESSURE

DIAMONDS ARE FORMED under 800,000 pounds per square inch of pressure and at a temperature of over 2,000°C. That is a lot of heat and a lot of weight. But the results are breathtaking.

Many people aspire to escape pressure, working extremely hard just to guarantee a retirement of leisure; others seek to avoid pressure earlier and find ways to minimise their responsibilities. Both ideas seem tempting at times, but nature shows us a different way. Nature says: it is the swaying in the wind and the storms that gives a tree its eventual strength; and it is the pressure upon the carbon that ultimately creates the diamond.

It leaves me wondering if we aren't designed to be at our best when we encounter a little bit of pressure. Rather than avoid it, there are mindsets and tools we can employ to help us manage it well. But if we are formed under pressure, then our aspiration can be, like the diamonds, to sparkle, and be bright, fully present and alive.

- *How would you describe your reaction under pressure?*
- *Do you think you could begin to see pressure as a creative opportunity?*

- *Looking back on your year, what are you most proud of?*

- *What outlook or mindset do you most want to carry forward into the year ahead?*

MENTAL HEALTH STIGMA

Stigma is defined as 'a mark of disgrace associated with a particular circumstance, quality, or person'. With mental health conditions, the stigma is often unseen and unintended.

Our language can play a big part in maintaining the stigma about psychiatric conditions. There are countless examples of language that we hear or use in our day-to-day conversations that may be harmful or hurtful to someone experiencing poor mental health – words like 'weird', 'crazy', 'nuts', 'crackers', etc.

The term 'bedlam', which is used to convey a sense of uproar and confusion, is in fact derived from the name of the historic mental asylum, the Bethlem Royal Hospital. Today, the ongoing underfunding and separation of mental and physical health services sustains the poor perception many people have of mental health. Many mental health units, for example, are located and operate apart from general medical hospitals.

Diagnostic labels can also feed into mental health stigma. For example, the term 'personality disorder' – which describes long-standing problems people have with their self-identity, their relationships with others and the regulation of their emotions – is often poorly explained or, worse still, used incorrectly to convey that someone going through a distressing time psychologically is simply 'not a nice person'. Labelling someone with alcohol dependence as an 'alcoholic' risks ignoring the complex biological and social factors that often result in the condition; instead, it makes them feel that the blame lies purely at their feet and harms their confidence in breaking the cycle of addiction.

Stigmatisation makes people who are experiencing mental health challenges feel ashamed and discourages them from seeking help. Minority communities that may be experiencing social or racial prejudices are particularly vulnerable to the impact of mental health stigma. This, in turn, leaves them less likely to access treatment at the early stages of mental illness and, therefore, more likely to need hospitalisation and longer-term support.

Workplace environments can also reinforce stigma. Excessive drinking and macho cultures (exemplified by the 'stiff upper lip' mindset) prevent people from having the psychological safety to open up about mental health difficulties and access the care they need. Such cultures can often be present in sectors where exposure to distressing situations is common, for example among healthcare professionals and emergency workers.

In overcoming stigma, storytelling by people who have experienced mental health difficulties can help to increase awareness about mental health conditions and challenge misconceptions about mental illness. Other steps that are likely to have a positive impact include the creation of spaces within society – such as the workplace and places of worship – in which conversations about mental health are less daunting, where there is non-judgemental curiosity about other people's mental wellbeing and where inappropriate phrases are challenged.

Mental health stigma is a real obstacle to treatment. But, if you are reading this book and think you may be suffering from mental distress of any kind, please believe me when I say that doctors and mental health professionals are here to help you and not stigmatise you. We will treat you with dignity and respect and try to help you to start your recovery journey.

Please don't hesitate to contact your healthcare provider in confidence to start the conversation.

Dr Chi-Chi Obuaya
Consultant Psychiatrist
Harley Street, London

WHEN IT GETS
REALLY TOUGH . . .

There are times when self-help isn't enough and we need professional support. This is as true in physical health as it is with
emotional and mental health. Even the strongest of us can sometimes meet an obstacle we cannot overcome alone.

The good news is that there is lots of good professional help
available. Exactly what you need will vary – sometimes we need
help RIGHT NOW; other times it is less urgent, but we know it is
something we need to invest some energy into at some stage.

If you need help now, please do not hold back. Most countries
have mental health help available twenty-four hours a day, and
they would prefer to see you sooner rather than later. It's never
a waste of time to them – that is just the little voice in our own
head trying to lead us off course.

Do seek urgent help if you have noticed any of the following:

- *A major, rapid change in your ability to function such that you
  cannot do your normal daily routine;*
- *Disturbance in more than one of the following: sleep,
  appetite and concentration;*
- *Persistent thoughts of not wanting to be alive anymore,
  especially if you have started thinking in detail about how to
  go about this.*

That last one is tough, isn't it. Life can be amazing and exciting,
but sometimes we get so tired we feel we can't carry on. We feel
others would be better off without us. We don't want to be a
burden anymore. But doctors know that these thoughts are actu-

ally symptoms of depression, that effective treatments are available and that people DO want to help.

Exactly how you seek help will also vary according to which country you live in. Your government national health websites will have the appropriate contact numbers on them. If in doubt, phone the emergency number for your country and ask for help – they will know how to route your call. Remember that you are not wasting anyone's time: you are precious, and worthy of getting the support you need. There are professional, experienced and kind people available and waiting for calls like yours.

For others, the problem is less urgent, but you feel you have exhausted self-help, friends and family. The problems seem so complex and deep-rooted. The good news is that medicine and psychology have tools for complex problems. We have been studying the brain intensely for the last one hundred years and we know a lot about how it works. Start with an appointment to discuss your experiences with your local GP or family doctor. They may be able to provide direct treatment or suggest a range of options for you to consider.

Some people may subsequently seek help from a psychological therapist, someone who is professionally accredited and has good testimonials. They may have a waiting list, and this may cost you some money – but think of it as an investment in your future, and one that is worth researching well.

Working with a skilled counsellor, psychotherapist or coach is often a transformational experience that helps people beyond their initial expectations or goals.

Remember that getting help is a sign of strength, not weakness. You matter, and your mental and emotional health matter too.

Dr Rob Waller FRCPsych
Consultant Psychiatrist
Edinburgh, Scotland

A FINAL NOTE

Your brain is amazing – pondering, processing and perceiving everything you need about what is going on around you, managing things from the past and the present as well as planning for the future. But it's also the filter through which you experience the world, and sometimes that filter leaves us feeling flat, frustrated or fearful.

Twenty-first-century life is non-stop, full of energy, stimulation and excitement. It can be tough trying to manage all the demands of life, and keep track of everything you need to pay attention to or remember. There's an ancient proverb that says, 'More than anything you guard, protect your mind, for life flows from it.'

The ancient Greeks loved feats of athletic strength and achievement. But they recognised that you needed more than just physical strength to win – you needed mental fitness. Success is about our mindset in the battle of life. Some of the best moments will challenge us emotionally, particularly when we put ourselves under pressure to dream big and aim high. Building mental fitness helps expand our capacity and releases the potential within us.

Sometimes the battle will feel more like a struggle. There will be seasons of life where we have to find a way through things we never expected or wanted. It's easy to think that emotional wellbeing means avoiding or eradicating painful emotions, but life just isn't like that. Emotions have a vital part to play in the healthy functioning of our minds, in helping us process and move through the tough stuff.

But in the low moments we all need some help with how to manage them, helping us hold our nerve until the storm settles.

It's about how to sleep well, deal with stress and hold anxiety without being pushed into panic. Those skills are vital in our lives because your mind really matters. You can learn these skills to support your emotional health – just as you might work out physically to support your physical health.

This book is about developing mental fitness, but also good perspectives to help you understand your mind better. It's not about changing who you are, or becoming a 'Teflon' person who is never affected by what is going on around them. It's about how making small changes can make a big difference – to help you not just SURVIVE the rough moments, but maybe even THRIVE through them.

Dr Kate Middleton
Psychologist and author
Hitchin, UK

THANKS

With thanks to: the creative and editorial team at Hodder Faith – Theodore Brun, Andy Lyon and Jessica Lacey; Caroline Michel and all at Peters Fraser and Dunlop; the Mind and Soul Foundation Team, psychiatrists Dr Chi-Chi Obuaya and Dr Rob Waller and psychologist Dr Kate Middleton; and the Mind charity, especially Jessica D'Cruz for mental health script advice.